ERIK H. ERIKSON

Also by Paul Roazen

Freud: Political and Social Thought
Brother Animal: The Story of Freud and Tausk
Sigmund Freud (editor)
Freud and His Followers

ERIK H. ERIKSON

The Power and Limits of a Vision

Paul Roazen

THE FREE PRESS
A Division of Macmillan, Inc.
New York

Collier Macmillan Publishers
London

The Free Press
A Division of Macmillan, Inc.
866 Third Avenue, New York, N.Y. 10022

Collier Macmillan Canada, Inc.

First Free Press Paperback Edition 1986

Printed in the United States of America

printing number
1   2   3   4   5   6   7   8   9   10

Library of Congress Cataloging in Publication Data

Roazen, Paul
    Erik H. Erikson: the power and limits of a
vision.

    Includes bibliographical references and index.
    1. Erikson, Erik Homburger, 1902-
RC339.52E74R6   150′.19′50924 [B]   76-10497
ISBN 0-02-927170-3

For Deborah, Jules, and Daniel

Contents

Preface

Since my own interests lie in the history of ideas, a book about the concepts of a living thinker seems to me to require a special justification. Erik H. Erikson's talents have been widely recognized. Sixteen years ago, in praising one of Erikson's books, W. H. Auden observed that it "is so full of wise observations . . . about human life . . . that no quotations could do it justice. . . ."; he saw Erikson as "that happy exception, a psychoanalyst who knows the difference between a biography and a case history."[1] Erikson's remarkable books and essays have been so influential, however, that they have often met with uncritical acceptance, among social scientists as well as the general reading public. He is broadly acknowledged as one of the foremost psychologists of our time; a long and wholly flattering book has been devoted to him,[2] and in a *Time* article on his latest work he was called "probably the most influential living psychoanalyst."[3] Even an unsympathetic writer recently observed: "He is at once the most resourceful, the most humane, and not coincidentally the most popular of all Freud's heirs."[4] In contrast to the relative barrenness of contemporary psychoanalytic thinking, Erikson has been unusually fertile in ideas.

Yet a writer of Erikson's impact deserves critical scrutiny. His concept of identity and his notion of the "identity crisis" have become well-established features of the contemporary climate of discourse. Educationists rely on his theories of childhood; historians turn to his work for biographical clues; and both philosophers and theologians have acknowledged his importance. Although his views on femininity have been disputed by writers in behalf of the women's liberation movement, on the whole Erikson's concepts have received relatively little criticism. Partly this has been because his developing approach has exerted a special charm hard for many to resist. And the elusiveness and ambivalences of his prose have made it exceptionally difficult to be certain where, on central issues, he has come to stand. So even though Erikson is unquestionably one of the most creative thinkers to have emerged out of the psychoanalytic movement, we would repay him poorly as a teacher if we allowed him to be loosely understood or inadequately challenged.

It is my hope that my own prior work on Freud and the early psychoanalysts,[5] and in particular on the implications of psychoanalytic thought for political and social philosophy,[6] will have enabled me to place Erikson's contributions in their proper historical context. Erikson has grown by moving beyond Freud's conclusions, and in the course of so doing he has succeeded in revitalizing the Freudian tradition.

An examination of Erikson's work, furthermore, gives us an opportunity to assess the strengths and weaknesses of Freudian psychology. Freud, of course, has had an enormous impact, not only on psychotherapy and child rearing, but more broadly on how we think about ourselves. In the face of the many criticisms Freud has been subjected to, we want to know what is of enduring value in psychoanalysis, and a study of Erik Erikson should help us in our quest.

The founder of psychoanalysis, we must remember, lived in a world very different from our own. Although Freud is often criticized for his cynicism about human nature, he could be curiously idealistic about sex. For who would have predicted, on traditional Freudian principles, that an energy crisis which shortened television-viewing hours in Western Europe would lead to an increase in baby-making? It would seem that sex rates lower in people's priorities than psychoanalysis might have led one to expect. Or would Freud have wryly regarded this debasement of human passions as simply another vindication of his low view of mankind?

I am once again grateful for the editorial help of my wife, Deborah Heller Roazen, who has repeatedly taken time from her own work to facilitate mine. I am also especially indebted to Michael Paul Rogin, not only for his critical reading of an early draft of this book but for an invitation to deliver a paper at a political science conference which enabled me to sort out my thoughts about Erikson's writings.[7] Presentations about Erikson to the Department of Psychiatry at Mount Sinai Hospital in Toronto, and to the Post-Doctoral Program in Psychology and Politics at Yale University, also were of assistance in clarifying my approach. Recent invitations to talk on Freud and the current state of psychoanalysis have helped to keep me on my toes; I am therefore grateful for what I learned from the give-and-take at the Department of Psychiatry of the Medical School of Syracuse University, the Queen Street Mental Center in Toronto, the American Institute for Psychotherapy and Psychoanalysis, the Department of Sociology at the University of Toronto, and the University of Chicago's Masters Program in Social Science. Finally, Robert Wallace of The Free Press has made helpful suggestions for improving my text; and I also want to thank Jack Lynch for his copy editing.

CHAPTER 1

Freud

Erikson entered Freud's circle in the summer of 1927. He was then twenty-five years old and was working as a painter of children's portraits, though he did not as yet have any firm professional goals. An old school friend, Peter Blos (later a New York psychoanalyst), was at that time the director of a small progressive school in Vienna run by Dorothy Burlingham and Eva Rosenfeld, both close friends of Freud's youngest daughter, Anna. Many of the children at the school were in psychoanalytic treatment, and a number of the parents were undergoing analysis. Blos suggested that Erikson might be hired to paint the portraits of Dorothy Burlingham's four children: as a member of the American Tiffany family she was immensely rich, she was currently in analysis with Freud, and her children had been among Anna Freud's first patients. Since Blos wanted to go on vacation, he also suggested that Erikson could replace him as a tutor in the school.

After a brief period of contact with the children, Erikson was asked by Dorothy Burlingham and Anna Freud whether he would consider becoming a child analyst—a profession he had not heard of before and which had at the time only a handful of practitioners. In 1909 Freud had written one of his most moving case histories, known subsequently as "Little Hans," about a small child; but Freud had not treated the boy in person; rather, the boy's father (Max Graf, a follower of Freud) brought Freud the material on which he based his interpretations. Later, others, notably Hermine von Hug-Hellmuth, Melanie Klein, and Anna Freud, developed their different ways of entering into therapeutic contact with children.

Although by 1927 Freud was world-famous, psychoanalysis still resembled a secret society. When Anna Freud accepted Erikson for analysis at the low fee of seven dollars a month, he entered a tight-knit movement that was still in conflict with the academic world (Erikson refers to his "truly astounding adoption by the Freudian circle" [1]). Freud resented the fact that the medical establishment, and in particular the psychiatric profession, continued to be dubious of the objective value of his findings. And so, despite the many popular successes of Freud's ideas, analysts still felt "proud to work underground." [2]

Erikson remembered the atmosphere in the Viennese psychoanalytic group as being "one of intense mutual loyalty and a deep devotion to a truly liberating idea, if often also of deeply ambivalent mental upset." [3] He read his first paper, "Psychoanalysis and the Future of Education," [4] before the Vienna Psychoanalytic Society on April 30, 1930. It was an era when analysts still hoped to achieve utopian changes in the upbringing of children—for instance, through enlightenment about sexuality and by avoiding unnecessary secrets between parent and child.

In the course of his training, involving many evenings in

small seminars and case discussions, Erikson absorbed a full measure of "the devotional atmosphere in which no clinical detail was too small and no theoretical insight too big to merit intensive presentation and debate." [5] Although Erikson also received a Montessori diploma, his psychoanalytic training remained his basic professional experience (later he emphasized the phase of discipleship as a "moratorium" for those who become innovators). As he said of himself in 1967, "I am primarily a psychoanalyst; it's the only method I have learned." [6] It may have been with his own background in mind that Erikson wrote of an early intellectual influence on Martin Luther: "the first discipline encountered by a young man is the one he must somehow identify with unless he chooses to remain unidentified in his years of need." [7] And in writing his book on Mahatma Gandhi, Erikson continued in this conservative vein, contending that a "man denies and abandons the visions and the disciplines he has already acquired only at the risk of historical and personal regression." [8]

Erikson came to his study of Gandhi, in the 1960s, through interviews with the great man's devoted followers; in his account of their allegiance to the transforming cause of non-violence, it is hard not to be reminded of Erikson's own early involvement with psychoanalysis. In Gandhi's case, Erikson proposed to study those who, when they encountered him, had not yet found their identities. Gandhi succeeded in instigating, according to Erikson, "such changes in people that meeting him remained *the* irreversible encounter of their lives." Erikson's own experience as a psychoanalytic convert helped him to appreciate in his Indian interviewees "the glow of a youthful memory, the memory of the beginning of a mission, a mission sanctioned and led by a great spirit." Like Freud, Gandhi had single-mindedly held his adherents to specialized purposes, and like Freud, Gandhi had fathered spiritual as well as natural children. Gandhians, like the early Freudians, had been "selected and seduced," though they thereby became "the heirs of both a political and a spiritual revolution." [9] Gandhi, once more like Freud, had been exceptionally proud of his independence, and this was part of his appeal to disciples.

By the time Erikson began his psychoanalytic apprenticeship, Freud was already afflicted with the cancer of the jaw that played so large a role in the last sixteen years of his life; and this perhaps accounts for Erikson's sensitivity in his work on Gandhi to "the morbid motivation in the lives of the daring innovator as well as his fanatic followers, not to speak of the anxiety and the perversity which fill the vacuum left by a weakening and dying leader. . . ." [10] Among Gandhi's followers Erikson admired those who had achieved some distance from their master; in one instance Erikson found a man's memories especially refreshing because he had never given himself unconditionally to Gandhi. Despite his admiration for Gandhi, Erikson could perceive his harshness toward the people closest to him, as he repeatedly threatened to repudiate those whose self-fulfillment might result in rebellion against him. Erikson wondered—possibly with his own life also in view—"who is the true representative of revolutionary advance—he who modestly continues the work of a giant and adapts it to less heroic circumstances, or he who continues to flex his muscles to see whether he may prove to have gigantic measurements himself." [11]

It is not clear how early Erikson felt dissatisfied as one of Freud's younger disciples. In the years of Freud's old age, most of his newer pupils in Vienna were welcomed by his daughter Anna; the more her father became an invalid, the more important she became in the psychoanalytic movement as a person close to him. Yet, like other newcomers in Freud's circle, Erikson felt that to some extent he functioned as a servant for the master: he took Freud for at least one long drive in Dorothy Burlingham's car.

In later years Erikson considered himself a bit delinquent for not continuing to practice the new nonmedical profession of child analysis for which he had been trained by Anna Freud. Although Freud's older pupils were patronizingly protective of her status in psychoanalysis, Freud's defense of the practice of "lay" analysis was at least partly designed to safeguard her future. Medical qualifications have been regarded as less relevant for therapists undertaking to treat children psychologically, and Erikson's contributions confirm Freud's hope that through lay analysis psychoanalysis would attract people with broad backgrounds.

As a student in analysis with Anna Freud, however, Erikson encountered some of the ambivalent aspects of a training analysis. Carl G. Jung had been the first to espouse the idea that all future analysts be required to undergo analysis themselves.[12] But this practice, which by 1925 had become a standard part of psychoanalytic training, was bound to have, besides its advantages, special drawbacks. For it proves surprisingly difficult for a student to avoid the subtle possibilities of suggestion, and to retain objectivity toward his own analyst's commitments. On the analyst's part, it is harder than one might think to guard against taking advantage of a patient's dependencies. If the course of psychotherapy is marked by its own difficulties, training can be an especially problematic issue.

Some psychoanalytic groups later tried to separate therapy from training, in order to minimize the stifling of individuality. For the analytic candidate may either overidentify with his analyst or needlessly repudiate a helping mentor. Erikson, for example, throughout all his years of involvement with Anna Freud, never became aware of the remarkable fact that her own analyst had been her father; he had loyally blinded himself to something that was bound to come as a shock when he eventually learned of it.[13]

Freud's school, in his declining years, was not, at least in Vienna, especially marked by intellectual vitality. The one trend in child analysis to rival Anna Freud's approach was that led by Melanie Klein, but Freud regarded her work as the first "heresy" to be held within the psychoanalytic movement. Melanie Klein's contributions might seem at an opposite pole from the point of view Erikson came to develop; she postulated the existence of inborn emotions of hate and envy in early infancy, had a penchant for deep interpretations of primitive impulses, and relied on Freud's death instinct in her clinical work. She had, many thought, constructed a new version of the Christian belief in original sin. Nonetheless, there were similarities between Erikson and Klein. Both relied on play constructions in nonverbal work with children, and both tried, by different theoretical routes, to get away from what they saw as the excessive egoism of the early Freudian concept of the mind. Erikson and Klein have emphasized a religious dimension to human experience, although at the time Erikson regarded Klein's work as alien ("arresting and disturbing"[14]) to his own outlook.

In Vienna, Erikson felt stifled by what he described as the maternalistic overprotection of the women analysts. Freud had failed to hold the farthest-seeing of his early male disciples, and by the end of his life he was surrounded predominantly by female followers. Erikson had been encouraged to enter child analysis precisely because in that era it was considered unusual for a man to be good at communicating with small children. But Erikson's initial efforts to express his own thoughts created tension with his seniors. He has recalled

a growing conservatism and especially a subtle yet pervasive interdiction of certain trends of thought. This concerned primarily any idea which might be reminiscent of the deviations perpetrated by those earliest and most brilliant of Freud's co-workers (such as Rank, Adler, and especially Jung) who had been separated from the movement before World War I.[15]

Although Otto Rank had in fact left Freud's circle only a short time before Erikson entered it, that so-called defection (actually encouraged by some who were jealous of Rank's closeness to Freud) had already become so secure a part of the Freudian mythology that Erikson could later mistakenly date it before World War I, while accurately placing it within the line of the "deviations" of Alfred Adler and Carl G. Jung. To sound like Klein, as Erikson was being accused in Vienna, was in that context as bad as to be likened to the other heretics in psychoanalysis; therefore Erikson could feel invigorated by the idea of leaving.

Nonetheless, Erikson's ambivalence was such that he never could feel comfortable about joining the revolutionary tradition in psychoanalysis. He thought that he was "inept in theoretical discussion" and that his "primary interest in the flux of phenomena left little impetus either to find safety in orthodoxy or escape in heresy." [16] However, Erikson did on occasion dare to turn psychoanalysis on some of Freud's own reported dreams. To Anna Freud, such interpretations amounted to lèse majesté. She has taken strong exception to the reminiscences of Theodor Reik and Felix Deutsch, as well as to at least one of the historical reconstructions of the Bernfelds.[17] She was disgusted at a paper of Erikson's which touched on Freud's worries about the growth of his family at the time his wife was pregnant with Anna.[18]

Erikson met Joan Serson in 1929, and married her on April 1, 1930 after he had completed his training analysis. An American student (Canadian born), she had been analyzed in Vienna and became a tutor in the small school where Erikson was working. She eventually helped convince him that if he wanted to fulfill himself he had to go abroad. (Later he credited her with having helped him become a psychoanalytic writer.) Born of Danish parentage, Erikson first made a brief and unsuccessful attempt in 1933 to establish himself in Denmark; then he tried the United States but was turned aside as unimpressive by Freud's leading American pupil in New York City, A. A. Brill.[19] By the end of 1933, however, Erikson had settled in Boston, Massachusetts. In those days European training in analysis was superior to anything to be had in the United States and it was assumed that any "export-ware" from European psychoanalytic institutes, even if like Erikson only recently graduated, would be far superior to other available talent. American analysts might be irritated by the situation, but they were usually willing to accept their European-trained colleagues.

Erikson enrolled in the Harvard graduate program in psychology, but he flunked his first course. His "failure" can be attributed to his unwillingness to accede to what may have seemed to him some of the unnecessary demands of academic psychology, and in later years the Harvard psychologist Edwin Boring was embarrassed about how Erikson had fared in his department. One can only wonder how different the situation would be today.

In 1936, when Harvard was holding its tercentenary celebration, the ceremonial arrangements were elaborate. One of the organizing committees, on which Henry A. Murray served, unanimously decided to offer an honorary degree to Freud. It did not occur to the members that he might refuse. Erikson, who had been welcomed as a worker at Murray's Psychological Clinic, informed Murray that the chances of Freud's accepting were nil. So the committee declined to proceed, for if its offer were rejected the recipient would be chosen by a different committee, and the psychologists wanted one of their own to get the honor, rather than risk the prize going to, say, an economist. (Instead of Freud, in the end Jung received the honorary degree.)[20]

Despite the tension within Erikson's work between the Freudian loyalist and the erring rebel, there is abundant evidence within the corpus of Erikson's writings to support a claim for his orthodoxy. In line with Freud's own fascination with psychological origins, Erikson has regretted that we still know so little of the earliest beginnings of mental life.[21] Freud had great ambitions for what his "science" might add to human knowledge; and Erikson—though he has been less than consistent in referring to psychoanalysis as "our science" rather than a "clinical art-and-science"—has argued that "we have, in the last few decades, learned more about the development and growth of the individual and about his motivations (especially unconscious motivations) than in the whole of human history before us (excepting, of course, the implicit wisdom expressed in the Bible or Shakespeare.)" [22] Like Freud, Erikson maintained as late as 1958 that "human nature can best be studied in the state of conflict. . . ." [23]

Freud preferred to think of psychoanalysis as a theory and technique relatively independent of the practitioner. Erikson has written of the neutral-sounding "application of the psychoanalytic instrument"; psychoanalysis is supposedly a system of thought which "verifies" observations, and Erikson has appealed to the nature of "everyday psychoanalytic work" for "the proof of the validity" of an approach of his.[24] "The experienced dream interpreter," Erikson has gone so far to say, "often finds himself 'reading' a dream report as a practitioner of medicine scans an X-ray." [25] And in his conversation with Huey Newton, the Black Panther leader, it was the method of psychoanalysis that Erikson hoped would be enlightening.

In attempting to persuade others of the advantages of

Freud's outlook, Erikson has insisted that the highest level of psychoanalytic abstraction, its metapsychology, involves "a method of cross-checking not easily appreciated by the untrained." The core of Freud's findings involve for Erikson what he calls "the rock-bottom concepts of repression and regression, transference and libido." In citing Freud's own cases and dreams, Erikson once commented that "all of us [analysts] know the material by heart. Beyond this, we always find in Freud's writings parenthetical data worthy of the attention of generations to come." [26]

Similar to Freud's own fragmentary approach to case material, Erikson's method also employs "case fragments," and —again like Freud—he has felt the need, in introducing evidence, of a clinical "specimen." [27] The early psychoanalysts believed that the abnormal can teach us about the everyday; Erikson has tried to understand psychological "laws and mechanisms" by means of choosing "cases which high-light in an unusually dramatic way the principles governing the usual." [28] In line with Freud's therapeutic dictum that "where id was, there ego shall be," Erikson once proposed that "the only remedy for this upset [mental] economy is to make unconscious material conscious. . . ." [29] Finally, in full accord with many of Freud's disciples' unwillingness to question the master's version of his own psyche, Erikson once observed of a dream of Freud's that "it will not be necessary for me to indulge in the sport of newly interpreting what might be presumed to have been unconscious to Freud himself." [30]

Since Freud used the imagery of domination and control in describing how a patient has to "submit" to an analysis, it may well seem that Erikson is stretching a point when he writes that "Freud . . . called for a strict equality between patient and doctor. . . ." [31] Yet Erikson is undoubtedly correct when he says that, compared with alternative therapeutic methods of its day, psychoanalysis looked "more like morbid co-meditation than a manly professional activity." [32] Freud's proposed self-scrutiny of instinctual life, Erikson notes admiringly, amounted to "a new kind of asceticism," "a heroic abnegation of the kind which produces new steps in moral awareness." [33] Freud's theory of neurotic hysteria did more than produce another diagnostic term, for it also inaugurated a new image of man. Psychoanalysis may be, Erikson suggests, "the principal modern form of systematic introspection and meditation." [34] But only if one ignores all of Freud's own clinical intolerances can one begin to agree with Erikson's optimistic judgment that "Freud's revolutionary and abiding respect for his patients has had a decisive influence on the honesty of 'dialogue' in all manner of relations among men." [35]

For Erikson, Freud was a revolutionary as a doctor, as well as a critic of Victorian society: "Society, he concluded, is too blindly autocratic in demanding impossible feats of sublimation from her children." [36] Erikson sees Freud as a great enlightening influence, and therefore no aspect of Freud's career is insignificant. He has paid extensive attention to the details of Freud's life, whether his love of the honesty of dogs or his railroad phobia. Yet he can make some curious biographical mistakes about Freud: he erroneously speaks of "the psychiatric beginnings of psychoanalysis," whereas Freud was a neurologist, not a psychiatrist; he mistakenly dates Freud's trip to the United States in 1907; and he claims that Freud's "early case histories were said to read like novels, which can be a compliment but was then an opprobrium," whereas the truth of the matter is that it was Freud himself who worried about his artistic side overcoming the scientist in him.[37]

It is likely, however, that Erikson's own view of the function of a ritual as a "sanction for sinfully original ideas" [38] can help explain why he has invoked Freud's name so often.

Erikson remarks that "sovereign creators of new ideas . . . are ceremoniously quoted to justify newer ones. . . . ."; and this principle helps explain why Erikson has repeatedly cited from Freud's speech to B'nai B'rith his declaration of his "clear consciousness of an inner identity" as a Jew.[39] In part Erikson has tried to understand Freud's career in its own terms; but it is hard not to think that by tracing the positive identity binding Freud to Jewishness and intellectuality, in contrast to the corresponding "negative identity he had to live down . . . something akin to the Jewish *Schlemiel* or the German *Dummkopf*,"[40] Erikson is also trying to establish within the corpus of Freud's texts a new concept of identity which becomes so important only within Erikson's own writings.

Freud's speech to his Jewish lodge had never before, to my knowledge, been cited within the psychoanalytic literature; Erikson tells us that he "had started to use the terms ego identity and group identity . . . before I (as far as I know) became aware of Freud's having used the term *innere Identität* in a peripheral pronouncement and yet in regard to a central matter in his life."[41] In striking contrast to the practice of other students of Freud (who were often accused of stealing ideas from their former teacher), Erikson's many citations of Freud's single mention of the concept of inner identity is an instance of a disciple trying to foist off an original idea onto the founder of psychoanalysis. Erikson has himself observed the difficulties creative people can have in achieving "the courage of their own originality."[42]

In recounting the saga of Freud's development, Erikson, like other loyal followers, has largely accepted and popularized Freud's own version of events and has contributed to an idealized view of the founder. For instance, Erikson has helped keep alive the myth that Freud's *Interpretation of Dreams* was ignored by book reviewers.[43] If Freud helped collaborate on a disappointingly bad, polemical book on

President Woodrow Wilson, then Erikson did his best to dissociate his hero from it;* it subsequently became the official policy of the *Journal of the American Psychoanalytic Association* not to discuss this book. Although Erikson might be aware of some central limitations in Freud's psychology, at times he has been so credulous in describing how Freud's mind developed as to sound propagandistic.[45]

When Freud's private correspondence began to be published, notably his letters to his friend Wilhelm Fliess, Erikson found it a jolt. But instead of looking for signs of neurosis in Freud, Erikson emphasized Freud's early struggles as an aspect of the beginnings of creativity. He has been strangely reluctant to perceive the autobiographical element in Freud's ideas. Erikson has recently reprinted his account of the Freud-Fliess correspondence, first published in 1955. He is still unwilling to consider that when Freud was theorizing about the sources of incomplete sexual discharge, and traced neurosis to childhood seduction, he was engaging in a special kind of self-deception. Instead of Freud's seeing the problem to be his own limited potency, or difficulties with his sexual partner (his wife), Freud characteristically escaped a current mental conflict by placing it in the past.

Erikson's need for a mythical hero obscures his historical vision. He cites again, as in 1955, a letter of Freud's in which he speaks in 1900 of having finished begetting children. At this point Erikson has added a new sentence: "The reference to his 'finished' procreative activities has suggested to some that, for Freud, who considered the then available contraceptives unbearable, this meant a cessation of marital rela-

* When he reprinted his essay, originally so prominently published that at the time it lent credence to the alleged inauthenticity of Freud's part in writing the manuscript, Erikson introduced major changes in his account of Freud's collaboration with William C. Bullitt. Although Erikson still thinks the Freud-Bullitt book a bad one, he is now willing to see more of Freud's hand in it. Yet he did not alert the reader to his changing ground.[44]

tions altogether." [46] But what evidence there is in the correspondence that the sexual relations between Freud and his wife came to an early end is found not in that 1900 letter, but in one from 1897, in which Freud writes that "sexual excitation is of no more use to a person like me." [47]

Other than touching on the issue of Freud's sex life, Erikson made relatively minor changes in reprinting his account of Freud and Fliess. Nonetheless, in connection with their falling out, it is worth noting that on the whole Fliess gets more charitably treated now. Considering that the Freud-Fliess correspondence was bowdlerized, and Freud's subsequently published volumes of letters tendentiously edited and censored (with the exception of those to Jung), it would have been helpful to have had the reader alerted to some of the new evidence. If it were not for Erikson's textual changes in his essay (explained merely by the needs of re-editing for publication in book form), he could justify this omission by the claim he makes (as in the case of his study of the Freud-Bullitt collaboration) to have republished an "original" [48] review.

In discussing Freud's theory of femininity,* Erikson has been reluctant to challenge Freud's point of view. For example, when it comes to Freud's well-known and controversial dictum that "anatomy is destiny," Erikson puts it in the most favorable light by suggesting that "Freud meant to contradict Napoleon the conqueror's motto that history is destiny." [49] (Nevertheless, Freud was at the same time identifying with the Emperor's coinage of sayings.) Erikson admits that "Freud's general judgment of the identity of women was probably the weakest part of his theory." Freud shared the patriarchal biases of his era; instead of interpreting women's complaints of deprivation as a sign of social injustice, Freud postulated penis envy as a biologically bed-

---

* For a discussion of Erikson's concepts about women in his studies of play constructions, see Ch. 9, pp. 142–48.

rock feature of female psychology. Nowadays we can see that any such aspect of femininity is defensive, secondary rather than primary. For penis envy is not an irreducible concept, but can symbolize powerlessness. Freud, however, upheld the dominant cultural norms of his time, which denied that "an upper-class woman could have passionate and active sexual wishes and yet be refined and intelligent." Despite the widespread influence which Freud's misconceptions have subsequently had, Erikson is still willing to argue that "the point is not to deny what Freud saw [in women] and generalized."[50]

Erikson has sought in Freud what can be of value today. Psychoanalysis succeeded, according to Erikson, in giving "new function and scope to such divergent endeavors as natural philosophy and Talmudic argument, medical tradition and missionary teaching, literary demonstration and the building of theory, social reform and the making of money."[51] Yet he has also limited the potential applicability of Freud's work by pointing out that any theory "is no more than the sum of the things to which it can give an initial order." In contrast to Freud, Erikson feels that it has little meaning scientifically to talk about energies that are not demonstrable. But when asked if he thinks that "had Freud been living today he would reformulate his libido theory to conform to recent developments in the field of biology, biochemistry, and physiology," Erikson somehow replied: "I'm reasonably convinced of that."[52] Here Erikson's response is at odds with his own conviction that a great man's utterances are "eminently surprising"; in writing about Gandhi, whom Erikson so often compares to Freud, Erikson remarks that "nobody can know what a man of such complexity *would* have said or done."[53]

Erikson is generous in seeing how Freud's single-mindedness was an essential constituent of his genius. Freud's approach was almost that of the artist, disproportioning reality in order to heighten our perception of certain aspects of it. If Freud's one-sidedness was necessitated by his need to establish once and for all that "sexuality does not begin in puberty but develops in distinct stages," Erikson is willing to undertake the task of putting the libido theory in the perspective of "the totality of human life." [54]

Freud, Erikson has decided, constructed his model of man primarily out "of the processes which he observed when, with such primeval courage, he looked into himself as he looked into his patients; but the model has no place for the judicious observer, the curious man. Science, morality, and himself Freud 'took for granted.' " [55] Erikson has even suggested that Freud, as a theorist of sex, can be balanced by Karl Marx, as a theorist of work. If Erikson has been ever tactful in amending Freud's conclusions, it is at least partly out of a gnawing fear of that kind of excommunication which he is aware takes place, not only among Marxists, but within psychoanalysis too.

CHAPTER 2

The Ego

Freud gave a central impetus to the development of ego psychology, yet the implications of this psychology have resulted in a surprising shift of mood among many analysts. Freud demanded more of mankind, as he encouraged people to master neurotic difficulties; but ego psychologists are likely to be as concerned with accounting for successful adaptation as with overcoming symptomatological failure. Freud's fascination with the abnormal and the apparently bizarre led him once, for instance, to dismiss a patient he did not care to work with on the grounds that he had no unconscious. To Freud this was a way of saying that the patient's conflicts were so submerged and out of reach as to render him uninteresting if not "worthless." Although Freud was half joking about why he felt displeased with this patient, the anecdote does tell us something about early psychoanalysis's consuming interest in the irrational.

Freud tended to take a stonyhearted view of human nature, and paradoxically this pessimism was one of his enduring strengths. He was a naysayer, not a lover of humanity; his negativism had the purpose of helping people to be different, to change, to overcome their infantile dependencies. Freud's whole system was designed to explain the motivation of people in conflict with themselves, when their egos have failed at integrative tasks. As a therapist Freud aimed to pull problems apart, releasing people from fixations; but his operative assumption was that an individual's ego would then be capable of putting the pieces back together again.

In my view the most significant direction psychoanalytic thinking has taken since the late 1930s has been the full-scale development of ego psychology. For all Freud's earlier concetration on the vicissitudes of instinctual life, the term "libido"—by which he referred to the psychological side of the sexual drive—has largely disappeared from the psychoanalytic vocabulary. Whereas analysts once spoke of the need to rely therapeutically on the strength of the id's strivings to release itself, analysts now tend to think in terms of their establishing an alliance with the patient's ego.

For Freud analysis was automatically synthesis, and therefore the constructive forces of the ego could be taken for granted; he was interested in self-deception, not self-healing. Recent psychoanalytic thinking has tried to correct this imbalance. When Freud wrote about the ego as an agency of the mind, he meant, not egotism or grandiosity, but that organizing aspect of the psyche which is responsible for testing reality, mediating between conflicting demands. According to Freud, the ego won what strength it had vis-à-vis other parts of the mind through maneuvers of trickery and bribery; and although in his very last years he conjectured that the ego might have psychological energy of its own, by and large his work remained stuck to the image of the ego as a rider on an instinctually energized horse.

Freud predicted that in the exploration of the psychology of the ego "it will be difficult to escape what is universally known; it will rather be a question of new ways of looking at things and new ways of arranging them than of new discoveries."[1] Freud distinguished between what the newer ego psychology could show and the already psychoanalytically "discovered" so-called facts of instinctual life. In keeping with this distinction, Erikson adopted a cautious view of his own contribution: as he put it in his first book, *Childhood and Society*, published at the comparatively late age of forty-eight, "I have nothing to offer except a way of looking at things."[2]

It is of course true that Freud had long relied on rational insight as a curative agent. In order to facilitate such insight, as Erikson was to put it, the analyst uses "the patient's own ego strength for his own transformation."[3] Despite Erikson's eagerness to see in Freud a therapist who treated patients as co-workers, in reality he excluded many more types of patients from therapy than would today's analyst. Erikson puts the best face on this narrowness by saying that Freud chose "his patients carefully so that he could trust their truthfulness."[4]

Erikson is right in thinking that at its best psychoanalysis aimed at enlightenment and human freedom. But one difficulty was that Freud saw the technique of therapy that was personally congenial to himself as, from the patient's point of view, wholly noncoercive; and therefore Freud overlooked in psychoanalysis many elements of old-fashioned suggestion. Another difficulty was that Freud tended to view mankind from the perspective of the analyst observing patients reclining horizontally on a couch; such a situation will induce regressions in patients (and, unacknowledged by Freud, foster illusions in analysts as well), which limits psychoanalytic therapy as a model for normal psychology. Recently Erikson has mentioned in passing that "psychoanalysis has . . . not quite taken care of the singular importance of verticality for the human ego."[5] Nevertheless, Erikson has held that Freud's "monumental work" was "the rock" on which the exploration of the adaptive (as opposed to the neurotic or defensive) ego must be based.[6]

Erikson is aware of the possibility of improperly reifying many concepts in psychoanalysis, "as though libido or the death instinct or the ego really existed."[7] In a passage added to the revised edition of *Childhood and Society*, Erikson noted: "When men concentrate on an uncharted area of human existence, they aggrandize this area to become the universe, and they reify its center as the prime reality. Thus . . . the 'id' was reified in psychoanalysis. . . ."[8] The ego, on the other hand, though mentioned even in Freud's earliest work, played a very minor role in his vision of the structure of human conflicts. It takes a good deal of textual ingenuity to argue that the ego which Freud first began to emphasize as an abstraction in the 1920s and 1930s really existed in his work of the 1890s. It is historically more accurate to say that post-Freudian writers like Erikson have chosen to elevate an ego aspect of psychoanalysis that was only scarcely there in Freud's own day. Erikson prefers to think that the ego part of Freud's work somehow is less appealing, and that therefore the problem has been that Freud's later ideas have not had the attention they deserve.[9] Yet implicitly Erikson seems to acknowledge the need for a shift in the focus of psychoanalysis, as he declares, with customary loyalty, that "the study of identity . . . becomes as strategic in our time as the study of sexuality was in Freud's. . . ."[10]

As Freud in his *Interpretation of Dreams* used the image of taking the reader on a walk, so Erikson has liked the idea of a "conceptual itinerary" for his *Childhood and Society*.[11]

If Erikson's point of departure was Freud and what Erikson chose to think of as the essence of "classical" psychoanalysis, there were also a few writers, well known in analysis before Erikson achieved any prominence, to whom he could look to sanction his own direction of thought. For example, Heinz Hartmann, who became dean of the theorists of orthodox analysis, is often cited by Erikson, as is Ernst Kris, one of the leading pupils of Freud's last years.[12] Hartmann, an analysand of Freud (and, before that, of Sandor Rado), had proposed the ability of the "autonomous" ego to resist regression as an index of normality. And Kris, an analysand of Helene Deutsch and Anna Freud (and also married to the daughter of an old friend of Freud's), had pointed out, like Carl Jung long before, how apparent regressions could later serve reintegrations at a higher level. In addition, Erikson has cited Paul Schilder and Paul Federn (but not Victor Tausk) as forerunners in the development of ego psychology.[13] But Erikson does not, for instance, cite any of the literature indicating Freud's own doubts about the respective paths Schilder and Federn were taking.

Erikson did once, however, highlight the implications of the differences between Hartmann's approach and that of Erikson's own analyst, Anna Freud. Erikson has claimed that in his years in the Vienna Psychoanalytic Society "the basic theoretical struggle at the time was between Anna Freud's clarification of the defensive mechanisms employed by the ego against the drives and of Hartmann's explorations of the ego's adaptive response to the environment."[14] Although child analysis, led by Anna Freud, had been Erikson's earliest analytic area of interest—and he has reiterated: "I am the kind of clinical worker in whose mind a few observations linger for a long time"[15]—Erikson became attracted by Hartmann's more philosophical line of approach. Yet in contrast to what was to be Erikson's own vivid use of clinical cases, Hartmann, an experienced clinician, never cited case material in the course of his exposition of an abstract theory almost metaphysical in character.

Erikson respects Anna Freud's *The Ego and the Mechanisms of Defense* for having conclusively organized the nature of the defensive ego.[16] The problem for Erikson was that Anna Freud had described the ego's functions in terms of warding off quantities of drives, whereas Erikson wanted to go further and extend his reach beyond mere defensiveness to adaptation. In an early (1936) review of another of Anna Freud's books, Erikson began to differentiate his own approach from that of "Miss Freud":

> Following the traditional route of psychoanalysis the book says much about what may limit and endanger the child's ego; it says little about the ego itself. Correspondingly psychoanalysis has so far been useful to pedagogy primarily as a basis of criticism of cultural progress and the dangers it involves for children. So far as further studies may illuminate the ego, psychoanalytic insight will be able to help education in its most specific problem: the strengthening and enriching of the ego.[17]

In accord with his original artistic nature, the sort of ego strength Erikson wanted to talk about had to be less formalistic than the kind of "mechanisms" Anna Freud had outlined. In 1945 she wrote about the possibility of "perfecting [ego] functions, . . . rendering them more and more objective and independent of the emotions until they can become as accurate and reliable as a mechanical apparatus." Here Erikson found an example of the modern tendency to over-identify with machinery: "If . . . the ego itself seems to *crave* mechanical adaptation we may not be dealing with the nature of the ego, but with one of its period-bound adjustments as well as with our own mechanistic approach to its study."[18]

Within psychoanalytic theory an excessively mechanical image of human nature has been allied to a Darwinian conception of the unconscious, which tends to see the child as a savage and man as a brute. Yet, as Erikson has protested, we do not attribute to animals "a certain built-in balance, a restraint and discipline."[19] He has been wary of what he calls "a faddish preoccupation with the more sordid aspects of childhood as though they were the final determinants of human destiny."[20] It is too easy to mistake a patient, child or adult, for his symptoms.[21] Erikson believes that we must clearly understand that "the central question is whether a person has a neurosis or the neurosis has him."[22] We should, for instance, recognize that fears are not the same as anxieties; the former apprehensions focus on realistic responses to dangers, whereas the latter, caused by upset inner controls, magnify obstacles without providing the means of mastery.[23]

Adaptive responses are bound to be neglected by a viewpoint which regards the ego mainly as a set of defenses against inner drives. "Early psychoanalysis . . . describes human motivation as if libido were the prime substance, individual egos being mere defensive buffers and vulnerable layers between this substance and a vague surrounding 'outer world' of arbitrary and hostile social conventions." [24] The key, according to Erikson, lies in a perspective which looks to the ego for the organizing capacities which are the source of "that strength which can reconcile discontinuities and ambiguities."[25]

Following Freud, Erikson believes in the ego as unconscious. But, like other post-Freudians, Erikson emphasizes that the ego has a unifiying function, ensuring coherent behavior and conduct; the job of the ego is not just the negative one of avoiding anxieties, but also the positive role of maintaining effective performance. The ego's defenses, then, are not necessarily pathogenic, for some may be adaptive as well as maladaptive. It is true that adaptation can be bedeviled by anxieties and guilts. And the outside environment will have inadequacies of its own. But Erikson would measure the ego's strength not by the earlier psychoanalytic standard of what in a personality is denied or cut off, but rather by all the extremes that an individual's ego is able to unify.

For Erikson the ego guards the person's indivisibility, and everything that underlies an ego's strength adds to its identity. Erikson obviously has a number of ideas in mind when he uses the term "identity," which he even once characterized as "a relatively unconscious conflict."[26] Identity refers not only to a conscious sense of individual uniqueness, but also to what Erikson stresses as the unconscious striving for continuity and sameness of experience. At the same time Erikson considers the sense of identity to be a criterion for the unspoken workings of ego synthesis. Freud could take identity for granted partly because of his special kind of patients. In a memorable passage, which assumes a change in clinical clientele, Erikson observes that "the patient of today suffers most under the problem of what he should believe in and who he should—or, indeed, might—be or become; while the patient of early psychoanalysis suffered most under inhibitions which prevented him from being what and who he thought he knew he was."[27]

Finally, for Erikson identity is responsible for the individual's maintaining an inner solidarity with the ideals and aspirations of social groups.[28] The ego has a general balancing function, keeping "things in perspective and in readiness for action. . . . it mediates between outer events and inner responses, between past and future, and between the higher and lower selves." Erikson's concept of ego strength accounts for the difference between feeling whole or fragmented, at best establishing "a sense of being at one with oneself as one grows and develops."[29]

In addition to a sense of continuity, each of us needs, according to Erikson, a feeling of newness ensured by the "leeway" that a secure identity provides. By leeway Erikson means the maintaining of a centrality in our experience, so that we can be capable of making meaningful choices. Certainly psychoanalysts have encountered in their consulting rooms "those who cannot stand the tension between polarities, the never-ceasing necessity of remaining tentative in order to be free to take the next step, to turn the next corner."[30]

At first Erikson called identity "ego identity," choosing a name analogous to Freud's concept of ego ideal.[31] As a "subsystem" of the ego, identity was held responsible for testing, selecting, and integrating the "self-representations derived from the psychosocial crises of childhood."[32] At the same time, identity has to be considered "more than the sum of the childhood identifications. It is the accrued experience of the ego's ability to integrate all identifications with the vicissitudes of the libido, with the aptitudes developed out of endowment, and with the opportunities offered in social roles."[33] In terms of the history of psychoanalysis, it had been too easy to ignore clinically the ego as "a selective, integrating, coherent and persistent agency central to personality function."[34] That inner synthesizer, silently organizing experience and guiding action, is what patients so often lack.

Here Erikson has drawn some implications for amending the principles he started out with; in contrast to some of his own earlier pronouncements, he now writes:

In psychoanalysis we repeat for our own encouragement (and as an argument against others) that human nature can best be studied in a state of partial breakdown or, at any rate, of marked conflict. . . . The ego, in the psychoanalytic sense of a guardian of inner continuity, insofar as it is in a pathological state is more or less inactivated; that is, it loses its capacity to organize personality and experience and to relate itself to other egos in mutual activation.[35]

Erikson has tried to argue that psychoanalysis's origins in psychopathology led it to describe positive states only in negative terms. To the extent that a sense of identity develops out of a gradual integration of all earlier identifications, "these processes are difficult to study in patients, because the neurotic self has, by definition, fallen prey to overidentifications. . . ." [36] The whole is different from the sum of its parts.

In conceding what so many early critics of psychoanalysis feared, Erikson does "not believe that we can entirely reconstruct the ego's normal functions from an understanding of its dysfunctions, nor that we can understand all vital conflict as neurotic conflict."[37] In psychoanalysis the experience of being a patient had come to be too central to its image of humanity; as Erikson noted,

some of us have inadvertently driven our children into an identification with our patients. At least, one little son of a psychiatrist recently expressed it in so many words; when this carefully and considerately brought up child was asked what he wanted to be when big and strong, he said, "A patient."[38]

Whatever the undoubted merits of Erikson's attempts to change the focus of traditional psychoanalytic thinking, the development of his ideas is consistent with some of the tensions in his own life; the subjective sources of his work will help explain both the strengths and the weaknesses of his key concepts. When he challenges the excessively mechanistic outlook of his predecessor Anna Freud, it is in keeping with his own original artistic nature. Yet one wonders how at the same time he can endorse the almost inhumanly abstract psychology of Heinz Hartmann.

Erikson has also maintained his continuity with a crucial strain in psychoanalysis that has emphasized the significance of the inner dimension of experience. A therapist, and most especially a psychoanalyst, has to work with the realities patients bring to the treatment setting. Although the past can never be undone, it can be reinterpreted; and although the present cannot be changed to match the heart's desire, conflicts in a patient's current life can be actively ameliorated. The future must remain unknown, but goals can be re-examined: Goethe once warned that young men should beware of their aspirations, for when they are old they will have attained them.

But Erikson's innovations are marred by his characteristic ambiguities. For in his effort to come to terms with the flux of experience he is overdoing the use (and meaning) of the word "sense"—sense of identity, sense of continuity, sense of leeway. Each of us may need to rely on at least some illusions, and some may develop elaborate myths about themselves. But there is still, however Erikson may avoid it, an important difference between truth and falsehood. A healthy ego needs not just a sense of mastery, but real mastery; and as we shall see, the critical difference between the two may determine whether or not the psychoanalytic concept of the ego is really able to bridge the gulf between the inner and outer worlds. We will want to question whether or not ego psychology need lead to a complacency which justifies the social status quo.

It may in fact be a sign of inadequacy for someone not to react to certain realities with pathology. Freud used to quote a saying of Lessing's: "A person who does not lose his reason under certain conditions can have no reason to lose." It is no sign of strength for an individual to need to deny or twist realities in order to shore up false continuities. In terms of

Erikson's own concepts of ego psychology, for instance, it would be out of ego weakness rather than repression that someone would need to evade his past.

Erikson's construction of an ego psychology can be an avenue to a fresh perspective on how we conceive of life. As psychoanalysis's model of human nature turns away from old-fashioned sufferers of neurotic complaints, trying to understand more normal functioning, it becomes possible to put clinical material in a new framework. What once might have been interpreted as evidence of the strength of human instinctuality can be looked at rather differently from an ego point of view. A symptom, for example, may represent a defense in behalf of identity formation: "What to the observer looks like an especially powerful manifestation of naked instinct is often only a desperate plea for the permission to synthesize and sublimate in the only way possible."[39] Erikson therefore sees ego identity as "the only safeguard against the *anarchy of drives* as well as the *autocracy* of conscience."[40]

Since he thinks that Freud's postulation of a primary destructive urge, the death instinct, represents an "essentially . . . philosophic" problem, Erikson minimizes Freud's mythology of primeval instincts, for example by interpreting rage as a response to a threatened loss of identity. Erikson even believes that "deprivation of identity . . . can lead to murder." Interference with an individual's identity can be responsible for opening "the floodgate of infantile urges."[41] Freud stressed the vicissitudes of instinctuality, the patterning of both sexual and aggressive urges. "But psychoanalysis has not charted the extent to which these drives . . . owe their intensity and exclusiveness to sudden depreciations of the ego and of material available as building stones for a future identity."[42]

To focus on ego capacities in contrast to instinctual urges does not necessarily mean a dryasdust conception of human nature devoid of impulses or feelings. Erikson is willing to assert that "in the social jungle of human existence, there is no feeling of being alive without a sense of ego identity."[43] In order to reach the feeling of being, as William James once put it, "most deeply and intensely active and alive," Erikson maintains that the ego needs not motionless rest but rather what James called "an element of active tension."[44] But Erikson's endorsement of the importance of the individual's search for the feeling of being "the real me" does contain an unspoken optimism about basic human nature. I am reminded of the report by a psychoanalyst who interviewed for treatment a former convict who had committed murder; when tactfully reassured by the therapist that it had not been the "real you" who committed the crime, the murderer said no, that was the terrible part, he had felt most like himself as he killed. (It may parenthetically be of interest that the analyst did not accept the patient for therapy.)

Erikson's ego psychology necessarily has had implications for the primary datum of psychoanalysis, the dream. According to Freud, dream images are to be interpreted primarily as expressive of warded-off instinctual wishes, whereas Erikson is apt instead to perceive them as symbols standing for threats to individual identity. From Erikson's point of view dreams can be looked at on the model of a regression in the service of the ego: "good sleep and effective dreaming are necessary conditions for the nightly restoration of the ego's active tension." The dream restores the vitality of essential ego functions: dreaming "must help us awake with a sense of wholeness, centrality, and competence—in other words, in an ego state of active tension." But then for Erikson the dream cannot be, as it remained for Freud, a model of psychosis; and Erikson has been led to wonder: "as long as the sleeper can thus relax, dream well, and wake ready for action, do we really have a right to say that his ego in the state of sleep was 'weak'?"[45]

Erikson has concluded that in the light of ego psychology other cherished views of Freud must be re-examined. Religion, for instance, ought not to be dismissed simply as a collective neurosis: "we all relive earlier and earliest stages of our existence in dreams, in artistic experience, and in religious devotion, only to emerge refreshed and invigorated."[46] Religions may confirm identity needs, providing a belief in immortality that overshadows the certainty of death. Rituals, through "re-enactment," may help transcend infantile curses; and for Erikson, in contrast to Freud, re-enactment can be a renewal, going "far beyond the dictates of a mere 'repetition compulsion' such as characterizes the unfreedom of symptoms and of irrational acts."[47]

As much as Erikson feels can be gained from his concept of ego identity, he has shied away from making it a static catchall for everything that might be humanly valuable. He has explicitly stated that "identity is by no means the highest and the last achievement of personality," and he has tried to counterpoint processes of identity formation with his concept of "negative identity" elements:

> We will call all self-images, even those of a highly idealistic nature, which are diametrically opposed to the dominant values of an individual's upbringing, parts of a *negative identity*—meaning an identity which he has been warned *not* to become, which he can become only with a divided heart, but which he nevertheless finds himself compelled to become, protesting his wholeheartedness.[48]

Fragments of an unconscious evil identity, the sum of everything we do not wish to resemble, are frequently an expression of images which a family has tried to avoid and suppress in its children. Members of oppressed minorities, for example, may find themselves compelled to identify with fragments of a society's negative identity.[49] But the more

Erikson commited himself to his ego psychological approach, the more he found it necessary to reconstruct not only psychoanalysis's attitude toward child development, instinct, dreaming, and religion, but, more broadly, its traditional view of social processes.

CHAPTER 3

Society

Erikson has called attention to the failure adequately "to integrate childhood and society"; in particular, he has pointed out the social naïveté of much clinical work: "in the traditional case history . . . the patient's residence, ethnic background, and occupation are the first items to be radically altered when it is necessary to disguise his personal identity. The essence of the inner dynamics of a case, it is judged, is thereby left intact."[1] Erikson believes that people not only have bodies, as Freud so notably insisted, but have egos as well and are, moreover, members of social organizations. Erikson has therefore explicitly tried to avoid the charge of "biologism" so often leveled against psychoanalytic thinkers. The inner developmental "laws" within an individual that Erikson had in mind are such that "create a succession of potentialities for significant interaction with those around him."[2] According to his conception of personality, it is impossible to abstract man from society: "the growing child must derive a vitalizing sense of reality from the awareness that his individual way of mastering experiences, his ego synthesis, is a successful variant of a group identity and is in accord with its space-time and life plan."[3]

Erikson's concept of ego identity, that sense of coherent individuality which represents man's capacity to unify his conflicts adaptively, is intended to be ineluctably social. (Increasingly Erikson has talked in terms of "psychosocial" identity, rather than the more isolated-sounding ego identity.) He has long believed that "only through a meaningful development of his individual childhood in line with one of the major trends of history can an individual find his ego identity. . . ."[4] By the same token, the loss of a sense of identity is marked by the absence of a feeling "of sameness and of continuity and the belief in one's social role."[5]

Earlier psychoanalytic thinking was unable to understand the concept of identity because, according to Erikson, of the inadequacies of its approach to the environment. The difficulty was that "psychoanalysis had, at first, little to say about the way in which the ego's synthesis grows—or fails to grow—out of the soil of social organization."[6] To isolate psychological drives, especially of an instinctual nature, can lead to a false dichotomy between the individual and society; and Erikson has regretted how "the so-called basic biological orientation of psychoanalysis has, it seems, gradually become (out of mere habituation) a kind of pseudo-biology, and this especially in the conceptualization of man's 'environment.' "[7]

It cannot be successfully argued that Freud ignored environmental considerations, for after all he was a leading critic of his era's sexual hypocrisy. When Freud talked about culture he often attacked society, seeing it primarily in terms of an unnecessary body of taboos; at the same time, however, he tended to assume the advantages of many civilized restraints. According to Erikson, "Freud stood for the primacy of insight, but he took state and civilization for granted. . . ."; but, when pressed, Freud would say that society necessarily supressed the individual—both sexually and intellectually.[8] It is largely for these reasons that Erikson has held that "the greatest difficulty in the path of psychoanalysis as a general psychology probably consists in the remnants of its first conceptualization of the environment as an 'outer world.' "[9]

When Freud did discuss the psychological links between the individual and society, for example in his concept of the superego, he regarded society as a "foreign burden . . . imposed on the ego." In Erikson's view of Freud's attitude toward society, "psychoanalysis came to emphasize the individual and regressive rather than the collective-supportive aspects. . . . It was concerned with only half the story." Erikson has not been content, as have many analysts since Freud's death, with "patronizing tributes to the existence of 'social factors.' "[10] In order to correct the imbalance in earlier psychoanalytic thinking, Erikson has tried, for example, to study "those adaptive social processes that must protect and support ego development in childhood and give strength and direction to adolescent identity."[11]

For Erikson, society guides and narrows the individual's choices, as it confirms members in "the right life plan."[12] The development of a young individual's positive identity depends on support from significant social groups. Erikson feels at odds with the earlier psychoanalytic outlook on society: "Instead of emphasizing what social organization denies the child, we wish to clarify what it may first grant to the infant, as it keeps him alive and as, in administering to his needs in a specific way, it seduces him to its particular life style."[13] Erikson has even discussed the way in which we may repress the need for such ego support: "infantile wishes to belong to and believe in organizations providing for collective reassurance against individual anxiety, in our intellectuals, easily join other repressed childhood temptations—and force their way into dreams." For some, like Freud, to acknowledge any dependence on social structure for our wellbeing seems to have been "experienced as a reflection on some kind of intellectual autonomy."[14]

Analysts since Freud's death who have tried to use his techniques in a wider variety of clinical settings than he would have deemed appropriate for psychotherapeutic influence have written of the need to expand the scope of psychoanalysis. Erikson in particular has called for a widening of social horizons: "societies lighten the inescapable conflicts of childhood with a promise of some security, identity, and integrity. In thus reinforcing the values by which the human ego exists societies create the only condition under which human growth is possible."[15] For Erikson nothing human can be secure in its psychological beginnings "unless it is verified in the intimate meeting of partners in favorable social settings."[16] Social organization, then, becomes a constructive necessity in the individual's development: "the ego can only remain strong in interaction with cultural institutions and can also only remain strong when the child's inborn capacities and potentials are developed."[17]

Erikson has therefore looked for social sources of ego strength. The environmental basis for individual wholeness may be a class, a nation, a culture, or a combination of these: "social institutions seem to provide the individual with continuing collective reassurances in regard to such anxieties as have accrued from his infantile past."[18] Yet Erikson does not emphasize here how often reinforcements that may be beneficial in terms of the internal dynamics of the individual are at the same time socially harmful and noxious: one has only to think of the positive role many racist institutions play in overcoming individual guilt and anxiety.* It has become a basic principle of Erikson's approach that ego strength depends on the support first of familial and then of social models.

Perhaps the most striking contrast between Erikson and Freud in their respective attitudes toward society comes in their characteristic treatment of religion. Freud saw religious beliefs as a superstitious remnant of man's infantile past, and he condemned such illusions on the ground that reality was in the long run the only safe recourse. It would not be going too far to say that Freud regarded psychoanalysis as a rival way of interpreting phenomena on which religion had once possessed a monopoly. Erikson, however, does not share Freud's utopian faith in what man might be like without religion. First of all, as a psychopathologist Erikson "cannot avoid observing that there are millions of people who cannot really afford to be without religion, and whose pride in not having it is that much whistling in the dark." More positively, "religion through the centuries has served to restore a sense of trust at regular intervals in the form of faith while giving tangible form to a sense of evil which it promises to ban." [19] (Once again, Erikson theorizes as a therapist: it is the "sense" of evil, not evil itself, which he is concerned that religion cope with.) According to Erikson, and here he is implicitly challenging Freud, "he who believes he can do without religion obligates himself to a new accounting for very basic human needs." [20]

Erikson realizes that organized religions have lived off mass infantilizations, and he acknowledges how "much cruel, cold, and exclusive totalness has dominated some phases of the history of religion." [21] He even concedes that Freud "has convincingly demonstrated the affinity of some religious ways of thought with those of neurosis," but he insists that

* For Erikson's later treatment of this matter under the heading of "pseudo-speciation," see Ch. 10, pp. 160–62.

we not use clinical terms to characterize group irrationalities.[22] It is Erikson's conviction that, partly as a result of ritual regimentation, religion serves a crucial function in that it "restores . . . a new sense of wholeness, of things rebound."[23]

Erikson's respect for religion does not entail complete social Pollyannaism. He has noted the existence of "ego-damaging social pathology," and observed the peculiar way in which collective supports may allow "the obedient adherent . . . [to] feel totally good as a member of a nation, a race, or a class blessed by history."[24] But he has been more cautious than some in applying diagnostic labels to society: "One can speak . . . of 'sick' institutions, but only as long as one specifies the adaptive mechanisms which have bogged down in mere repetitiveness; and as long as one does not indulge in the assumption that psychiatric enlightenment as such will heal society." Unlike so many who use terms for madness interchangeably, Erikson has pointed out "the systematic differences between the inner state of insane individuals and the social conditions conducive to mass irrationality."[25]

Erikson has chosen to expand upon what he takes to be one of Freud's fundamental insights, the conviction that "human childhood provides a most fundamental basis for human exploitation."[26] But according to Erikson it was only in the course of his clinical work, when he "found social interpretations inescapable," that he "slowly became aware of the depth and cruelty" of American social conflicts.[27] He has written that

should a child feel that the environment tried to deprive him too radically of all the forms of expression which permit him to develop and to integrate the next step of his identity, he will defend it with the astonishing strength encountered in animals who are suddenly forced to defend their lives.[28]

On the basis of his own experience Erikson believes that it is possible for insightful clinicians to discern in historically dominant neuroses shifts in psychosocial processes. Underlying that search would be the hope that such social understanding will ultimately aid therapy.[29]

Erikson's optimism may have been encouraged by his emigration to America and the heightened perspective it gave him on the role played by social variables in personality development. The impact of his own removal from European culture was further magnified by his willingness to expand his clinical awareness through anthropological field work. It had been one of the cardinal features of the Freudian system to aim for introspective truth in behalf of self-enlightenment, with the understanding that major differences in cultural varieties were merely "surface" (superficial) matters, epiphenomenal as compared to the individual's "depths."[30] Freud insisted on psychological unity; for him, national character studies retained their late-nineteenth-century racist connotations. (Though he did not deny his Jewishness, Freud, it could be said, was trying to escape from doctrines of cultural separateness.[31])

As Erikson remembered his field work, "I set out to study and compare two American Indian tribes at a time when it was still fashionable to liken collective 'primitive' idiosyncrasies to the 'neurotic' symptoms of 'civilized' individuals like you and me."[32] (Such views were still fashionable mainly in psychoanalytic writings; modern anthropology was already being emancipated from ethnocentrism.) In time Erikson had to qualify the dictum which looked for similarities to neurosis in the nonliterate: "it is not the 'savage' in his unified and communal world who resembles our neurotics, but rather modern neurotics who, in their failure to master discrepancies in their environment and in their values, become lonely caricatures of our primitive ancestors." On the other hand, Erikson does not seem ready to accept his departure from the earlier psychoanalytic view of the relationship between the neurotic and the "savage," for he continues: "That is, neurotic symptoms are not only partial regressions to infantile stages, in ontogeny, they are also diffuse retrogressions to mental and emotional mechanisms belonging to mankind's more magic and homogeneous past."[33] Still, Erikson's interest in the ego had accompanied a new appreciation of social forces, and led to at least a qualified denial of the equivalence of neurosis and so-called primitivity: "the study of the ego—and that is, to me, the study of the interdependence of inner and social organization—must as yet determine the function of magic thinking in different human states."[34]

The field work Erikson undertook in the 1930s was with two American Indian minority groups, the Sioux in South Dakota and the Yuroks in California. He sought to understand the social tragedy of race relations, in the hope of attaining "some simplified demonstration of the laws man lives by." Inevitably Erikson carried over his clinical approach to his new area of inquiry. He wrote about one informant as he would of a patient: an internal contradiction in a story was understood by Erikson as a confession. In the end he found that, as in other instances of social victimization, those whose communal integrity had been destroyed ended by identifying "with the very destroyer himself."[35] (Here he was following the concept of identification with the aggressor initiated by Anna Freud.)

In the relatively homogeneous culture of the Sioux, Erikson traced the sources of the prevalent apathy, passivity, and depression to the loss of a group identity. The Sioux had originally been buffalo hunters, and the distant past remained a powerful psychological reality in what remained of their identity. According to Erikson's observations, "it becomes inescapably clear only in puberty that what initiative has been salvaged will not find an identity. Emotional withdrawal and general absenteeism are the results."[36] The future for the Sioux seemed "empty except for dreams of *restoration*," and in the face of the white man's recent efforts at reform "the passive fortitude of Indian children seemed as infuriating as it was incomprehensible."[37] Confronted with both traditional generosity and truancy, "the administrator and teacher cannot possibly know when they are dealing with an old virtue, when with a new vice."[38]

In the culture of the Sioux, property was disregarded and competition avoided. Such values could not persist without institutional support: "the cultural demand for generosity received its early foundation from the privilege of enjoying the nourishment and reassurance emanating from unlimited breast-feeding." But since the conquest by the white man "the integrative mechanisms of child training have not been encouraged to sustain a new promising system of significant social roles, as they had done once before when the Dakota became buffalo hunters." The Sioux girl was still socialized to be a helper and mother for a future hunter. As a result of the discontinuities between past and present, the weakest human tie seemed "to be that between the children and their fathers, who cannot teach them anything and who . . . have become models to be avoided."[39]

The world image of the Yuroks was quite different from that of the Sioux; they exhibited "folkways of stinginess, suspicion, and anger," and "the acquisition and retention of possessions is and was what the Yurok thinks about, talks about, and prays for." In both cultural instances, however, Erikson shied away from committing himself to anything as seemingly changeless as "their respective 'basic character structures.' Rather, we have concentrated on the configurations with which these two tribes try to synthesize their concepts and their ideals in a coherent design for living." [40] Erikson did his field work in the heyday of the culture and personality approach in anthropology. He therefore tried to show how cultural values infused and gave meaning to particular elements in child training: "the training methods and the systems of education in various cultures," Erikson concluded, "are not senseless instruments of chastisment and exploitation, as was often assumed in early psychoanalysis. . . ." [41] Values cannot endure unless they work. [42] "Good" was "whatever seemed 'virtuous' in a 'strong' man or woman in that culture," [43] and this perspective eventually contributed to Erikson's later elaboration of the basic human strengths of the life cycle.

As Erikson pondered cultural varieties, and gained more distance from his own particular psychoanalytic training, he was forced to conclude that a clinical concept of human nature demands historical self-awareness. He began to wonder about the social determinants of psychoanalysis's concepts. Psychoanalysis has been, in his view, "always in danger of becoming part of the disease it meant to cure. . . ." Psychoanalysts may have started out as an underground movement, but they not only survived the Nazi holocaust but "succeeded in establishing power spheres in the cities of their choice." [44] And Erikson has been aware that "psychoanalytic power under certain historical conditions can corrupt as much as any other power. . . ." [45]

If psychoanalysis has been used as "a tool of history," Erikson has, with his penchant for playing with words, also proposed that psychoanalysis be used as "a historical tool." [46] He has assigned to it a role "for the detection of that aspect of the total image of man which in a given historical period is being neglected or exploited, repressed or suppressed by the prevailing technology or ideology—including hasty 'psychoanalytic' ideologies." [47] Erikson has also looked for the creation of "a psychoanalytic critique of society," while fearing the danger of "falling back into mystical or moralistic philosophizing." [48] He has even gone so far as to suggest that "maybe it is time to study political sequences as psychological continuities rather than as accidental fatalities," [49] as if those were the only alternatives available.

But despite such a suggestion, fully in accord with Freud's most grandiose hopes, Erikson has shifted from early psychoanalysis's interest in resistances stemming from the individual unconscious to the social sources of self-deception; the earlier view can itself be considered a resistance: "partial acceptance of painful unconscious determinants of human failure and [the] . . . emphasis on individual treatment even where the patient seemed anything but introspective and verbal can . . . be seen as a widespread resistance against the awareness of a failure of social mechanisms under radically changing historical determinants." [50] Erikson believes that there are now "resistances" against acknowledging the existence of social symptoms arising out of specific historical sources. [51] He even goes so far as to maintain that a therapeutic interpretation of a religious pattern, for example, can be "as violently resisted as an id content." [52]

Erikson has noted the influence on his own early work of the political and social climate of New Deal America: "my first book was written during the Roosevelt era, when the whole American enterprise, foreign and domestic, seemed to be going in . . . an antitotalitarian and antiracist direction, especially in the eyes of a recent immigrant." People like him could not forget the menace of Hitler, and therefore would "never be able to use the word 'fascism' as casually as it is sometimes used in radical circles today." Somehow, partly because FDR was President when Erikson came to America, he argues that "it certainly would never have occurred to me at the time of my immigration as a refugee from European fascism to suspect any fascist potential in the American system." [53]

Yet others of Erikson's refugee contemporaries did not share his blinders. It is not necessary to adopt Freud's own prejudices about America to justify a rational concern for potential trouble in American power. The failure of Erikson's insight here may be a signal to look for some conservative trends in his psychology. Erikson had started out as an artist, leading "an anti-Establishment way of life." [54] During the period of Senator Joseph McCarthy's power in the United States, when the junior senator from Wisconsin had, as Erikson remembered it, "succeeded in creating in almost all Americans a fear of radical thinking. . . . ," Erikson played an untarnished part in a University of California loyalty oath controversy: he was fired in his first year of teaching, and then "reinstated as politically dependable," but he resigned "because of the firing of others who were not so judged." [55]

Though Erikson in 1960 accepted a prestigious professorship at Harvard, his feeling that he lacked "the usual credentials" [56] for academic life seemed to deprive him of the necessary distance from the status quo. For example, in reflecting on a partisan report about Negro family life, Erikson could naïvely observe: "whatever the methods employed, Patrick Moynihan's intentions could not be doubted." [57] Out of his concern that radical historical change may pose "the threat of a traumatic loss of ego identity," Erikson has stressed, like many earlier conservative thinkers, the "costly" side of revolutions.[58]

Erikson's whole ego approach might well have disturbing conformist implications. On clinical grounds, for example, he has claimed "the necessity for a new unity of the outer . . . environment and the identity needs of man." [59] His emphasis on the need for an identity confirmed by social institutions may give undue weight to conformist values: "the conscious feeling of having a *personal identity* is based on two simultaneous observations: the immediate perception of one's self-

sameness and continuity in time; and the simultaneous perception of the fact that others recognize one's sameness and
continuity." [60]

But does the individual derive no advantages whatsoever
from personal discontinuities, if not outright alienation? Indeed, how much creative work could ever go on if society's
recognition is always demanded or expected? To be at one
with oneself, must one necessarily, as Erikson thinks, have at
the same time "a sense of affinity with a community's sense
of being at one with its future as well as its history—or mythology"? [61] If, as Erikson proposes, "a sense of identity implies
that one experiences an over-all sameness and continuity extending from the personal past . . . into a tangible future;
and from the community's past . . . into foreseeable and
imaginable realities of work accomplishment and role satisfaction," [62] then there may be disadvantages to having a
secure sense of self. Géza Roheim, an early analyst with
anthropological experience, was perhaps the first to point out
that Erikson's approach contained the seeds of conformism:
"Roheim objected strenuously to Erikson's softening of
Freud's critical terminology. . . . 'Some anthropologists and
evidently also Erikson seem to think that whatever a "culture" demands must be "good" and the main thing is "cultural synthesis." ' " [63]

On clinical grounds there may be good reason to entertain
Erikson's view of the uses of society, as opposed to the early
Freudian negativism. (To Freud positive social feelings
were basically homosexual in nature.[64]) Erikson holds that
"ultimately, children become neurotic not from frustration,
but from the lack or loss of societal meaning in these frustra-
tions." [65] But in a broader perspective one has to question
whether he has not put too much trust in the benign functions of the social order.

In particular, the value and function of continuities merit

critical examination. For what if the price of social sameness has to be self-deception and evasion? Let us look at some twentieth-century cultural myths that have unsavory connotations. The "stab in the back" legend helped bring Hitler to power. And then later in Germany the Adenauer regime relied on myth to deny that Hitler had been supported by most Germans; the country may have thereby been helped to recover from its terrible past, but it was at the expense of letting war criminals go unprosecuted. In the Soviet Union, Nikita Khrushchev was able to pretend that Stalinism was merely the consequence of the "cult of personality."[66] (According to a counterculture legend, someone is supposed to have been brave enough to shout during his Twentieth Party Congress speech: "Where were you?") Finally, many Americans today like to pretend that their politics have degenerated in the second half of the twentieth century—as if a nobler group of politicians once regularly governed. It may be useful to appeal to the finest elements in any political tradition, but one wonders how desirable in the long run such distortions of the past will be.

One can concede the utility of at least some social mythology. However much we might like to believe ourselves to be freethinkers, obviously if all possible social options had to be considered in every case, the result would be anarchy. It may help ensure stability, for instance, when the U.S. Supreme Court uses legal interpretations to pretend that the country is still living under the intentions of the constitutional document framed by the Founding Fathers, or that the authors of the Fourteenth Amendment really meant what it is now said to imply. But Erikson does not want to examine the costs of any such mythifications. Illusions, however, are not necessarily socially valuable, any more than they are in private life.

But Erikson has recently, in the vein of a conservative thinker like Edmund Burke, talked about the "genius of culture," as though all cultures were equally worthy of praise: "to fathom the genius of culture it is necessary to trace the implanting of the dominant value system into each newborn member of a primitive community. . . ." Again, in reflecting on his anthropological field work, Erikson claims that "one must acknowledge a certain genius in the cultural assimilation to each other of somatic, social, and personal patterns and in the creation of a communal identity which, in turn, is indispensable to any individual identity."[67] It is doubtful whether anyone even minimally at odds with his own culture could be happy with Erikson's recent statement that "man's higher self receives meaning from, as it gives meaning to, the elite of his polity. . . ."[68]

Erikson has, however, explicitly approved of Freud's objection to psychoanalysis becoming a "glorification of 'adjustment.' "[69] Erikson insists that "psychoanalysis will have to go beyond adapting individuals to the status quo. . . ." [70] But when he writes that "identity awareness may have to do with matters of an *inner emancipation* from a more dominant identity. . . .," one uneasily recalls Hannah Arendt's ironic denunciation of those Germans after World War II who reported their prior "inward" opposition to Hitler's regime.[71] Erikson does acknowledge that too often psychoanalysis "has let itself be drawn into modern attempts to neutralize powerful inner and outer forces by making man more superficially and more mechanically adjustable."[72] But whatever the danger that it might lend itself to "such vain streamlining of existence," for Erikson psychoanalysis "in its origin and essence . . . intends to *free* man for 'ultimate concerns.' "[73]

Erikson has also tried to stress the urgency of adapting the social environment to fit human needs. One of the misconceptions about his identity concept, he believes, is to think that "a sense of identity is achieved primarily through the individual's complete surrender to given social roles and through his unconditional adaptation to the demands of social change."[74] Yet a critic would not have to have in mind such "complete" surrender, or such "unconditional" adaptation, in order to be entitled to be uncomfortable. Erikson tries to confine his argument to the dependence of ego development on social models; and he insists that health consists in altering pre-existing social forms to fit new needs, and it is thus that he thinks that society gets kept alive.

But instead of highlighting tension, Erikson has concentrated on describing the integrative relationship between the individual and his society. True, he does argue that "we, the adjusted, repress in ourselves our worst potentials and our best, in order not to endanger our adjustment," and he has lamented "excessive and irrational conformity," as well as the "increasing demand for conformity, uniformity, and standardization which characterizes the present stage of this, our 'individualistic' civilization."[75] Yet he remains characteristically ambivalent: "even as we must refuse to be technicians of adjustment, we should abjure being the harbingers of maladaption," [76] as if such so-called neutrality did not have conservative implications all its own.

In some of what Erikson has written about America he has accepted Cold War mythology. It is not so much that as late as 1959 he was still writing about the Russians as "our adversaries," and that in 1963 he thought "they are our cold, our dangerous adversaries today."[77] More importantly, in speculating how American family life can be said to train its children for democracy, Erikson uses his psychology for the sake of buttressing political ideology; speaking in the conventional piety of post-World War II America, he found in the American family

an automatic prevention of autocracy and inequality. It breeds, on the whole, undogmatic people, people ready to drive a bargain and then to compromise. It makes complete irresponsibility impossible, and it makes open hate and warfare in families rare. It also makes it quite impossible for the American adolescent to become what his brothers and sisters in other large countries become so easily, uncompromising ideologists. Nobody can be sure he is right, but everybody must compromise—for the sake of his future chance. The analogy here to the two-party system is clear. . . .[78]

It is especially remarkable how Erikson, in writing about the impossibility of "complete irresponsibility," can so readily forget America's destruction of its Indians. Can Erikson really prefer American adolescents to what he sees as the "uncompromising ideologists" of other large countries? Even as late as 1971, in his conversation with the Black Panther leader Huey Newton, Erikson was naïve enough to ask, at the end of their talks: "Huey, what do you think of the two-party system?" [79]

Erikson has admired America's "strangely adolescent style of adulthood—that is, one remaining expansively open for new roles and stances. . . ." [80] As an immigrant he accepted too uncritically America's hopes for itself. To him, in the United States, "historically . . . the 'self-made' idea and the technocratic vision fused into an idealized image of a man who almost literally made himself, created himself, manufactured himself, invented himself." Erikson allows himself to be so carried away here as to even speak of someone's "choice of parents." [81] It should go almost without saying that no one ever gets to choose his own parents. Erikson's wishing away of the inevitable coerciveness of family life appropriately comes up in the context of his idealization of America, and is a part of his personal history.*

To be sure, Erikson does not believe that the American was ever in reality self-made: "I am talking about the *image* he had of himself and the way that image fed into his ideal

---

* For a discussion of Erikson's biography, see Ch. 6, pp. 93–101.

identity." [82] But he does not seem to realize that he has been taken in by propaganda, and how close his psychology comes to adding to the pervasiveness of public-relations image-consciousness. It takes a parochial perspective of world history and geography to ask:

> Is there any other country which continues to ask itself not only "What will we produce and sell next?" but ever-again, "Who are we anyway?" which may well explain this country's hospitality to such concepts as the identity crisis, which, for better or worse, now seem almost native to it. [83]

American mythology took a beating in the course of the war in Southeast Asia. Yet Erikson, throughout the Vietnamese disaster, remained publicly silent and aloof from the antiwar movement. Even as late as in an essay reprinted in 1975, Erikson allows himself to refer to difficulties with only "what seemed to be a senseless war." [84]

The chief source of Erikson's admiration for America lay not in its specific commitments to civil liberties, but in its myth of respect for human freedom. He has, however, commented on some of the less attractive features of a culture officially dedicated to choice; for example, "it was the fear of becoming too old to choose which gave old age and death a bad name in this country." Whatever its ideals, Erikson has sometimes also observed the presence of "autocratic trends in this country and in any other land." In particular, he has regretted the characteristic American tendency to "make 'functioning' itself a value above all other values." [85] He may balk at referring to this century's American "Empire," but it is because he "would rather call America a World Technocracy which imports to her world markets also a technocratic identity." [86]

Machines, as many others have pointed out, have acquired a life of their own, and "far from remaining an extension of the body, destine whole classes to become extensions of machinery. . . ." [87] In Erikson's view of the Western world it is to be regretted how the tendency to unconsciously identify with machinery has influenced our concept of humanity. But in his opinion these less admirable features of modern society have, paradoxically, been responsible in particular for the well-known success of Freud's ideas in America: psychoanalysis "promised to the self-made man a tool to remake in himself what he had brought along by dint of his origins . . . psychoanalysis seemed to promise more efficient self-management. . . ." [88]

In his ability to see how such apparent opposites—introspective psychology and mechanistic conformism—can go hand in hand, Erikson was a true representative of the depth-psychology tradition. It was precisely in order to avoid too flat and uniform an account of national "character" that Erikson preferred to talk in terms of elements of national identity. In the case of the United States, for example, he argued that the dominant identity left the blacks "the most 'opposite' group in this self-made business, not only because they didn't come over here of their own free will but also because their color marked them as a most recognizable 'other' species." [89] The experience of the Negro was exceptionally painful precisely because of the discrepancy between the dominant American values and the restricted opportunities to share in them. Any group sense of identity is bound to have its "unconscious evil identity (that which the ego is most afraid to resemble) . . . composed of the images of the violated (castrated) body, the ethnic outgroups and the exploited minority." [90] In a do-it-yourself culture, "otherness would be characterized by an inability . . . to help *oneself*. . . ." [91] Social oppression gets internalized in the oppressed to the extent that "the suppressed, excluded, and exploited unconsciously believe in the evil image which they are made to represent by those who are dominant." [92]

Such a process of self-inflicted damage can, according to Erikson, help account for Hitler's success in Germany. For, to Erikson, Hitler embodied the German negative identity: "Everything that the world had always criticized as 'German,' the Nazis made to appear positive and pretended that it was what they really wanted to be." [93] However complacent Erikson may sometimes be in his description of normal psychology, in practice he—unlike some others—refused to stick pathological labels on Hitler. It would be reassuring to stigmatize Hitler as abnormal, instead of seeing him as a representative of a universal human potential for evil. Of much of the psychiatric terminology applied to Hitler, Erikson concedes that "at times, he undoubtedly was all of that. But, unfortunately, he was something over and above it all. His capacity for acting and for creating action was so rare that it seems inexpedient to apply ordinary diagnostic methods to his words." [94] But Erikson was evidently aware of claims that Hitler sought psychoanalytic treatment for individual symptoms. [95]

Erikson's treatment of the Hitler phenomenon, however, involves him in social fatuousness. For in raising the question why Hitler failed, Erikson asks: is "his failure the only evidence for the argument that he was bad? I'm sure some Germans today still feel that his only mistake was that his plans didn't work." Instead of rejecting such nefarious pragmatism root and branch, Erikson proceeds to restate the view of "some" Germans within his own psychological terms. For he doubts whether Hitler's plans could possibly have worked: "I think there was really no possibility for their fulfillment in long-range actuality. I do not think that his ideas ever had a chance to activate a future." [96] However valuable Erikson's social revisions in traditional psychoanalysis, in an examination of the implications of his position we can not ignore certain striking weaknesses in his approach.

CHAPTER 4

Post-Freudianism

Psychoanalysis succeeded as a profession in providing, according to Erikson's terminology, multiple opportunities for fulfilling individual identities. But as he itemizes the various elements that fused into the new identity of the psychoanalyst, one wonders if he is not being critical of his field: they were "identities based on talmudic argument, on messianic zeal, on punitive orthodoxy, on faddist sensationalism, on professional and social ambition."[1] Many have observed that the majority of analysts, whose task Freud thought was enlightenment, have been Jews; and in describing the unconscious conflicts in people of Jewish background, Erikson noted how the new "Letter may have become political or scientific dogma (socialism, Zionism, psychoanalysis) quite removed from the dogma of the Talmud, yet quoted and argued in a way not unlike the disputation of passages from the Talmud in the tradition of their ancestors. . . ."[2] (It is of interest that when he first published this passage,[3] he did not include the illustration of "socialism, Zionism, psychoanalysis"; he inserted the parenthetical words thirteen years later, which may suggest how his views have changed, or how he has grown more outspoken.)

Erikson, like others, has noted the way psychoanalysis has become a surrogate religion. He compares the training of an analyst to the novitiate of a monk: psychoanalysis has, he believes, "its monkhood, its monkishness, and its monkery."[4] He has seen how a supposedly scientific creed is capable of being transformed into an ideology. He has drawn attention to "a new form of dogmatic and ritual association (the psychoanalytic technique, the 'psychoanalytic movement,' and psychoanalytic institutes)" and "the common dogmatic conspiracy of calling only that real which happens to fit into a past ideological state of the theory or into a particular local or regional trend in the political organization of psychoanalysis itself."[5] And he believes that psychoanalysis, like any other method of investigation, "can serve the drive for power and the need for a sharp if seemingly unbloody weapon."[6]

In considering the hidden biases in psychoanalysis, Erikson suspects that any "special method bares truths especially true under the circumstances created by the method...." He is here tactfully suggesting that one should beware of generalizing about material that comes out of "the venting in free association of hidden resentments and repressed traumata."[7] He considers it unfortunate that clinical evidence has been "increasingly" used to confirm Freud's original theories, which has led to "a gradual estrangement between theory and clinical observation."[8] Erikson would like to think that these difficulties with psychoanalytic evidence are new ones. He is aware, though, that this problem has always been complicated by the therapeutic aim of the practitioner. In psychoanalysis the earliest work was done by clinicians who were trying to understand and relieve suffering. Erikson would therefore limit the situation of analyst and patient to being "merely a model of 'competent' behavior considering the subject matter it must deal with." [9]

Erikson has sometimes expressed the view that since psychoanalysis originated as a form of therapy, its theories can be of only limited usefulness for an understanding of normal psychology: "the cumulative experience of being and becoming a man or a woman cannot, I believe, be entirely dependent upon fearful analogies and fantasies." [10] Furthermore, despite the psychoanalytic goal of enlightenment, Freud's influence has often led to fatalistic attitudes toward the ontogenetic past. Even since the growth of ego psychology, it is still true that "psychoanalytic theory is heavily weighed in favor of insights which make dysfunction plausible and explain why human beings, at certain critical stages, should fail, and fail in specific ways." [11]

Yet Erikson remains hopeful that psychoanalytic "theory will eventually make adequate or superior human functioning dynamically plausible as well." [12] As part of his initial effort to minimize the extent of Freud's collaboration with Bullitt on their controversial book about Woodrow Wilson, Erikson tried to refute what he suspects is the widespread view that Freud would knowingly use his concepts to belittle a person, and he has repudiated what he considers the "totally un-Freudian bias" of the book, which caused "the 'facts' reported consistently to disintegrate into a petty denigration of the man under study." [13]

Despite his efforts to defend Freud, Erikson concedes that clinically he is apt to perceive as "fluidity" what might once have been deemed pathology. [14] It is perhaps an inevitable misfortune that "psychiatric thinking sees the world so full of dangers that it is hard to relax one's caution." [15] Erikson has instead emphasized the recuperative capacities of the ego, and dwelt on instances of individuals who recovered from psychic distress. From the point of view of ego psychology, "what under prejudiced scrutiny may appear to be the onset of a neurosis often is only an aggravated crisis which might prove self-liquidating and even, in fact, contribute to the process of identity formation." [16]

Erikson has taken exception to some of Freud's imagery, which helped lead many to see the individual as the plaything of unconscious drives: "Man is not organized like an archeological mound, in layers; as he grows he makes the past part of all future, and every environment, as he once experienced it, part of the present environment." [17] In contrast to Freud's insistence on the way the past persists unaltered in the present, Erikson has described how the individual can transform his previous experiences by a process of organic growth: "in any healthy change the fresh opportunities of the new relationship will outweigh the repetitious insistence on old disappointments." [18] An affirmative mood pervades Erikson's writings.

He now thinks that in the early days of analysis "regressive pulls in human life were then much more emphasized than what pulls a child out of the past, out of the family and out to wider experiences." [19] And, as a matter of therapeutic technique, he holds that "we must do our best to overcome clinical habits which make us assume that we have done our part if we have clarified the past." [20] In keeping with his attempt to counteract the negativism of early psychoanalysis, he has focused on "what, in man's total existence, leads *outward* from self-centredness to the mutuality of love and communality, *forward* from the enslaving past to the utopian anticipation of new potentialities, and *upward* from the unconscious to the enigma of consciousness." [21] But one must ask how much success his ideas have had clinically; for often when he attributes a point of view to early psychoanalysis, it would still as a matter of practice be endorsed by many analysts today.

As we noted in our discussion of Erikson's ego concepts, his approach entails a special perspective on dreaming. For Freud each dream could be considered a miniature psychosis. Erikson still believes that dreams can be conceived as "the most sensitive indicators of an individual's continuing struggles with earlier crises. . . ." [22] But while conceding that structurally a dream corresponds to a neurotic symptom, he points out that dreams have a recuperative function, since dreaming itself is both healthy and necessary. Although he accepts the regressive component in dreams, Erikson believes that any successful dream leads forward as well. But it would be hard to reconcile Freud's position, and his general distrust of the nonrational, with Erikson's view that dreams are "those gifts of nature which permit us to commune with our unconscious and emerge clear-eyed." [23]

For Erikson dream interpretations represent a "multidimensional task" which is to be approached "not by an immediate attempt at 'going deeper' than Freud did, but, on the contrary, by taking a fresh look at the whole of the manifest dream." Erikson regrets that so many in psychoanalysis "mistake attention to surface for superficiality, and a concern with form for lack of depth." Although Freud would not have taken the manifest content of dreams as seriously as Erikson proposes, Freud could have conceded that suggestion can play a role in the composition of a dream: "different schools of dynamic psychology and . . . different analysts," Erikson writes, "manage to provoke systematically different manifest dreams, obviously dreamed to please and to impress the respective analysts. . . ." [24]

Erikson has naturally looked at dreaming within his own categories. Dreams should be understood with psychosocial interpretive purposes in mind, and not just from the perspective of psychosexuality; just as, according to Freud, a dream can be taken to represent a regression to earlier stages in libidinal development, so can it be understood as retracing various steps in psychosocial development.[25] Not wholly content with Freud's theory of dreams as wish fulfillments, Erikson believes that broader needs have to be taken into account to arrive at satisfactory generalizations. As he put it in discussing one of Freud's own dreams, "what Freud first demonstrated in reporting this dream was the power of the infantile wish over the inner life of the adult." But Erikson has had society in mind, and he claims that Freud failed to "take account of the alignment of the dream's wish-fulfillment with the actuality of the dreamer's total life space." [26]

Of another of Freud's dreams Erikson writes in the kind of teleological terms which Freud had tried to combat: "this dream may reveal more than the basic fact of a disguised fulfillment derived from infantile sources; . . . this dream may . . . carry the historical burden of being dreamed in order to be analyzed, and analyzed in order to fulfill a very special fate." In contrast to Freud's id orientation, Erikson holds that the ego, by returning the dreamer to securities once available in childhood, helps to ensure successful dreaming and restful sleep. More generally then, for Erikson dreams "not only fulfill naked wishes of sexual license, of unlimited dominance and of unrestricted destructiveness; where they work, they also lift the dreamer's isolation, appease his conscience, and preserve his identity, each in specific and instructive ways." [27]

Part of what Erikson has tried to accomplish has been purely terminological. Thus "fixation" sounds too fatalistic to Erikson, who would prefer to talk in terms of a "point of arrest." [28] The technical term "object," used by analysts to describe a loved one, seems to him "unfortunate" [29] and doubtless it does have too cold a ring. When it comes to Freud's postulation of an oral phase, Erikson would substitute "incorporative"; instead of anality Erikson hypothesizes "autonomy"; and conflicts over "initiative" and "guilt" can encompass the Oedipus complex. Erikson therefore speaks of having restated Freud's theory of infantile sexuality.[30] Through his psychosocial terms Erikson hopes to have humanized the so-called biologism of much Freudian theory.[31]

But Erikson's shift in terminology also implies a change in orientation. He once wrote: "I could begin to repay my debt to the Freuds . . . only in my own currency." [32] (Yet his imagery reflects his ambivalences; he himself has stressed the low fee for which he was analyzed.) There is often a vagueness, even a woolliness, to Erikson's writings, which seems in part calculated to protect a mythic continuity with Freud. Even in the midst of Erikson's attempts at innovations, he pauses to note that "all of this . . . seemed to me always implicit in Freud's own writings. . . ." [33] When Erikson is willing to concede the contrast between the content of his work and that of Freud, he tries to discern a stylistic similarity. (Freud's writing was, however, extraordinary for its clarity.)

Erikson considers himself one of "those who are carrying on Freud's work and recognize its fundamental grandeur even where it is most dated and open to question." [34] He is confident, as he put it in an interview published in 1967, that Freud "always transcended his own theories":

> When I started to write extensively about twenty-five years ago, I really thought I was merely providing new illustrations for what I had learned from Sigmund and Anna Freud. I realized only gradually that any original observation already implies a change in theory . . . One can follow such a man only by doing likewise, and if one does so, one differs.[35]

But Erikson also maintains that his own differences from Freud were inevitable outgrowths from within psychoanalysis: "the psychoanalytic method itself demands that the record proceed from case history to the life history, from the symptoms of human conflict to the signs of human strength, from man's adaptive and defensive maneuvers to his generative potentials." [36]

This mixture of tact and self-deception has permitted Erikson to become, as he himself put it, a member of "the Freudian establishment." [37] He has kept the faith insofar as he still believes that the psychoanalytic perspective remains concentrated on what is unconscious in mental life. [38] Instead of characterizing himself as a neo-Freudian (even Erich Fromm does not like that label applied to himself) or, perhaps worse still, a revisionist, Erikson has chosen the more neutral term of post-Freudian. He has been eager to avoid the risk of being excluded from the ranks of psychoanalysts, which would mean being omitted from the reading lists of professional training institutes, and he has deliberately ignored the possible links between his work and that of other innovators.

Just because some of the psychoanalytic "revisionists" have, to my mind, taken unnecessary chances with . . . [the] foundation (discussing ponderously as scientific differences what were ideological ones), I have not been able to give much thought to the question of how my methodological and terminological suggestions may or may not fit theirs. [39]

But he has implied that he prefers to use identity concepts rather than the terms employed by revisionists like Fromm or Abram Kardiner. [40] In Erikson's view, "eminent psychoanalysts, generally called neo-Freudians," have bypassed ego psychology, overadjusting "some basic Freudian notions to a new climate of discourse." [41] Nonetheless, he now acknowledges "a significant shift of focus from the classical psychoanalytic outlook to newer perspectives such as my own." [42]

As with other analysts trained in the Freudian school, Erikson's work shows little awareness of the writings of the so-called heretics of the early days of analysis. However, Erikson has written, in the tradition of Alfred Adler, about the significance of inferiority feelings (in Erikson's terms, a "sense of inferiority"), and he has alluded to Adler's concept of "masculine protest." [43] Erikson has also noted that "the question of the 'admission' of social considerations into 'official' psychoanalysis has had a stormy history ever since the publication of the work of Alfred Adler. . . ." [44]

Erikson has had more to say about Carl G. Jung. Jung's ideas are considered "controversial" by Erikson, but he has held that on important occasions we "meet face to face the clinical facts on which Jung based his theory of inherited prototypes ('archetypes')." Mentioning, at least in passing, such Jungian clinical concepts as "anima," "animus," and "persona," Erikson has cited Jung's work as "ideological regression," and alluded to his association with the Nazis as "weakly denied . . . reactionary political acts." [45] Following Freud's own rigid conception of the contrasting role in science of theories as opposed to facts, Erikson has commented upon the widespread ignorance of Jung's work among his colleagues: "As though in fear of endangering a common group identity based on an identification with Freud's personal greatness, psychoanalytic observers chose to ignore not only Jung's excesses but also the kind of universal fact he had, indeed, observed." [46] Erikson has recently even referred to "depth psychology, Jungian and Freudian," [47] as if giving equal weight to both schools of thought.

In contrast to the most well-known dissenters in analysis, Erikson would still hold that basic childhood conflicts endure within adulthood: "The earliest steps are preserved in the deepest layers." [48] Yet Erikson, in fact, differentiates his own position from the early Freudian one in that he has criticized the attempt to infer meanings from origins; he has called "originology" that "habit of thinking which reduces every human situation to an analogy with an earlier one, and most of all to that earliest, simplest, and most infantile precursor which is assumed to be its 'origin.'" [49] This attitude toward psychological beginnings can be "as great a fallacy as teleology," [50] which Freud had fought in Adler's approach.

Erikson has been unwilling to deal with current problems as pre-empted by the past, and has raised (like the most famous dissenters in psychoanalysis) the issue of personal and historical potentialities. For without an orientation toward the future psychoanalysis remains retrospective, a "'traumatological' psychology." [51] (Erikson's own early clinical writings were quite traumatological. [52]) The early analysts' interest in traumatic origins may be due to the way in which psychoanalysis became a substitute for abandoned orthodoxies; Erikson considers the exceptional place of psychoanalysis in American cities as an illustration of the search "for a new and orthodox parentage on the part of the intellectual diaspora." [53]

Freud's quest for origins was accompanied by what Erikson considers an unnecessarily simplistic conception of cause and effect. In discussing one clinical crisis Erikson has denied the applicability of the notion of "cause" at all: "instead we find a convergence . . . of specific intolerances which make the catastrophe retrospectively intelligible, retrospectively probable." [54] (Here Erikson assumes a distinction between retrospection and traumatology.) Terms such as "transference" and "defense mechanism" seem too starkly mechanistic to Erikson (yet he himself has talked about "laws" of development); when they are used for explanatory assumptions they are "apt to become not only reductionist but also accusatory as well as excusatory. . . ." [55] As an alternative to Freud's approach to causality, Erikson would prefer to talk instead in terms of configurational fits between the various components of a situation.

In keeping with Freud's own conception of his central contribution, Erikson has focused on Freud's theories on sex: "mature genital sexuality, he concluded, is the end product of an infantile sexual development, which he consequently called *pregenitality.*" [56] Erikson thinks that "what Freud first had in mind was a reconstruction of early sexuality, that is psychosexuality. . . ." [57] But here Erikson is, like others, mistakenly depriving Freud's thought of its full original radicalism. For Freud was contending that the child has, not a sex-like life, but a sex life. At a pre-World War I meeting of the Vienna Psychoanalytic Society, one member, evidently without contradiction by Freud, talked about the existence of orgasms in children. [58] In those years Freud was himself not sure, in discussing infantile sexuality, whether orgasm was the special characteristic of sexuality, or whether sexual pleasure could be equated with pleasure in general. But Freud considered the "most reliable proof of infantile sexuality" to be neurosis. [59] It is often overlooked that the peculiar nature of what Freud meant by infantile sexuality was one of the sources of his differences with Jung. And to compound the problem, Freud, at least in the years of the great controversies in psychoanalysis, tended to treat neurosis as a product of infantile sexuality almost as a matter of definition.

Instead of accepting the differences between the historical Freud and what would be considered scientifically acceptable today, Erikson has chosen to describe how Freud erroneously formulated his ideas in terms of the imagery of a transformation of energy: "To express the fact that libidinization withdrawn from the genitals . . . manifests itself elsewhere, Freud used the thermodynamic language of his day. . . ." But, Erikson reassures us, "great innovators always speak in the analogies and parables of their day. . . . True insight survives its first formulation." [60] For Freud, neurotic symptoms could be understood on the model of an already aroused energy, first suppressed and then finding devious expression.

But Erikson has claimed that "the whole energetic viewpoint means rather little" to him, whereas the configuration approach is more attractive. He would rather talk about behavior which is observable in a variety of contexts than speculate about energies which cannot be demonstrated. [61] On the grounds of historical perspective Erikson tends to minimize Freud's concept of resistance by treating it as part of the "physicalistic" terminology of Freud's day. [62] Once more Erikson can innovate while suggesting that Freud had not gone far enough in shifting from received wisdom, in this case away from physiological concepts to pure psychology. [63] Erikson has, in his special way, tried to put psychoanalysis into its social context.

No aspect of the Freudian conception of the unconscious has had more notoriety than the Oedipus complex. Yet here again Erikson takes a healthy-minded approach; in writing about Luther, Erikson comments:

> most certainly we would ascribe to Luther an Oedipus complex, and not a trivial one at that. We would not wish to see any boy—much less an imaginative and forceful one—face the struggles of his youth and manhood without having experienced as a child the love and the hate which are encompassed in this complex. . . . [64]

The oedipal stage of development has its clinical importance, for example in explaining the growth of the potentiality for guilt; but Erikson thinks that such guilt can be alleviated by the reassertion of a unique identity. He notes that "following Freud we have obediently persisted in referring to the origins of the rebellious complex in childhood as the Oedipus complex," [65] but Erikson is apt to stress the oedipal problem as a reaction to a certain kind of father. He observes that "we always talk about the Oedipus complex as if only the boy's hostility was involved. But we never talk about Laius. . . ." [66] (Laius' feelings toward Oedipus were brought up in psychoanalysis at least as early as 1914.[67])

Although Western middle-class family life has radically altered since World War I, psychoanalysis at the time of its beginnings (and in the hands of a contemporary of ours like Ronald D. Laing) stood for an attack on aspects of customary family life. Although in the short run Freud's ideas often reinforced traditional patriarchal culture, over the long haul psychoanalysis has helped to highlight some of the specific weaknesses of the culture Freud cherished. To see what a world away from our own time was the psychoanalysis of pre-World War I days, we have only to recall the clinical vignette in which Freud stressed "the influence on the child's behavior of the parents' presence or absence. A boy of four or five years is on very good terms with his father if the mother is not present." In connection with Freud's proposition about what might explain a good relationship between father and son, it took a particularly warmhearted analyst to relate "the case of a three-year-old boy who was affectionate toward the father because the latter behaved in the same way [toward him]." [68] What sounded innovative among analysts then has by now become acceptable common sense.

Like the revisionists, Erikson prefers to look at the Oedipus complex within the context of Freud's culture; and in line with Erikson's own interest in ego processes, he is apt to desexualize the oedipal conflict. According to Erikson, even when the choice of a marriage partner is governed by unconscious incestuous wishes, it ought not to be necessarily regarded at pathological.[69] He also thinks, as Jung did

earlier, that a revived oedipal struggle should not be interpreted as mainly a sexual conflict, but rather seen in terms
of a wish to be reborn.[70] Erikson looks upon the oedipal
crisis in relative terms—as a specific phase in personality
development characteristic of certain historical periods.

From Erikson's point of view it is essential to modify
the classical psychoanalytic concept of instinct derived
from the model of sexuality. According to him, the only
way to defend the Freudian view is to see drives as culturally modifiable; to this end he sets up a contrast between
the biologically "instinctive" and the socially "instinctual."
As in his treatment of the Oedipus complex, Erikson wishes
to put Freud's libido theory in perspective: "It was clear to
him," Erikson claims for Freud, "and it becomes clearer
to us—who deal with new areas of the mind (ego), with
different kinds of patients (children, psychotics), with new
applications of psychoanalysis (society)—that we must
search for the proper place of the libido theory in the
totality of human life." [71] If Freud believed in an untenable
doctrine like the death instinct, Erikson is willing to put
the best possible face on this belief: Freud must have been
blaming a socially sanctioned "instinctual" craving for
destructiveness.[72]

As part of their dissatisfaction with Freud's outlook,
analysts such as Carl Jung and Otto Rank had long ago
emphasized the non-oedipal aspects of the relationship
between mother and child, instead of interpreting it ex-
clusively as a sexual tie. Similarly, analysts such as Harry
S. Sullivan and Donald W. Winnicott have identified legitimate dependencies in early childhood. Erikson has noted
in recent psychoanalytic thinking the recognition of the
significance of benevolent mothering care. Freud thought
that the primary tie of the infant boy, for example, was
first established by identifying with his father, but Erikson

has stressed the importance of the mothering sanction. The presence of attentive maternal activity was an aspect of child psychology that Freud took for granted.

Just as earlier writers in the history of psychoanalysis (such as Jung) did not so much repudiate Freud's concept of the unconscious as adopt a different version of it, Erikson has called attention to special features of childhood that Freud tended to overlook. Erikson wonders, for example, about the traditional view of the child's ego as weak (as he had questioned the supposed weakness of the dreamer's ego):

> does it really make sense to speak of an infant's rudimentary ego as being "weak" and then to liken it to what is weak in an isolated adult's neurotic dependence? . . . the infant, while not yet able to grasp and to test what we call our reality, is competent in his actuality.[73]

Erikson attributes to childhood, however, the source of one of his own special difficulties: the "tendency to always search for an older figure who will sanction whatever license he takes." [74] As part of Erikson's integration of his view of childhood with a broad conception of human nature, he is afraid that our prevalent unconscious identification with the machine may lead to depersonalized child rearing.

Despite his more general pronouncements, Erikson has maintained that he is "primarily a clinician." [75] As a therapist he is interested in questions of technique, not only from the point of view of effecting a cure or accelerating a recovery but also from the standpoint of making sure that the analyst minimizes the harm he can cause. High on his list of therapeutic mistakes comes "diagnostic name-calling," since for Erikson there are "malignant implications" to a "fatalistic diagnosis." [76] He warns, for example, that youth is especially impressionable, and that a young person may try to become exactly what is socially expected of him.

Erikson has tried to stress how a person's potentialities for uniqueness can be burdened by a diagnostic curse. He believes that even criminals can be artificially made. People should not be confirmed in any of their negative identity fragments, lest these become dominant. The very success of psychiatry has "tended to make patienthood a self-defining, self-limiting role prison. . . ." [77] There is a realistic danger that patients, by assuming roles diagnostically suggested, may find their identities in neurosis.

In contrast to the pretensions to scientific exactness shared by many orthodox analysts (Erikson himself once referred to "the psychoanalytic microscope"), he is now willing to say that "therapists of different temperament and of various persuasions differ as to what constitutes an interpretation. . . ." [78] Erikson believes that the existence of different psychiatric schools of thought today testifies to a demand for an ideological orientation. In any psychotherapeutic encounter there has to be "the element of subjectivity, both in the patient's complaints and in the therapist's interpretations," which "may be vastly greater than in a strictly medical encounter, although this element is in principle not absent from any clinical approach." [79] Hence the requirement that all analysts be themselves analyzed, lest blind spots in therapists needlessly interfere with their efforts to help their patients.

Erikson has questioned the legitimacy of many traditional features of psychoanalytic treatment. The use of the couch may have led not only to "some sadistic and faddish exploitation," [80] but also to a self-deceptive illusion of objectivity. Unlike those analysts for whom a couch has been the touchstone of a proper therapeutic encounter, Erikson has had some patients sit across from him in an easy chair. There is an inherent inequality between the therapist and patient which may not need the reinforcement of the contrast be-

tween a reclining and a sitting position. As for dream interpretations, Erikson feels that "even a periodic emphasis on
dreams today is wasteful and may even be deleterious to
therapy." [81] And he has protested against the psychoanalyst's
traditional reliance on the strength of rational, intellectual
insight. Too often analysts have seen regressive tendencies
in patients, overlooking the need in adulthood of a "detour
through the archaic." [82] (Jung had written about the significance of what he called the night journey.) Unlike others,
Erikson is willing to acknowledge that the psychoanalytic
"method may make some people sicker than they ever
were . . . especially if, in our zealous pursuit of our task of
'making conscious' in the psychotherapeutic situation, we
push someone who is leaning out a little too far over the
precipice of the unconscious." [83]

Initially specializing in child analysis, Erikson adopted
techniques suitable for that clinical situation, such as drawing with children. And long ago he wrote that it was his
practice before accepting a child as a patient to share a meal
at the family's home. For adolescents in particular, Erikson
has stressed that ego bolstering is a legitimate therapeutic
maneuver: "Rehabilitation work can be made more effective
and economical if the clinical investigation focuses on the
patient's shattered life plan and if advice tends to strengthen
the resynthesis of the elements on which the patient's ego
identity was based." [84] From his therapeutic success he has
concluded that analysts must not only clarify past drives but
also support present developmental strengths. For at every
stage of the life cycle, Erikson believes, an individual has not
only special vulnerabilities, but some new powers as well.

In view of what he has seen of clinical practice, however,
Erikson has recently said that he believes that "psychoanalysis is the preferred method for fewer types of patients than
are now undergoing psychoanalysis." [85] He hopes this observation is in line with the view of others; he reports that when

he first started out in America and wrote about his cases to Anna Freud, she replied that some of them would not have been considered suitable for analysis in Vienna.[86] In keeping with his own reservations, Erikson has defended variations in traditional psychoanalytic therapeutic technique; he would assess cases not only from the perspective of the patient's so-called analyzability, but also from that of his potentiality for adaptation, "his chances of re-establishing active ego tension in his actuality."[87] The therapist, despite what many have seen in Freud's teaching, cannot afford to ignore the manifest clinical material of patients: "one must learn to listen to what they *are* saying, and not only to the symbolism implicit in their message."[88]

Erikson's skepticism about the therapeutic value of the analyst's sitting out of sight behind a reclining patient, what he calls "the asceticism of the 'expendable face,' " has wide ramifications throughout his work:

> when a devotional denial of the face, and a systematic mistrust of all surface are used as tools in a man's worklife, they can lead to an almost obsessional preoccupation with "the unconscious," a dogmatic emphasis on inner processes as the only true essence of things human, and an overestimation of verbal meanings in human life.[89]

The ideal of analytic impersonality implied a standardized analytic procedure, but Erikson claims that any routine neutrality would be untrue to Freud's intentions.[90]

Too rigid an implementation of analytic neutrality can, according to Erikson, induce in the patient a fear that he may lose his identity. Erikson believes that "we can help him grasp reality only to the extent to which we, within our chosen method, become actual to him."[91] The analyst must accept a patient's irrational transferences as meaningful, while refusing to become unduly drawn into them. But any analytic reconstruction of the past "presupposes patients strong enough to learn by introspective insight. So even the most passive therapeutic attitude is action. . . ." [92]

There is widespread agreement that "to Freud and his followers the consulting room has always been not only a healer's sanctuary but also a psychologist's laboratory." [93] Unlike others, however, Erikson has defended Freud's assertion that he was mainly motivated by scientific curiosity, not therapeutic ambition: "This may sound a little cold-blooded, but he meant it as a useful warning that many people by an exaggerated wish to cure, may do more harm than good." [94] But one must have some doubts about just how uncontaminated a laboratory the analyst works in.

Let us assume the so-called classical psychoanalytic setup, in which the patient cannot see the analyst. Erikson wondered as late as 1972: "if vision is . . . the basic organizer of the sensory universe and if the beholding of one person's face by another is the first basis of a sense of mutuality, then the classical psychoanalytic treatment situation is an exquisite deprivation experiment." [95] More recently, in his Godkin lectures, Erikson has been bolder: instead of calling psychoanalysis an "exquisite" deprivation experiment, he has said it can "only" be called a visual deprivation experiment since the eyes of therapist and patient are unable to interplay with each other.[96]

This was an original statement for a psychoanalyst to make—that psychoanalysis involves sensory deprivation. But if, as I think, he is right, then there is a good deal more to be said. It is Freud's own best scientific spirit to pursue these implications, since he was convinced of the eventual cultural triumph of the truth: "The voice of the intellect is a soft one, but it does not rest till it has gained a hearing. Finally, after a countless succession of rebuffs, it succeeds." [97] Erikson's suggestion implies that a patient's ability to thrive in a situation of sensory deprivation tells us little about psychological normality. Such success may require, not introspective or verbal strength, but credulity toward authority figures combined with a need for isolation. The illusionary intimacy of treatment can be less threatening than involvement with people in real life.

But how are we now to understand transference, and the other so-called "rock-bottom" concepts that Freud evolved from the psychoanalytic situation? Supposedly, transference, the patient's bond onto the person of the analyst, is made up of idealization as well as suspicion, and is to be traced to the patient's irrational conflicts stemming from the past. By means of the analyst's coolness and distance, the patient is permitted to develop his own fantasies and expectations about the analyst; the analyst's job is then to interpret such transferences, helping the patient to understand his difficulties in terms of his pre-adult past. On the basis of his clinical experience Freud generalized grandly:

> It must not be supposed . . . that transference is created by analysis and does not occur apart from it. Transference is merely uncovered and isolated by analysis. It is a universal phenomenon of the human mind, it decides the success of all medical influence, and in fact dominates the whole of each person's relations to his human environment.[98]

At times, even now, Erikson accepts Freud's doctrine that transference is the mainspring of psychoanalytic work. [99] (Jung was prescient about the dangers involved in evoking transference reactions; for to have the power to activate conflicts does not necessarily entail being able to help channel them constructively.) Yet elsewhere Erikson says that transference is in part produced by the technique of using a couch,[100] which might make it an unreliable guide to the nature of the patient's past history.

Erikson once defined transference as "the patient's wish to exploit sickness and treatment for infantile and regressive ends." [101] But his more recent formulations mean to me that the regression in transference feelings can also be understood as a reasonable response to the peculiarities of the psychoanalytic setting. Psychoanalytic therapy may turn out to be manipulative as a technique precisely because of its hidden suggestive elements. The usual silence, for instance, ensures a disproportionate weight to each of the analyst's remarks. The use of a couch may arouse so much regression and dependency in a patient that he is unable to cope, and the traditional analyst is ill equipped to meet the patient at such a level. In the midst of uncanny and magical feelings, it is little wonder that dogma comes in as a needed crutch.

One has to question how neutral a research tool psychoanalysis can ever become when so many of its supposed findings are predetermined by its technique. Any patient's past has momentous significance; but an artificial treatment situation is incapable of guaranteeing genuine and unslanted reliving. Erikson has himself not followed up on the range of questions that emerge when analysis is seen as sensory deprivation, but he has declared that the analyst "can really learn only a method which is compatible with his own identity." Elsewhere Erikson writes about the general urgency of widening cultural identities. But in the concrete context of psychoanalytic therapy, he has been content to lend support to the status quo, claiming that "it isn't just a question of which method is best for patients, but also of which method the therapist feels most at home with and creative in." [102]

CHAPTER 5

Psychohistory

Erikson may be best known as an early advocate of psychohistory; yet he has recently warned that he does not want to be associated with everything that gets done in the name of that term.[1] His special interest in this area has been in using psychology to enrich the art of biography. Erikson has observed how even anti-psychological biographers function with an implicit psychology. Whatever the conservative implications of Erikson's work, in each of his major biographical studies he has chosen to examine the life of an ideological innovator. His heroes have been those who have succeeded in making the environment adapt to their special demands.

In trying to bridge the traditional gulf between the perspectives of the historian and the psychologist, Erikson has had in mind a two-way street in which the practitioners of the respective crafts would have something special to gain. On the one hand, Erikson feels that Freud's teachings can contribute to the clarification of psychological obstacles, arising from the past, that obstruct present thinking and decision making. And at the same time Erikson has welcomed the impact of history on psychoanalysis, in the expectation that it would provide a much-needed perspective on concepts that all too often are seen as universal rather than time-bound.

In trying to evolve a common method for psychoanalysts and historians, Erikson has highlighted the way a clinician necessarily interacts with his evidence, thereby affecting it; the analyst influences what he observes, and therefore becomes a part of what he is studying. For Erikson "the first rule of a 'psycho-historical' study" must be "that the author should be reasonably honest about his own relation to the bit of history he is studying and should indicate his motives without undue mushiness or apology." [2] In his own book on Gandhi, for example, Erikson wrote extensively about his personal interaction with the data he gathered. A good deal of ambivalence is bound to underlie almost any historical work.

Erikson has cited Freud's concept of countertransference to help explain his own experience of emotional involvement in historical research: "Freud . . . discovered . . . that *psychological discovery is accompanied by some irrational involvement of the observer, and that it cannot be communicated to another without a certain irrational involvement of both.* Such is the stuff of psychology. . . ." [3] Although Freud pointed out the logic of countertransference, he wrote virtually nothing about the phenomenon. He assumed that, not only he himself, but properly trained analysts as well, would be in control of such feelings. And although Erikson pays tribute to Freud's insight on this matter, Erikson implicitly acknowledges this gap in traditional psychoanalysis when he turns to pay tribute to Harry Stack Sullivan's understanding of the psychoanalytic method as a "participant" technique.[4]

Erikson's anthropological field work gave him further insight into the ways an observer necessarily participates in the lives of his subjects. What a field worker finds out is in some way determined by the limitations of his personality, and anthropologists have learned that one's personality is an important instrument of research. Therefore Erikson has set down another rule of psychohistorical study: "that there be at least a rough indication of how the data were collected." [5] In his own *Childhood and Society,* he made it clear that his book dealt not just with "facts," but with his experiences in coming upon those "facts." [6]

In addition to pursuing his biographical and methodological interests, Erikson has tried, in the course of studying great men, to come to terms with the phenomenon of greatness itself. (The theme of greatness was one of Freud's last preoccupations, or at least his *Moses and Monotheism* can be interpreted that way.) Erikson says he wants to cut across frontiers of academic discipline and moral prejudice; he notes that "one would like to believe that great men of other, more 'abstract' aspirations—in science or technology, say—are totally removed from any comparison with men of political and of destructive military action." [7] Erikson aims to study not only the origins but even some regularities in the growth of certain kinds of genius. For instance, he proposes that they share a basic zeal to settle an infantile account or curse. In his effort to fathom the nature of "historical greatness," he has hypothesized that such people had especially powerful childhood consciences, and commonly appeared old in their early years. [8]

It is, on the face of it, highly dubious to think there is any common core of greatness at work in scientists and politicians. Actually, by greatness Erikson means effective leadership and success, which might well exclude many writers or artists who failed to achieve immediate recognition or had no significant impact on their era. In terms of his background, however, Erikson has been trying to get away from the negativistic aspects of the Freudian heritage. For example, he tells us that "the whole ecology of greatness . . . transcends many of the assumptions which clinical work has suggested regarding the inner economy of a person." [9] Erikson is right in thinking that greatness is often "based on an excessive restatement of some previous overstatement, usually made by others, often by the master himself." [10] In exploring what he regards as the ambiguities of greatness, Erikson proposes to examine the crucial problem of creativity. He has insisted on the differences between a clinical case history and a life history; for patients are undermined by their neurotic conflicts, whereas in history such human problems add an essential ingredient to all extraordinary effort. [11]

Erikson sees a focus on historical greatness as a way of examining and emphasizing ego strength, "how a person managed to keep together and to maintain a significant function in the lives of others." [12] Yet in studying the youth of one great man, Erikson insists that how such a person copes with the conflicts that inhibit others has to be understood according to other than traditional psychoanalytic principles. And this is because Freud "primarily described the conscience which inactivates ordinary people, and neglected to ask aloud (except, maybe, in a cryptic identification with Moses) what permits great men to step out of line." [13]

However one adapts Freud's framework, it is often rightly pointed out that historical material will elude psychological categories to the degree that one cannot check interpretations as one can hope to in a clinical context. Historians have often wondered about the problem of verifying psychological hypotheses, and in particular, what could count for or against any particular interpretation, and Erikson has made some effort to discuss the nature of psychohistorical evidence. Yet in the past people are likely to have been more open, and less self-conscious, about inner conflicts than they are today. For one of the unintended consequences of the Freudian revolution has been that nowadays people have a whole armory of new defenses drawn from modern psychology, enabling them to deceive themselves by means of fancy terminology.

One of the dramatic means by which Erikson tried to revivify the personality of Martin Luther for the modern temper was to compare him with Freud. For Erikson both Luther and Freud were men who "endeavored to increase the margin of man's inner freedom by introspective means applied to the very center of his conflicts; and this to the end of increased individuality, sanity, and service to men." [14] (Freud would no doubt have been surprised at the comparison, and in his old age might have growled at the effort to see him as a benefactor to humanity.) Sometimes the analogies in the lives of Luther and Freud that Erikson finds are more specific: for example, both men felt uncomfortable when someone looked them directly in the eye.[15] But often Erikson only hints at the likenesses in his pictures of Luther and Freud; for example, he described in Luther what we know to have been true of Freud too: the "ability to hate, as well as an inability to forgive those who in his weaker years had, to his mind, hindered him, he shares with other great men." [16] Above all, perhaps, Luther, like Freud, who had followers as well as enemies, helped transform his era's image of what it might mean to be human. As the first psychoanalyst, Freud was "the father of it all," and Erikson has written that this was "a fact which I probably tried to objectify in my later studies of great men." [17] But describing Luther in terms of Freud also served Erikson as a way of hiding from himself discontinuities in his own development.

Luther has received a special degree of attention from psychoanalytic writers; both Erich Fromm and Norman O. Brown, for example, have shown an intense interest in the significance of his writings.[18] In Erikson's case Luther fits into the special needs of his own work. For it is partly as a psychologist that Erikson admires this great religious figure. He thinks highly of Luther's descriptions of shame, doubt, vanity, and guilt, and the borderline between the psychological and the theological remains, for Erikson, a flexible one. "What we today explain as meaningful slips, he simply called the devil's work." [19]

In justification of the associative way he sometimes presents his version of Luther, Erikson recalls the experience of a clinical case conference; he treats his readers as if they were participants in a seminar at which clinical material has been tentatively put forward. Erikson knows that what has come down to us about Luther's early life is necessarily sketchy; it takes a creative imagination for anyone to extract, from an ounce of recorded fact, a pound of credible historical interpretation.[20] It is, however, above all "the youth of a great reformer" that he set out to describe, since he believes that—as in the case of his own life history—"the difference between the young and the old Luther is so marked." [21]

As we shall see, Erikson thinks that ideology has a special psychological function for adolescents; and in Luther's life, he stresses how an abrupt conversion brought his young academic career to a sudden halt, as he determined to become a monk. According to Erikson's account, Luther "only records that *something in him* made him pronounce a vow before the *rest of him* knew what he was saying." His training as a monk was a form of "indoctrination," yet only that discipline gave Luther the breathing space, in Erikson's view, in which to find himself. The conversion had been "necessary so that Martin could give all his power of obedience to God, and turn all his venom of defiance against the Pope"; but the delay, the "moratorium" of monkhood, was also "necessary to provide time and a seemingly wrong direction, so that Martin (as Luther put it later) could really learn to know his true historical enemy, and learn to hate him effectively." In Erikson's terms, Luther chose a negative identity when he undertook to be a monk; "and he soon indulged in further contrariness by trying to be a better monk than the monks." [22]

In keeping with the characteristic psychoanalytic emphasis on the importance of the singular event, Erikson begins his interpretation of Luther's character with an account of a fit he is supposed to have had in the choir of his monastery during his early or middle twenties; falling to the ground, Luther is said to have raved: "It isn't me!" according to the German version, or "I am *not!*" according to the Latin one. Erikson uses this fit in the choir as a means of understanding Luther's identity problems:

> Today we would feel that such an attack might be the internal result of stored rage in a young man who is trying to hold on to his obedient, pious self-restraint, and has not yet found a legitimate outer object to attack or a legitimate weapon with which to hit out about him.

In Erikson's view, Luther was struggling to solve an extended identity crisis, and this became that "trauma of near defeat" which "follows a great man through life." [23]

Not until almost a decade after this fit does Luther, in 1517, nail his ninety-five theses onto the church door in Wittenberg. But for Erikson it is characteristic of original thinkers to experience long delays in impressions and reactions. Then, around the age of thirty—"an important age for gifted people with a delayed identity crisis"—Luther's distinctive theology emerges. Once Luther has outlined his theology, he loses interest for Erikson's presentation of identity theory: in 1517 Luther "became a celebrity . . . Then it became politics and propaganda; it became Luther as most of us know him. But we are interested here in beginnings. . . ." [24]

If Erikson seems to be repudiating his own ideas about the inadequacies of the search for origins, the inconsistency is an indication that his purpose was to propagandize only a partial aspect of Luther. The year 1517 marked the occasion of Luther's "official identity, the moment when life suddenly becomes biography," and as far as Erikson is concerned, what happened to Luther "after he had acquired a historical identity is more than another chapter. . . ." Erikson feels he has described what he sees as Luther's self-cure, even though, in terms of Erikson's conception of the life cycle, "a completed identity is only one crisis won." [25]

Erikson is also interested in the ethical substance of Luther's religious solution to the problem of identity. One reason why Erikson is so fascinated by the early Luther is that here he is able to concentrate on Luther's ideals and does not have to confront him in action as a historical leader. Erikson sees Luther as having provided "new elements for the Western male's identity." For Erikson, Luther's basic contribution was to reformulate Christian doctrine. Luther's concept of justification by faith was what he reported as the "revelation in the tower"—that faith must precede deeds. The hierarchy of the Catholic Church was for Luther no longer necessary. Relying on the self-evidence of the Scriptures, Luther proclaimed the priesthood of every believer. Erikson admires Luther for his Christian egalitarianism, and for his rediscovery of "the passion of Christ in each man's inner struggles." [26]

Freud had seen psychoanalysis as an assault on Gentile culture, and on Christianity in particular; he even insisted that the maxim "love thy neighbor" was both undesirable as an ethical principle and psychologically unrealistic as a human expectation.*[27] Whereas Freud sought to transform traditional theology into a scientific psychology, Erikson has looked to theology for psychological guidance. Despite Erikson's displeasure with Freud's pessimism, he never cites Freud at his most utopian; for in *The Future of an Illusion*, published in 1927 (the same year Erikson entered Freud's circle), Freud lyrically described what a world without religion might be like. In contrast to Freud's atheism, Luther is a hero for Erikson precisely because the Reformation marks a memorable point when Christ became the heart of the identity of Christians: "Christ is today here, in me." [28]

Erikson believes that Luther also succeeded in giving a new emphasis to individual conscience. Luther insisted on the momentous significance of inward intent: religiously one has to mean what one does. Luther felt that "a man without spirituality became his own exterior," and therefore he "re-emphasized the spirit in which a thing is done from the start for its own sake." Although Luther may have "ignored the Renaissance," which is for Erikson the period of "the ego revolution *par excellence*," he nevertheless did "the dirty work of the Renaissance, by applying some of the individualistic principles immanent in the Renaissance to the Church's still highly fortified homeground—the conscience of ordinary man." [29]

Clinically Erikson has observed that people with well-adapted egos do well at work if they can mean what they do. Here Erikson looks at things individualistically, not socially. For he maintains that "many individuals should not do the work which they are doing, if they are doing it well at too great inner expense." But Erikson does not question

* See Ch. 10, pp. 156–57.

work from society's point of view. The spirit in which work gets done may matter little if the work's social purpose is questionable. But for Erikson it was "Luther's new emphasis on man in *inner* conflict and his salvation through introspective perfection" that marks his contribution as "a decisive step in human awareness and responsibility." [30] And just as Freud had his special method of free associations, Luther too, Erikson emphasizes, had his technique—prayer.

For all his admiration of Luther, Erikson does not ignore the psychoanalytic principle of noting his hero's special afflictions. Throughout his life Luther suffered from constipation and urinary retention, and viewed sexuality as an "eliminative" function. Erikson discusses the course of Luther's passions—for example, conjecturing about the role in his youth of spontaneous ejaculations—as well as his lack of feelings. Luther produced great oratory, but also had a terrible temper and a powerful capacity to hate. If, in Erikson's view, Luther contributed to the growth of human consciousness, he also, "alas, inadvertently helped to increase and to refine authoritarianism." [31] Luther took a vindictive stand during the Peasants' War, and Erikson reminds us how a great revolutionary is capable of turning into a notorious reactionary. But Erikson does not dwell on this side of Luther, nor does he explore his anti-Semitism.[32] He argues that, as in Freud's own battles against so-called defecting followers, Luther's struggle had to "continue (as any great man's must) exactly at that point where his word is perverted in his own name." Yet, like Marx, who reputedly disavowed that he was a Marxist, Luther "was not a Lutheran; or, as he said himself, he was a mighty bad one." [33]

Even though Luther repudiated his followers' rebellion, for Erikson he remains "a rebellious theologian," a "great reformer." [34] For some reputable historians, however, Erikson's whole interpretation of Luther's character will not wash: "He did not rebel against the Church. As a loyal son he was cast out of the Church. He did not set out to found a church of his own." [35] Yet all heretics have, at the beginning of their careers at any rate, insisted on their devoted loyalty to the establishment. And in Luther's case, against the criticism that Luther did not become a monk out of rebellion against his father, Erikson reminds us that when at last Luther married he stated as his main reason that "it would please his father." [36]

Yet Erikson has not reduced Luther's life to the status of a neurotic case; on the contrary, he argues that Luther was great precisely in his struggle "to lift his individual patienthood to the level of a universal one and to try to solve for all what he could not solve for himself alone." [37] Erikson has held that the main purpose of any psychohistorical study should be to attempt to fit the identity conflicts of a particular leader with the identity problems of a historical era.[38] This task requires an understanding of what was excessive as well as what was typical in any life, taken in conjunction with the social environment; and it often involves an examination of social mythology.

In Erikson's conception of greatness there are "transforming functions of the 'great man' at a certain juncture of history." [39] In understanding the relationship of the individual life to collective history, Erikson proposes that we see how a leader is "prototypical for his time" and also fulfills "specific needs in the lives of those who followed him." [40] The interplay between leaders and followers has been of central concern to Erikson; and, to an extent unusual in a psychoanalyst, he has tried to see Luther in the social context of his time.

In his treatment of historical material, however, Erikson is bound to seem a bit cavalier.[41] For example, Luther himself never mentioned that fit in the choir, which was reported by "three of Luther's contemporaries (none of them a later follower of his)" Yet Erikson is willing to concede:

> If some of it is legend, so be it; the making of legend is as much part of the scholarly re-writing of history as it is part of the original facts used in the work of scholars. We are thus obliged to accept half-legend as half-history, providing only that a reported episode does not contradict other well-established facts; persists in having a ring of truth; and yields a meaning consistent with psychological theory.[42]

Erikson's attitude, unsettling though it be, may be justified at least insofar as even the most well-established historical data have survived owing to a past era's "sense of the momentous."[43]

In his treatment of Luther, as in his essays on Freud, Erikson is as much a mythologist as a historian. The psychologist in Erikson is really more comfortable "talking about myth rather than history, about the way men mythologize the facts of history as they develop newer and wider identities."[44] Two of Erikson's most convincing pieces were written about the legend of Hitler's childhood and the legend of Maxim Gorky's youth. Every historical actor, perhaps each individual, needs a myth about himself, and Erikson has referred in his *Young Man Luther* to "retrospective dramatization, which I will call *historification* in order to avoid calling one more process 'projection.'"[45]

In his tolerance for the human need for legend, as in his respect for the idealization of heroes, Erikson is at odds with Freud's own negative view of the function of illusions and, in particular, of religion. Erikson is right in believing that myths can be a means of mastering our anxieties, and of finding external support for our aspirations. But it would have been better to distinguish between a myth and a deception, for had he acknowledged the moral shock of a lie, he would have better appreciated the limitations of fable. It remains to be seen what the psychohistorical trend in the end will amount to. But the specific examples of Erikson's biographical use of psychohistory, to the degree that he himself has gone in for "historification," are bound to leave skeptical scholars unsatisfied.

CHAPTER 6

Youth and Identity

Erikson has had a long-standing special interest in the psychology of youth. In his view, youth is the time when an individual's positive ego identity becomes established, even though that phase may seem to some to be a "no-man's-land between childhood and adulthood more or less derisively called adolescence." [1] Many of the psychological changes ushered in by puberty have been known to previous psychoanalytic writers. But Freud himself tended simply to contrast childhood and adulthood as alternatives, and even his daughter Anna, in her memorable account of puberty, dealt primarily with the defensive side of its primitive features. [2]

Erikson has characteristically stressed the adaptive side of youth. He has complained that those who emphasize the child who lives on within the adult have not adequately taken account of the persistence of adolescent traits. Although Freud's libido theory allowed for an early period of developmental delay after the height of the Oedipus complex (the so-called latency years), it did not adequately account for what Erikson considers a second phase of delay, protracted adolescence.[3] Nevertheless, in Erikson's treatment of youth it is not exactly clear whether he considers it "the last and concluding phase of childhood," or whether, as he elsewhere writes, he believes that "with the advent of puberty, childhood proper comes to an end." [4]

Erikson has, however, consistently tried to examine, on a cross-cultural basis, the way societies provide what individuals need as youths, "more or less sanctioned intermediary periods between childhood and adulthood." [5] For some people this intermediary phase may take the form of an apprenticeship or discipleship, while for others it may be characterized by temporary patienthood or even delinquency. In Erikson's account of Luther, as we saw, a "moratorium" preceded his historical identity as a reforming preacher. It is Erikson's conviction that in one way or another societies must offer young people this kind of way station, "a span of time after they have ceased being children, but before their deeds and works count towards a future identity." [6]

Erikson considers the suspended period between childhood and adulthood so important that he is willing to assert that "the adolescent mind is essentially a mind of the *moratorium*. . . ." [7] Delay in the form of a psychosocial moratorium is, in Erikson's view, structured into the pattern of human development. The prolongation of this interval may become almost a separate adolescent way of life, as youth needs the social sanction under which to search for "a new sense of continuity and sameness." [8] In permitting the postponement of adult commitments, the moratorium leaves the individual with the leeway to experiment and to test, without assuming all the responsibilities of the future. This sanctioned phase of delay in functioning as an adult may also provide "a period for meeting one's neurosis . . . the inhibitions and anxieties of the moratorium may protect the novice against false and premature successes. . . ." [9]

It is impossible to doubt Erikson's admiration for young people, especially gifted ones. Perhaps no phase of life is better known for its discontinuities; and despite his commitments to sameness in other areas, Erikson tends to idealize youth's disharmonies. "The chosen young man extends the problem of his identity to the borders of existence in the known universe," whereas "other human beings bend all their efforts to adopt and fulfill the departmentalized identities which they find prepared in their communities." [10] When Erikson writes that "the creative mind seems to face repeatedly what most men, once and for all, settle in late adolescence," it is reminiscent of Goethe's maxim that genius is the capacity for having repeated puberties. [11] For Erikson the "greatest advances in human consciousness are made by people who demand too much." [12] So he can respect what he calls "the protests of humanist youth." [13] A friend of protest, Erikson is nonetheless suspicious of rebellion: "What is driven out by young rebellion is always reinstated by the dogmatism of middle age." [14] He is dubious about the legitimacy of the young in claiming amnesty for their deeds, almost before consummating them. Although Erikson likes the sportiveness of the young, and wants to educate them without violence, nevertheless he believes that we can commit violence by withholding proper guidance. [15]

Youth is an age marked by "the inability to settle on an occupational identity," and, like many others, Erikson considers this hardly surprising. [16] Adolescence is that phase of uprootedness in life when a certain amount of isolation and uncertainty is to be expected. A young person has "good inner reasons to escape premature commitments"; but specific conditions may force "a transitory adolescent regression on the individual as an attempt to postpone and to avoid . . . a psychosocial foreclosure." [17] (Erikson's banking imagery—

ego strength "accrues," adolescents require various "moratoria," and, adults are in danger of "mortgaging" their life choices—may seem surprising in a former artist, but it is in keeping with Freud's own commercial metaphors.) In Erikson's terms, a premature "forfeiture" of a moratorium could be a great loss, for youth is that period in life when instinctual demands force people to confront their preconceptions. As Anna Freud pointed out in 1936, intellectuality as a defense can be seen dramatically in puberty.[18]

Probably Erikson's most famous concept has been that of the identity crisis, which was designed to point to the central conflict of adolescence: "each youth must forge for himself some central perspective and direction, some working unity, out of the effective remnants of his childhood and the hopes of his anticipated adulthood. . . ." A young person must find some resemblance between what he perceives in himself and "what his sharpened awareness tells him others judge and expect him to be."[19] In their need for objects of allegiance, young people experiment with systems of thought which may cure, or sometimes may aggravate, their identity problems. Erikson has called what youth searches for in religion or other comprehensive systems of thought an "ideology." By "ideology" he is referring to what he considers an important source of identity strength. All religions and political systems, as well as scientific ones, have underlying tendencies toward a world-view. Sometimes Erikson is willing to settle for "a convincing world-image."[20] He believes that without this kind of commitment to an ideology, however tacitly expressed, youth will suffer "a *confusion of values.*" Erikson obviously finds attractive the young person's "search for something and somebody to be true to," even though he thinks lasting "confusion" to be self-evidently bad; and he holds that a comprehensive ideological orientation is ultimately fruitful.[21]

From clinical observations made in the 1950s, Erikson assembled a syndrome of problems occurring in patients from about sixteen to twenty-four years old. At first he labeled these difficulties "identity diffusion," but later replaced that term with "identity confusion." The symptoms include "a split of self-images, . . . a loss of centrality, a sense of dispersion and confusion, and a fear of dissolution." [22] Such identity dilemmas not only involve a breakdown in the ability to concentrate, but also are accompanied by a withdrawal from perceived competitiveness. In the face of threatened identity loss, rage can accumulate because of "unfulfilled potentials." [23] (Here Erikson joints Erich Fromm, who long ago saw destructiveness in terms of a response to "unlived life." [24]) A young person's role experimentation can involve not only confusion but also destructive playacting. In the midst of a moratorium sometimes excessively prolonged by identity confusion, "every adolescent . . . knows at least fleeting moments of being at odds with time itself." [25]

In his overall effort to concentrate on adolescence as an adaptive phase of personality development, Erikson admits his tendency to overlook the negative: "in my endeavor to understand identity confusion as a developmental disturbance, I neglect the diagnostic signs which would mark a malignant or more irreversible condition." [26] He is acutely sensitive to the pessimism which seems to be habitual to clinicians. To Erikson "adolescence is not an affliction but a normative crisis, i.e., a normal phase of increased conflict characterized by a seeming fluctuation in ego strength as well as by a high growth potential." [27]

The adolescent ego has to enlarge, and therefore needs diffusion, as the self's boundaries expand to encompass a broader identity. Though Erikson is well aware of all the obstacles to identity formation, what obviously impresses him is the extraordinary recuperative capacities of youth. In contrast, "neurotic and psychotic crises are defined by a certain self-perpetuating propensity, by an increasing waste of defensive energy, and by a deepened psychosocial isolation. . . ." [28] But it is, according to Erikson, a characteristic of an adolescent "to test rock bottom and to recover some of his as yet undeveloped childhood strengths." [29]

In keeping with his psychosocial orientation, Erikson insists that the identity crisis be considered both psychological as well as social. It is, for example, societies which confirm an individual in ideological frameworks, and assign roles in which he can find himself—as well as feel recognized.[30] Socially sanctioned rites of passage—such as religious communions and inductions—may limit the young to a particular identity, threatening penalities for specified transgressions; yet Erikson tends to emphasize the constructive side of such institutions: "of the social institutions which undertake to channel as they encourage such initiative and to provide atonement as they appease guilt, we may point . . . to initiations and confirmations. . . ." [31] For Erikson, achieving "a sense of free choice" is the outcome of "ritual regimentation."[32]

As religion is, in Erikson's view, the social institution which ensures basic trust, so ideology becomes the guardian of identity. Each person needs to have his ego imagery reinforced in times of stress, and such ideals can be "personified in . . . youth by genuinely adult and competent figures."[33] Since Erikson sees the growth of the ego as a process of "mutual affirmation," he has held that "the *outerworld of the ego* is made up of the *egos of others* significant to it."[34]

Erikson has been trying to counteract what he sees as the original Freudian "biologism." But he does not adequately comprehend the possible dangers inherent in his subjectivistic approach. The picture he paints of a model of human growth seems unduly conformist, dependent on the expectations of others. Ideal "images" may be very different from authentic ideals. In all his talk about world-views and images, he does not seem to realize that to be caught up in pseudo-realities can in the end be as damaging as any other lack of genuine meaning.

The specific ego problem Erikson posits at the end of adolescence consists in the development of a firm identity, able to outbalance the potential power of the demands of the childhood conscience. In order successfully to integrate previous self-conceptions and identifications, the young person has to create for himself a wider identity. The upheavals of puberty are a key stage in the development of the ego's strength, and for Erikson identity "connotes the resiliency of maintaining essential patterns in the process of change." Such wholeness need not imply, Erikson claims, a static conception of the mind, but rather can involve "a sound, organic, progressive mutuality between diversified functions and parts within an entirety, the boundaries of which are open and fluent."[35]

Erikson does not regard this sense of identity as a constant set of traits or roles, but as "always in conflict with that past which is to be lived down and with that potential future which is to be prevented."[36] The ego for Erikson has an "active . . . choosing role which is of the essence in a sense of identity as a continuity of the living past and the anticipated future."[37] Adolescence, with all its vulnerabilities, is a critical transformer of society; it is the young who give meaning to the past. Erikson sees identity formation as a process that continues throughout life, though its specific crisis occurs in adolescence. At the same time Erikson would put identity problems in a larger perspective:

> Identity does not first emerge in youth and it is not the aim and end of development. Our times emphasize identity as a predominant concern. If the relation of father and son dominated the last century, then this one is concerned with the self-made man asking himself what he is making of himself. Yet, this cannot be the last question.[38]

Erikson also recognizes that it is no accident that identity problems have become especially important to American psychologists. His concept of the identity crisis immediately became popular in America—so much so that Erikson once reported that he found himself "asking a student who claims that he is in an 'identity crisis' whether he is complaining or boasting." [39] He thinks that the direction his thought took after coming to America was linked to problems peculiar to the United States in the 1930s. He has gone so far as to say of that era that it was "the time when *it* entered into something of an identity crisis, just because it had tried to make out of the descendants of so many different pseudospecies one new one."[40]

Erikson's ideas have flourished primarily in the United States, and he has thought of himself as adopted by America. He had left Central Europe before the largest wave of analytic refugees to the New World. Though, obviously, psychoanalysis could be practiced almost anywhere, the demand for analysts was greatest in America. Therefore he considered himself especially fortunate as an immigrant. Erikson thought he had "found a loving stepfather in an adoptive country." [41] Like other members of a self-styled revolutionary community, he chose a new name in his new home. Although he had published papers and held posts at Harvard and Yale as Erik Homburger, when he became an American citizen in 1939 he changed his name to Erik Homburger Erikson. This choice of a last name may have represented an identification with the Norwegian discoverer of America.[42]

But Erikson's feelings for America have made it easier for him to "historify" his own past, retrospectively smoothing over disharmonies to create a fresh identity. But such self-creation has its own tensions. Erikson has alluded to the "pathological side" of his own youthful identity confusion, placing it on "the borderline between neurosis and adolescent psychosis." And he admits: "No doubt, my best friends will insist that I needed to name this crisis and to see it in everybody else in order to really come to terms with it in myself."[43] (In a revised version Erikson suppressed an earlier reference to "psychosexual" difficulties.[44])

To make new contributions to depth psychology one has to work from one's own experiences. And this is both a great strength and an underlying weakness of the Freudian approach. But to go in for explicit autobiography, as Erikson has done, inevitably lays one open to attack. Freud's attempt at honesty in *The Interpretation of Dreams* gave his critics all the ammunition they would ever need. It requires bravery to engage in self-confession. In the case of Erikson, the subtle alterations in the two printed versions of his autobiography made it more revealing of himself than he can ever have intended. Autobiographical candor, however, can be in its own way deceptive, and Erikson has camouflaged the testing of his own rock bottom that went to make up his adult sense of self.

Erikson was born in Frankfurt-am-Main on June 15, 1902, and he tells us that he

> grew up in Karlsruhe in southern Germany as the son of a pediatrician, Dr. Theodor Homburger, and his wife Karla, née Abrahamsen, a native of Copenhagen, Denmark. All through my earlier childhood, they kept secret from me the fact that my mother had been married previously; and that I was the son of a Dane who had abandoned her before my birth. . . . As children will do, I played in with this and more or less forgot the period before the age of three, when mother and I had lived alone.[45]

Now, a principle of Eriksonian psychology is that one cannot accept at face value any event autobiographically recounted. And one problem with Erikson's own version of his origins is that at a conference in 1955 he had declared: "my father died around the time of my birth, and my mother and I seemed to have travelled a lot." [46] Erikson's earliest clinical papers were published under his stepfather's name, Homburger; then why, one wonders, when he decided to take a new name, did he not revert back to his natural father's name? Erikson is silent in his autobiographical comments on his choice of a last name. He does, however, say that "a stepson's negative identity is that of a bastard . . . ," [47] a claim so strange as to hint that the issue of legitimacy may have played a key role in Erikson's life.

Erikson has written in connection with Gandhi that "autobiographies are written at certain late stages of life for the purpose of re-creating oneself in the image of one's own method; and they are written to make that image convincing." [48] Erikson is now a believing Christian; it would be impossible to understand either his interest in Luther and Gandhi or his specific contributions to clinical thinking without appreciating the depth of his ethical commitment to Christianity. But what was he throughout childhood? Marshall Berman, reviewing the book in which Erikson's autobiographical essay was reprinted, noted that Erikson's mother's name sounded Jewish and that Erikson had been disguising a Jewish past. [49]

If one examines Erikson's autobiographical reflections, the accusation of evasiveness seems justified. We are told that his mother was "a native of Copenhagen, Denmark," and that his real father was "a Dane." But Erikson says his stepfather came from "an intensely Jewish small bourgeois family." Why describe his parents by their geography and nationality, and the stepfather by his religion and class? Erikson does report that he came "from a racially mixed Scandinavian background," but in its context that inevitably sounds enigmatic. When he says that he "was referred to as a 'goy'" in his stepfather's temple, while to his schoolmates he was a "Jew," one would hardly guess that his childhood family was entirely Jewish.[50]

In the biography by Robert Coles, Erikson's early years begin with a wandering Danish woman coming to live with her son in a Jewish doctor's home in Karlsruhe. Coles quotes Erikson as saying that both his parents were Danish, while the stepfather is described as Jewish. We are told by Erikson that "my mother's family was Jewish."[51] But in discussing her ancestry a Jewish relative is balanced against a Christian one. (In Coles's book Erikson states that his parents were "separated" before he was born. One cannot overestimate the social stigma associated with being born out of wedlock in Central Europe at the turn of the century.)

Erikson has not described his conversion to Christianity. He does tell us of his adolescence: "like other youths . . . I became intensely alienated from everything my bourgeois family stood for";[52] but he has never clarified what he was rebelling against. Erikson has constructed what Freud would have called a "family romance" about his upbringing, which is particularly disappointing in one who writes in such an ethically high-minded fashion. One has to remain skeptical when Erikson is reported by Coles to have said: "Jewishness as such has meant little to me. . . ."[53] (Leaders of the Marxist Frankfurt school of critical sociology are also reported to have strongly rejected "the meaningfulness of Jewishness in their backgrounds."[54])

Berman has asserted, without contradiction, that Erikson "grew up in a home where both parents were actively devout,"* that evidently Erikson's stepfather was president of the Karlsruhe synagogue, and that after Erikson left home the family moved to Palestine. In Coles's book Erikson says

---

* Erikson does report of his mother: "her ambitions for me transcended the conventions which she, nevertheless, faithfully served." But since he had not told us of her Jewishness, he failed to "be descriptive in order to let the cast of contending identity elements announce themselves."[55]

that he considers "some of the Jewish elements in psycho-analysis ancestral in my work." [56] But he has been trying to work himself free from many traditional psychoanalytic formulations. In his discussion of his ego psychology he reminds us of "the historical Jewish identity of invincible spiritual and intellectual superiority over a physically superior outer world," [57] but it is an identity with which Erikson himself has not been comfortable; in his account of the problems characteristic of those of Jewish origin, he does not acknowledge his share in those difficulties. Furthermore, when he describes himself as a "favored" immigrant to America, "both in occupational and in racial terms," [58] he maintains the confusion about his origins; he was born a Dane, and his wife was Gentile, but this reference to his race should not obscure the fact that he was a German citizen and politically disadvantaged as a Jew.

Perhaps Erikson's firm belief in the psychological importance of continuities has encouraged him to mythify his personal past. His conservatism may be an implicit acknowledgment of the pain involved in breaking with his origins. But Erikson does not seem to realize that his method of disguising the simple facts of his family religion damages the authenticity of his commitment to Christian ethics; for it is bound to seem that he was not only attracted by the merits of Christianity but also repelled by the religion of his childhood. (Whatever Freud's own ambivalence about being Jewish, he—like a whole generation of emancipated Central European Jews—felt forced, once it had become a disadvantage, to insist on his Jewishness.) According to Erikson's own principles, any such self-won ideology is certain to be an insecure guardian of identity. There are limits, then, which Erikson does not often enough acknowledge, to how active and choosing an ego can be in ensuring continuities.

In a "memorandum" privately circulated by Erikson after

the publicity in *The New York Times* about his treatment of his origins, he stated that his mother was a Danish "Jewess," his original father a non-Jewish Dane. And we are now told that his stepfather was "German-Jewish." But this is the first time Erikson has straightforwardly discussed his mother's religion, a key matter in the traditional Jewish definition of a Jew. It leads one to question the meaning of Erikson's conception of bigotry; for he had declared to Coles: "one's sense of identity should not be restricted to what one could not deny if questioned by a bigot of whatever denomination." [59] It is noteworthy that in this same "memorandum" Erikson has for the first time mentioned his stepfather also by nationality.

Although he sees himself as belonging to a racially and religiously mixed background, German became Erikson's native language. Artistically inclined, he has said that he was first attracted to Freud's ideas by the magnificence of his German prose. Erikson believes that "psychoanalysis appealed above all to people who had lost their origins in soil, ritual, and tradition"; and he tells us, in connection with his initial contact with Freud, already regarded as a living legend, of his "search for my own mythical father." [60] We have seen how Erikson's need for a hero played a part in his construction of false continuities between his own ideas and Freud's work.

Even after his "adoption" by the Freudian circle, Erikson considered himself still fatherless. His choice of a last name is obviously significant. One story has it that his children were troubled by the American tendency to confuse "Homburger" with "hamburger," and that he asked one of his sons for an alternative; being Erik's son, he proposed Erikson. For Erikson's children such a name would be in accord with Scandinavian custom; but for Erikson it connoted that he was his own father, self-created. The name also harked back to his identifying with the Danish father who had abandoned him; such an identification had to be conflicted, and Erikson later made a special ideal of "generativity."

Whatever else this name change may have meant to him, it was also an act of repudiation of his German-Jewish stepfather, as well as the mother who had secured a legitimate name for her son. Erikson's recent "memorandum" about his past states that his choice of a new name was a family decision, taken with his stepfather's approval. Erikson has felt that as a child analyst he was partly fulfilling a tie to his pediatrician stepfather. But when Erikson says that he has "kept my stepfather's name as my middle name out of gratitude . . . but also to avoid the semblance of evasion," [61] he does not realize how hollow this rings. Perhaps Erikson suffered from ill-treatment about which he has been unwilling to write. At any rate, although he signed his prefaces to both *Childhood and Society* and *Young Man Luther* with his full name, Erik Homburger Erikson, the mere initial "H." on the title pages of all his books seems less than an expression of straightforward fidelity or love.

Erikson's professional beginnings are as elusive as his family origins. Once, at the same meeting in 1955 when he stated that his father had died around the time of his birth, he said of his analytic training: "I was trained as a child analyst under Anna Freud and August Aichhorn. . . ." [62] Time has passed, however, and Erikson's work has moved away from strict Freudianism; and Erikson has indulged in some of the "half-legend" and "half-history" that he described in *Young Man Luther*. For he has since 1955 stressed Anna Freud's part in his past as a child analyst, at the same time singling out Aichhorn (for his specializing in problems of adolescence and, in particular, delinquency) among an increasing number of other teachers in Erikson's psychoanalytic training. [63] In a moving essay about the identity conflicts of Shakespeare's Hamlet, Erikson described him as "an abortive leader, a still-born rebel," whose "words are his better deeds . . . he can say clearly what he cannot live. . . ." [64] Erikson too has felt a rebellious urge; unwilling to talk openly about his increasing divergencies from "classical" analysis, he prefers to mythify autobiographically in order to safeguard his credentials as a psychoanalyst. For to have been analyzed by Freud's daughter Anna might sound next-best to having been analyzed by Freud himself.

In writing about adolescence Erikson has been engaging in a kind of self-understanding. In telling us about youth, he is also telling us something about himself. In adolescence "you are constantly conscious of your own appearance and with your impression on others. . . ." And Erikson then hypothesized that there had to be "a certain vanity of some creative people, a preoccupation with their own biography." [65]

If, as Erikson declared in his study of Luther, thirty is an important age for gifted people suffering from a delayed identity crisis, it is fair to ask at what stage Erikson was himself by 1932. It is easier to believe that Erikson was then suffering from identity problems than to go along with him in thinking of America in the midst of the Depression as having an identity crisis. Erikson had met his future wife in 1929, and at thirty years old was awaiting graduation by the Vienna Psychoanalytic Society. He was "elected" a member on May 31, 1933.

Although Erikson, like other early analysts, has cherished the image of once having worked as part of an underground movement, there were great rewards for him, young and otherwise untrained, in the opportunities of this new profession. But in choosing to become a psychoanalyst he was confirming in himself a perpetually uncertain identity. For the peculiar question arose of who was and who was not entitled to the legitimate use of the name analyst. Freud had repeatedly (against Adler, Jung, and Rank most notably) declared former students of his to be no longer proper analysts. As much as psychoanalysis had become a spiritual home for Erikson, he continued to think of himself as "a habitual stepson," one who might "use his talents to avoid belonging anywhere quite irreversibly. . . ." [66] As Erikson became, in turn, a historian, a professor, and a preaching philosopher, he re-enacted the same pattern of being an outsider to the profession he worked in. He has written that his "positive stepson identity . . . made me take for granted that I should be accepted where I did not quite belong." [67]

Whatever its origins in his own experience, Erikson's concept of the identity crisis was eventually welcomed in America "because it helped," he tells us, "to glorify the drama of youth, with all its dangers, as a semipermanent state quite desirable on its own terms." [68] He has tried to assess the American preoccupation with the adolescent stage. His conception of youth includes some negative features not easy to idealize. Adolescents, in complementing their desire for devotion, have a need to repudiate something; and this conflict, like others, is apt to be heightened in puberty. According to Erikson, "it belongs to the characteristic of a severe identity crisis . . . that it vastly increases the need to delineate what one is not, and to repudiate what is felt to be a foreign danger to one's identity." [69] Here the young person has to struggle with conscious as well as unconscious negative identities, debased self-conceptions and social tasks. In the midst of the worst confusion, "youth sometimes prefers to be nothing and to be that thoroughly than to remain a contradictory bundle of identity fragments." [70]

To adopt a negative identity may seem better than to have none at all. It may be "easier to derive a sense of identity out of a *total* identification with that which one is *least* supposed to be than to struggle for a feeling of reality in acceptable roles which are unattainable with the patient's inner means." [71] Self-determination is vital to the ego's survival: "many a sick or desperate late adolescent, if faced with continuing conflict, would rather be nobody or somebody totally bad or, indeed, dead—and this by free choice—than be not-quite-somebody." [72]

Erikson and other post-Freudian analysts have been less suspicious of regressions than Freud would have been, emphasizing instead the adaptive side of apparent personality retrogression. Still Erikson is aware of potential danger as the troubled young person plays with fire, deliberately searching for his own "base line." [73] Erikson has called the adolescent's most urgent self-testing "the rock-bottom attitude." [74] In an effort to find themselves, youths can desperately, even intolerantly, search for a "totalistic" explanation or self-definition. Out of their all-or-nothing approach, they may feel that only by merging with a great leader can they be saved. By "totalism" Erikson means to refer to a specific quality of adolescence, the potentiality for "an inner regrouping of imagery, almost a *negative conversion,* by which erstwhile negative identity elements become totally dominant, making out of erstwhile positive elements a combination to be excluded totally." [75]

Adolescents are "transitory existentialists by nature" since they are on the brink of separating off as independent persons; but they can react totalistically to their acute conflicts and isolation. [76] Erikson finds this human tendency for totalization merely hinted at by the Freudian concept of transference, and he feels that the significance of his own larger category "ill fits the intellectual contempt for fellow humans dependent on cosmologies and deities, monarchies and ideologies." [77]

Erikson's concern for the ego needs of youth conflicts with the more instinctivistic orientation of earlier analysts, and in particular with the endorsement of "free love" by Wilhelm Reich. Although Erikson knows that in genital activity people may be using each other as a source of stability, he holds that "an invitation to sexual freedom can only aggravate an already present identity conflict." [78] He warns against separating sexuality from love, and considers it "a real question whether early freedom in the direct use of his sexuality would make man freer as a person and as a guarantor of the freedom of others." [79] Among the consequences of Freud's taking a strong ego for granted is that he did not spell out the firm sense of self that must precede falling in love.

For Erikson, "at any time in history, in order to lose one's identity, one must first have one. . . ." [80] And in order "to be really intimate a rather firm identity has to be at least in the making." Here Erikson makes it clear that when he refers to "intimacy," he does not mean "intimacies." [81] He comes close to early psychoanalytic puritanism when he insists that "the sex act, biologically speaking, is the procreative act, and there is an element of psychobiological dissatisfaction in any sexual situation not favorable in the long run to procreative consummation and care. . . ." [82] But a procreative intention has strains of its own, and one might consider that modern contraceptive devices have fulfilled Freud's hope for the possibility of a less conflicted kind of sexual pleasure. But Erikson is evidently mainly worried about "an all too ready belief that . . . genital and procreative instinctuality . . . can be divided . . . without new kinds of emotional repressions. . . ." [83]

Although Erikson thinks of himself primarily as a clinician, he does not consider identity confusion a proper technical diagnosis. He believes, however, that the concept has its practical value, for if adolescents "are diagnosed and treated correctly, seemingly psychotic and criminal incidents do not have the same fatal significance which they may have at other ages." [84] For instance, he treats the existence of delinquents as a sign that we have failed them—"and if we fail to recognize this fact, we lose them." [85] In a young person psychiatric pathology may be "aggravated by acute identity confusion, which is relatively reversible if the confusion can be made to subside." Erikson is convinced that in youths with "gifts for language, histrionics, and personal warmth, a 'delusion' is very different in nature and prognosis from a truly psychotic condition." [86]

Erikson is aware of the parallels between the identity crisis of adolescence and diagnostic categories associated with the onset of schizophrenia, but he is hopeful that seeing the young person's troubles "as part of a life crisis may reduce the fatalism of some diagnoses." [87] He advocates an approach which would emphasize the life task common to everyone at a particular phase of the life cycle. It is possible, for instance, to design a hospital community for patients sharing the problem of identity confusion. Erikson thinks that "there are certain stages in the life cycle when even seemingly malignant disturbances are more profitably treated as *aggravated life crises* rather than as diseases subject to routine psychiatric diagnosis." [88]

Erikson suggests that the specific problems of youth require adaptation in the classical psychoanalytic treatment model designed by Freud. Although he has never made clear how far he would go in altering the traditional Freudian setup, Erikson does contend that in the treatment of young patients the therapist encounters "a specific exaggeration of trends met with in all therapies." [89] Resistances to cure, for example, may come not from instinctual sources, but as a response to perceived threats to ego identity. An adolescent may "fear that the analyst, because of his particular personality, background, or philosophy, may carelessly or deliberately destroy the weak core of the patient's identity and impose instead his own." [90]

In behalf of changes in psychoanalytic technique, Erikson has cited the pioneering work of his special teacher, August

Aichhorn: "As Aichhorn has taught us, in working with late adolescents, it isn't enough to interpret to them what went wrong in their past history. The present is too powerful for much retrospection." And then, having cited Aichhorn for confirmation, Erikson goes on in his own characteristic vein: "they often use that kind of interpretation to develop a florid ideology of illness, and actually become quite proud of their neuroses. Also, if everything 'goes back' into childhood, then everything is somebody else's fault, and trust in one's power of taking responsibility for oneself may be undermined." [91] Since a youthful patient needs the "identity-giving power of the eyes and the face," Erikson holds that "young people in severe trouble are not fit for the couch. . . ." [92]

Erikson has examined Freud's case history of "Dora" in order to highlight the ego approach to therapy: "Dora's neurosis was rooted in the developmental crisis of adolescence." [93] (It is possible, however, to see Dora's problems in terms of the culture of her era.[94]) Erikson suspects that at every phase of life what may appear pathological can actually represent a tentative reaching out for ego verification. Whereas Freud, in treating Dora, had refused to abandon his ideal of a relatively impersonal, nondirective approach, Erikson insists that young patients are in special need of finding a mentor in their psychotherapist. He respects the human quest for sanction, confirmation, and support: "If we call such fathers 'father-surrogates,' we empty an important function of its true significance in an effort to understand its potential perversion; this may lead us, as therapists, to cut off our own noses in order to present impersonal enough faces for our patients' father-transferences." [95]

The conclusion Erikson comes to for the therapy of the young is that "ideally speaking . . . our work of rehabilitation should at least provide a meaningful *moratorium,* a period of delay in further commitment." [96] This is one of those instances where Erikson believes that a human developmental need is met by social recognition; for, in the past, secondary schools,[97] colleges, service on the frontier or in the colonies, and *Wanderschaft* have been socially sanctioned moratoria.[98] Nowadays, at least in some Western countries and among certain classes of people, psychiatric treatment has come to fulfill just such a need for delay; to the degree that psychoanalytic treatment can help people escape from the standardization and mechanization of modern society, to that degree, Erikson believes, it succeeds in its enlightened aim. It is, however, a characteristic failing of Erikson's thought that he does not examine the extent to which societies may unnecessarily prolong youth, for excessively extended dependencies may have deleterious effects for later stages of life.

CHAPTER 7

The Life Cycle

One way of assessing Erikson's contribution would be to look at all his work from the perspective of the life cycle, whose pattern he has taken so much care to elaborate. For a central point of his has been that psychology in the West has not looked at the full range of the life cycle. In contrast to someone like Carl Jung, for example, who studied conflicts associated with middle age and still later phases of the life cycle, Freud had restricted himself to understanding the beginnings of a patient's life. Despite his narrowness Freud's approach had humility; it implied an appreciation for the richness of the potential diversity of future human choices. For all Freud's grandiosity of intent, his work could be genuinely modest, and he sometimes liked to emphasize how little psychologists can know.

Early on Erikson adopted what he has called the "epigenetic" principle, derived from the embryological model of the uterine growth of organisms. He coined "epigenesis" out of "epi" (meaning "upon") and "genesis" (emergence").[1] In fetal development each aspect of the fetus has a crucial time of ascendancy or danger of distortion. In human development Erikson interprets his epigenetic outlook to mean that "anything that grows has a *ground plan,* and . . . out of this ground plan the *parts* arise, each part having its *time* of special ascendancy, until all parts have arisen to form a *functioning whole.*"[2] At each stage of life a new strength is "added to a widening ensemble and reintegrated at each later stage in order to play its part in a full cycle. . . ."[3] Growth must take place not only step by step, but at a proper rate and in normal sequence; and "steps must not only be fitted to each other, they must also add up to a definite direction and perspective."[4]

Erikson believes that to approach human development from the perspective of stages is to have an alternative to either an animalistic or a mechanistic conception of human nature—a child is neither an animal to be controlled nor a machine to be programmed, but a growing creature with its own schedule of development. The growth of human strength takes place in a sequence of stages, representing the patterned development of the various parts of a whole psychosocial personality. It is characteristic of Erikson to stress the prospective features to the life cycle; in early psychoanalysis retrospection and instinct theory went together, whereas Erikson believes that "when future growth becomes unfulfillable, a deep rage is aroused in man comparable to that of an animal driven into a corner. . . ."[5]

In contrast to Freud's emphasis on scientific understanding, Erikson stresses the clinician's "restorative" responsibility; whereas psychoanalysis's "interpretations are based on reconstruction," Erikson insists that "every acute life crisis also arouses new energies in the patient."[6] In the midst of a developmental crisis an analyst's interpretation becomes a social act of intervention. Erikson aims to study "the whole life-cycle as an integrated psychosocial phenomenon," rather than to try to get at meanings derived from reconstructing infantile origins.[7] Erikson fears unnecessary fatalism, for he believes, in a mood akin to a long line of anarchist thinkers, "if we will only learn to let live, the plan for growth is all there."[8]

If Erikson sounds unduly optimistic about the process of human growth, his crisis terminology unnecessarily alarms many people. For he conceives of every stage in the life cycle as marked by a specific psychosocial "crisis," for each of which he is willing to provide a clinical specimen as illustration. He uses the word "crisis" in "a developmental sense to connote not a threat of catastrophe, but a turning point."[9] Luther's identity crisis took almost a decade to resolve— which renders the term "crisis" a highly unusual one in the context of everyday English.

In the end, Erikson's crisis talk turns out to be curiously reassuring. He reminds us that "in medicine a crisis once meant a turning point for better or for worse, a crucial period in which a decisive turn *one way or another* is unavoidable."[10] Any life crisis may be neurotically aggravated in a patient, yet from a developmental point of view it may be considered normal; therapists should avoid confirming patients in diagnostic roles. Therefore Erikson feels free to rely for his data not only on material brought out in the treatment of patients but also on developmental studies of so-called normal people; in fact, Erikson thinks that understanding the latter may enrich the handling of the former, a reversal of Freud's position, since Freud began with the study of pathological processes in order thereby to shed light on normal development.

Erikson denies that his epigenetic viewpoint means that all development is "a series of crises: we claim only that psychosocial development proceeds by critical steps—'critical' being a characteristic of turning points, of moments of decision between progress and regression, integration and retardation." [11] The various steps in the life cycle exhibit, according to Erikson, a tendency toward self-overcoming. And this is perhaps the most optimistic aspect of his life-cycle theory. For all "such developmental and normative crises differ from imposed, traumatic, and neurotic crises in that the very process of growth provides new energy even as society offers new and specific opportunities according to its dominant conception of the phases of life." [12]

Erikson is willing to interpret dreams as reflecting a particular stage in the dreamer's life cycle. For each step in the life cycle presents "a new life task, that is, a set of choices and tests which are in some traditional way prescribed and prepared for him by his society's structure." [13] At issue is whether an ego will prove strong enough "to integrate the timetable of the organism with the structure of social institutions." [14] Once again, Erikson characteristically sees growth in terms of the achievement of integration, not alienation. For he believes it is possible to define certain psychosocial crises "by the potentialities and limitations of developmental stages . . . and . . . by the universal punctuation of human life by successive and systematic 'life tasks' within social and cultural institutions." [15]

Erikson has tried to work out a schedule of unifying strengths as they are called forth by a developing life cycle. Each of these new strengths has the task of resolving a crisis in growth, and every resolution involves both psychological and social dimensions. He has hypothesized "the laws of the *ego* as revealed in ego pathology and in normal childhood play." And therefore he presents "a chart of psychosocial gains which are the result of the ego's successful mediation between physical stages and social institutions." [16] When he applies the term "basic" to an aspect of the growth of the ego's strength, he implies neither a conscious process nor a strictly unconscious one; he means that "neither this component nor any of those that follow are, either in childhood or in adulthood, especially conscious."[17] As a matter of epigenetic principle, "each basic psychosocial trend . . . meets a crisis . . . during a corresponding stage . . . while *all* must exist from the beginning in some form . . . and in later stages . . . must continue to be differentiated and reintegrated with newly dominant trends."[18]

In describing ego strengths, Erikson uses the terminology of "virtues." He has had in mind, he tells us, the Latin meaning of virtue: "the Romans meant by it what made a man a man, and Christianity, what added spirit to men and soulfulness to women."[19] Erikson contends that the meanings of virtue and spirit were once interchangeable, and that therefore his own use of virtue can capture that active, pervading quality of efficacious strength which is for him the essence of a strong ego. It is regrettable, he thinks, that so fundamental a matter as the constituents of a "strong" personality has up till now been left to moralizers, philosophers, and men of God. He would claim that "the negative of this kind of virtue cannot be vice; rather, it is a weakness, and its symptoms are disorder, dysfunction, disintegration, anomie . . . the particular rage which accumulates whenever man is hindered in the activation and perfection of . . . virtues. . . ."[20] In Old English, Erikson tells us, "the word 'virtue' could be used to describe the strength of a medicine. . . ."[21] It was in what Erikson likes to think of as "a militant mood" that he "called these strengths basic virtues," but he "did so in order to indicate that without them all other values and goodnesses lack vitality."[22]

Erikson has formulated eight stages of man. The first, and one of the most widely accepted psychiatrically today, has to do with the virtue of hope. During the earliest months of life, the stage Freud called oral but Erikson incorporative, the child develops its basic sense of trust and mistrust, which remains the source of "both primal hope and of doom throughout life."[23] Here Erikson, like others who have tried to talk about conflicts in nonverbal stages of child development, indulges in a mythology incapable of either verification or refutation. Nevertheless, it is hard to challenge the idea that "hope is the basic ingredient of all strength."[24] It is consistent with Freudian theory to think that such an essential constituent of the ego must come first developmentally. And there is some experimental work with animals that supports the primary significance of the first years of life for later mental health.

While psychoanalysis may have us too ready to assume that psychosis necessarily involves a "regression" to the earliest infantile phase, Ronald D. Laing and others may have gone to the opposite extreme of romanticizing the advantages of so-called mental illness. It is true, however, that the psychotic demands to be accepted and leveled with in an almost childish way. According to Erikson, psychoanalysis first came upon the primary significance of basic trust through its study of psychopathology in adults. He thinks that

> we do find in potentially psychotic people that the very first relationships in earliest childhood seem to have been severely disturbed. We could speak here of a psychosocial weakness which consists of a readiness to mistrust and to lose hope in rather fundamental ways . . . Frieda Fromm-Reichmann was a doctor who doggedly sat down with psychotics as if saying, "I'm not going to give up until you trust again."[25]

If the primary conflict at the outset of life centers on the problem of trust, society has an intimate role to play. For it is Erikson's conviction that "each successive stage and crisis has a special relation to one of the basic institutionalized endeavors of man for the simple reason that the human life cycle and human institutions have evolved together."[26] His principle that individual strength and the spirit of institutions interact in the course of development leads to a conclusion surprising for one coming from the Freudian school: Erikson has repeatedly urged that "it is organized religion which systematizes and socializes the first and deepest conflict in life. . . ."[27] In turn, the hope of an infant can inspire faith in adults; it is characteristic of Erikson to see individual life cycles interacting with each other, awakening new strengths. If the institution of religion successfully ritualizes the restoration of human faith, for adults as well as children, Erikson can acknowledge as well how it uses human weakness for the sake of its own worldly power; yet he also finds that it succeeds in "giving concerted expression to adult man's need to provide the young and the weak with a world-image sustaining hope."[28] For Erikson trust "becomes the capacity for *faith*—a vital need for which man must find some institutional confirmation."[29] And he believes that it is organized religion which ensures the faith that will support future generations.

Erikson's second stage of the life cycle postulates a conflict of autonomy versus shame and doubt, out of which should emerge a sense of self-control and will. As Erikson points out, the stage which Freud's libido theory characterized as anal can also be seen from an ego point of view to establish psychosocial independence. Erikson substituted "incorporation" for Freud's "orality," and in the battle for autonomy Erikson highlights what he calls the *"retentive-eliminative modes."*[30] In line with the traditional Freudian "originology" Erikson claims to have repudiated, he holds that "if in some respects you have relatively more shame than autonomy then you feel or act inferior all your life—or consistently counteract that feeling."[31] Put more cautiously, Erikson believes that "from a sense of *self-control without loss of self-*

esteem comes a lasting sense of autonomy and pride; from a sense of muscular and anal impotence, of loss of self-control, and of parental overcontrol comes a lasting sense of doubt and shame." [32] As Erikson thought that the social order, through organized religion, ensures hope, so the social institution which he believes secures the enduring gains of this second stage of the life cycle is "the principle of *law and order*." [33]

Erikson's third stage, involving a conflict over initiative and guilt, was designed to supplement Freud's oedipal stage, a crisis which "in its habitual connotations . . . is only the infantile and often only the neurotic core of an existential dilemma which . . . may be called the *generational complex*." [34] Therefore, for Erikson oedipal problems are the infantile or neurotic manifestation of generational conflict, which is unavoidable in human beings who experience life in terms of successive generations. [35] Instead of Freud's "phallic" stage in his concept of infantile sexuality, Erikson emphasizes "the intrusive mode" which characterizes this phase, whose basic virtue consists in purpose. According to Erikson's schema,

> the play age relies on the existence of some form of basic family, which . . . teaches the child by patient example where play ends and irreversible purpose begins. . . . Social institutions . . . offer an ethos of action, in the form of ideal adults fascinating enough to replace the heroes of the picture book and fairy tale. [36]

The fourth phase of the life cycle, and the last period of childhood, comes during latency, when the child reaches school age. Here "a sense of competence . . . characterizes what eventually becomes *workmanship*." [37] Industriousness develops at this time, although in conflict with feelings of unworthiness. "The danger at this age lies in the development of a sense of inadequacy." [38] Accordingly, Erikson considers an inferiority complex to be "the stubborn shadow of the school age." [39] The competence that emerges is aided by "a sense of the *technological ethos* of a culture" that arises at this time.[40]

We have already discussed Erikson's conception of adolescence, his fifth stage, marked by a conflict between identity and role confusion. "Youth can be the most exuberant, the most careless, the most self-sure, and the most unselfconsciously productive stage of life" [41]—and yet it can be very different for divided souls in search of a second birth. From the point of view of the individual, ideology comes to meet the youthful striving for fidelity, confirming identities; but from society's point of view, it is the young who rejuvenate its institutions.

While in 1945 Erikson had regarded adolescence as the last of the epigenetic crises, subsequently he enlarged his conception of the life cycle to include adulthood, which he divided into three stages: conflicts about intimacy, generativity, and integrity.[42] The post-adolescent struggles against isolation and self-absorption as he seeks affiliation and love. Then the middle-aged person has to confront the danger of stagnation; in his Luther study, and later in his work on Gandhi, Erikson discussed how the crisis of middle age "occurs when an original man first stops to realize what he has begun to originate in others." [43] As the young adult develops love, and middle age is the time of care, in old age the essential virtue is wisdom. This is the time of the conflict between integrity and disgust, as the individual must accept "one's one and only life cycle and of the people who have become significant to it as something that had to be and that, by necessity, permitted of no substitutions." [44]

In Erikson's view, there seems to be little healthy place for genuine regret, atonement, or remorse, for he holds that the frustration of wisdom is despair: "despair indicates that time is too short for alternate roads to integrity: this is why the old try to 'doctor' their memories." [45] The despair of old age may take many forms, and "is often hidden behind a show of disgust, a misanthropy, or a chronic contemptuous displeasure with particular institutions and particular people —a disgust and a displeasure which (where not allied with constructive ideas and a life of cooperation) only signify the individual's contempt of himself." [46]

This final stage of the life cycle, about which Erikson has written relatively little,* seems least satisfactory of all. Why should wisdom be defined by the acquiescence in the inevitable? It can just as well be argued that wisdom should also lead to dissatisfaction, even rage, at past personal mistakes, unfortunate chance, or uncorrected social injustices. Any old person is likely to be emotionally less elastic than in younger years. Not all development results in gains. As a matter of fact, there would be something peculiar if aging did not involve depression—not only does an older person lose some of his powers, but loved ones die. Whatever satisfactions can be foreseen in what has been, in Erikson's terms, generated for the future, death is lonely and often painful. Erikson's view of old age seems to define wisdom in an unduly self-satisfied way: it *"is the detached and yet active concern with life itself in the face of death itself, and . . . it conveys the integrity of experience, in spite of the decline of bodily and mental functions."* Even when it comes to acknowledging grief in old age, Erikson accentuates the positive: old people, he tells us, "learn" to mourn. [48]

But by his use of the concept of the life cycle Erikson hopes to express his conviction that the best unit of psychosocial observation should be a generation, not any individual. [49] Also, through the image of a cycle of life, he "intended to convey the double tendency of individual life to 'round itself out' as a coherent experience and at the same time to

* Erikson has, however, recently published an interesting interpretation of Ingmar Bergman's motion picture *Wild Strawberries*. [47]

form a link in the chain of generations from which it receives and to which it contributes both strength and weakness." [50]

Nevertheless, having reviewed his epigenetic schedule of emergent virtues, Erikson has properly been "concerned over the probability that this ascending list will be eagerly accepted by some as a potential inventory for tests of adjustment, or as a new production schedule in the manufacture of desirable children, citizens, and workers." He is justifiably worried that "an attempt to construct a ground plan of human strengths . . . could be accused of neglecting human diversities, of contributing to the fetish of deadly norms, and thus to the undermining of the individual. . . ." [51] Although Erikson has referred to a stage in his epigenetic chart as a "criterion of mental health," still he tries to maintain that he has "no interest in proposing a new list of norms, norms which would facilitate our giving ourselves or our fellow men good or bad grades in mental health." [52]

As Erikson would like to see it, "each person must translate this order into his own terms so as to make it amenable to whatever kind of trait inventory, normative scale, measurement or educational goal is his main concern." [53] As Erikson himself has used his version of the life cycle, he has demonstrated considerable latitude in applying his concepts to developmental phases: Luther is described as having had an identity conflict around the age of thirty. But Erikson does not claim any special advantages for such unusual, out-of-sequence conflicts. (It might be interesting to consider that Freud too was out of tune with age-appropriate experiences throughout much of his life, and though the source of a good deal of pain this also helped ensure his alertness and productivity.)

Erikson has also tried to combat a further possible misuse of his approach in "the connotation that the sense of trust (and all the other *positive* senses to be postulated) is an

achievement, secured once and for all at a given stage." [54]
Erikson finds it unfortunate that people often ignore the
negative aspects of his life-cycle crises (mistrust, doubt,
guilt, etc.) in order to make a neat uniform scale of achievement. Erikson would argue that "to learn to mistrust is just
as important," and therefore "a certain ratio of trust and
mistrust in our basic social attitude is the critical factor." [55]
But whatever his occasional protestations, Erikson is indubi-
tably trying to emphasize the positive; he believes that "what
the child acquires at a given stage is a certain *ratio* between
the positive and the negative which, if the balance is toward the positive, will help him to meet later crises with a better chance for unimpaired total development."[56] In arguing in
behalf of that balance toward the positive, Erikson's life cycle is in danger of confirming psychosocial smugness.

Erikson admits that he tends to view optimal personal
development as a sequence of steps successfully overcome.
One can only wonder what place human tragedy can find in
his schema. For are there not emotional conflicts in life
which lead in no "healthy" direction at all? The very essence
of some crises, in so-called normal people, is that they constitute a thoroughgoing waste of human feelings and impulses. Erikson's terminology cannot easily be used in order
to suggest that people might ever have been capable of
better things. His attempt to correct the excessively retrospective orientation of traditional psychoanalytic theory may
have led him to an opposite extreme, according to which
one is supposed to search in even the worst human losses for
some remnant of a saving grace.

A final danger in Erikson's life-cycle thinking lies in the
possible naturalistic fallacy, that is, the naïve effort to impute
to history the intention of developing what we might ethically prefer for the future. Erikson is aware that Heinz Hartmann has warned against "hidden preachers" in psychoanalysis, but this has not deterred Erikson's own quest for what
he considers "the bases in human nature for a strong ethics." [57]

What Erikson has in mind are what he calls developmental necessities: "we have attempted . . . to account for the ontogenesis not of lofty ideals but of an inescapable and intrinsic order of strivings, which, by weakening or strengthening man, dictates the minimum goals of informed and responsible participation."[58]

As Erikson has described these strivings: "somewhat challengingly, I called them basic 'virtues,' in order to point to an evolutionary basis of man's lofty moralisms." Even though "many people are dubious of the attempt to tie anything which sounds like virtue or strength to an evolutionary process," he has contended: "I'm not speaking of values; I only speak of a developing capacity to perceive and to abide by values established by a particular living system." [59] In this way he hopes to have redressed a bias in earlier psychoanalysis, by understanding what may balance the kind of psychopathology traditionally recognized by analysts, and therefore he has tried to account for "what may be the positive goals built into each stage of development." [60]

There need be nothing wrong with moralizing per se; and as we shall see, one of the merits of Erikson's approach is that it implies a far more explicit answer to the quest for a theory of individualism, a vision of what a fully developed human being might be like, than earlier psychoanalytic thinking. The problem is that Erikson does not seem sufficiently aware of the logical dilemma in moving from empirical statements to value judgments, in inferring an "ought" from an "is." On behalf of the "virtues" that go to make up ego strength, Erikson contends that "without them, institutions wilt; but without the spirit of institutions pervading the pattern of love and care, instruction and training, no enduring strength could emerge from the sequence of generations." [61]

But look at the terms Erikson has chosen for his "virtues": in infancy, faith; in early childhood, will power; in the play age, purposefulness; in the school age, efficiency; in adulthood, responsibility; and in old age, sagacity. If these "virtues" are "also criteria of ego strength," [62] then ego strength has all along been as much an ethical as a clinical concept. For all Erikson's tentativeness, it seems clear that he has committed himself to a version of the life cycle which is not so much an account of what does happen as an ideal of what he would like to come about.

Erikson is aware of the possibility of being called an "idealist," but he does not adequately recognize that when he refers to symptoms as "vices" [63] he undermines his effort to defend his own account of the special meaning of the "virtues" of ego strength. If Erikson's concept of the life cycle is in good part an ideal, one has to question how it might compare with other alternatives. For there is a wide diversity of human potentialities that might be fostered.

One of the sources of the appeal of Erikson's concept of the life cycle has been its degree of comprehensiveness; if it does have an ethical as well as a descriptive side to it, if it tries to tell what life could be like as well as how it can run into trouble, this has only strengthened the attractiveness of his approach. For we live in an era when previous systems of thought are under a cloud—though people are still in search of a new system, if not a secular religion. It may seem less important to study Erikson's categories of thought than to see how he uses these concepts in practice; yet it is the full-scale quality to his work which has helped ensure its impact. Nonetheless, we should be aware that what he has presented us with is a set of theories, not facts. And it is partly because of his own acknowledged lack of theoretical-mindedness that many of his readers come away with the belief, despite his declared intentions, that he has uncovered an ineluctable piece of science rather than constructed a valuable point of view.

CHAPTER 8

Gandhi's "Nonviolence"

UnlikeWestern psychology, Hinduism has had its traditional conception of the life cycle; and so it was appropriate that Erikson chose Mahatma Gandhi, the leader of an oppressed people, as a vehicle by which to enlarge the Freudian heritage. Drawing on this tradition of thought, Erikson explores a variety of psychological means by which certain groups in societies can be kept in subordinate positions. He thinks that people find reassurance in the belief that there exist others who are below themselves at their worst. He points to the "propensity to bolster one's own sense of inner mastery by bunching together and prejudging whole classes of people," and to the tendency of man to "do everything in his power to keep unchanged, and . . . to deepen in others inferiorities which are so essential to his own superiority."[1]

Erikson has been increasingly aware of the degree to which many identities thrive at the expense of degrading others, and he explains this in terms of the projection of negative identities: everything that is felt as inferior and threatening to one's own sense of identity can be relieved and gotten rid of by suppressing racial or ethnic minorities.[2] And it is by this avenue that what Erikson calls "the fanatic religionist" gains his "license to view and to treat others as if they were no better than the worst in himself. . . ."[3]

Erikson's concept of negative identity also helps explain how the defenseless, on their part, can accede to their oppressors' judgment. It is surprisingly easy to expect little of oneself. Erikson rightly finds it fearful how "any group living under the economic and moral dominance of another is apt to incorporate the world image of the masters into his own—largely unconscious—self-estimation. . . ."[4] He concludes that any lack of freedom—whether for blacks, women, or young people—cannot be "resolved by the mere promise of political and economic equality—although of course, [it is] impossible without it."[5] He thinks that an inner emancipation from oppression, aside from revolutionary action, may be required.

Erikson studied a revolutionary in his *Gandhi's Truth*. In the terminology of his ego psychology, by the doctrine of passive resistance Gandhi succeeded in transforming a negative Indian identity of weakness into an active and positive political technique. Biographically, Erikson sought to understand Gandhi's ideological innovation in the context of his middle age. The characteristic crisis of mid-life, according to Erikson's theory of the life cycle, is that of generativity, defined as "primarily the concern for establishing and guiding the next generation."[6] In his *Young Man Luther* Erikson had already proposed the concept of a generativity crisis. But only in his study of Gandhi did Erikson try to deal extensively with a crisis of a middle-aged great man.

Throughout this account of a great spiritual leader and professional revolutionary, Erikson had a comparison with Freud in mind. Erikson reminds us, for example, of Freud's aspiration in his early years to become a political leader (elsewhere Erikson has called attention to Freud's "own militant, over-sized handwriting" [7]). To make the reciprocal relationship between Freud and Gandhi more congruent, Erikson reports that Gandhi had once had the ambition to become a doctor. Freud evolved a new form of introspection, while Gandhi developed new ways of nonviolent action. But if Gandhi helped to liberate the Indian people, Erikson informs us that in Freud's early practice "certain classes of mental patients were unjustly treated by others, including doctors, as though they were possessed by evil or doomed genetically—were a separate species, as it were." [8]

Repeatedly Erikson compares the methodologies of Freud and Gandhi, for he sees similarities between psychoanalysis and Satyagraha. He objects to translating Satyagraha as "nonviolence," since that seems too negative a term: "Satyagraha constitutes the faith that he who can face his own propensities for hate and violence 'in truth' can count on a remnant of truth in the most vicious opponent, if he approaches him actively with the simple logic of incorruptible love." [9] Similarly, the method of psychoanalysis, Erikson tells us, involves the confrontation of "the *inner* enemy nonviolently." For Erikson, Freud and Gandhi are "the two men who invented two corresponding methods of dealing with our instinctuality in a nonviolent manner." [10] Both men help to change our view of humanity.

Yet the individual convictions of Freud and Gandhi remain radically different. As an advocate of more permissive sexual reform and as a theorist of the inevitability of human instinctuality, Freud thought violence was a permanent part of the human condition; but Gandhi, the proponent of nonviolence, "believed to the last in the potentially malignant nature of sexuality." [11] As a matter of principle, Gandhi came to abjure sexual activity altogether. Like earlier religious fanatics in history, Gandhi advocated asceticism; it was a necessary condition, he thought, for practicing nonviolence. Leaders in nonviolence had to commit themselves to absolute chastity. As a Freudian, Erikson complains to Gandhi's spirit: "not once, in all your writings, do you grant that a sexual relationship could be characterized by what we call 'mutuality.'" [12] (Erikson has defined mutuality* as "a relationship in which partners depend on each other for the development of their respective strengths."[13])

Erikson prefers to think, however, that Gandhi gave up personal intimacy for a wider communality. Like Freud, Gandhi was an advocate of self-control; but Gandhi wanted to achieve self-mastery through the avoidance of both sexual intercourse and killing. Freud thought that man was by nature a wolf to man, and that hostility not discharged outwardly had to be turned against the self, whereas Gandhi proposed nonviolence as a constructive form of self-suffering. It is in keeping with Erikson's post-Freudianism to see in Gandhi's program "a new kind of ritualization of conflict, one which poses an alternative to the cynical view of human nature." [14]

As early as his first edition of *Childhood and Society* Erikson had cited Gandhi, along with Jesus, as an upholder of ideals Erikson especially cherished; but there were also intensely personal reasons behind Erikson's interest in Gandhi. In line with his own conception of himself as an outsider, Erikson recounts that Gandhi too "was born on the periphery of his future 'domain'. . . ." And Erikson says explicitly: "my transference to Gandhi no doubt harbored an adolescent search for a spiritual fatherhood, augmented by the fact that my own father, whom I had never seen, had taken on a mythical quality in my early years." [15]

---

* For a discussion of mutuality, see Ch. 10, pp. 157–60.

But, above all, Erikson has stressed the potential Christian significance in Gandhi's approach to nonviolence. Evidently "Gandhi would not even contemplate as an adversary anybody with whom he did not already share a communality in a joint and vital undertaking. . . ." Therefore, according to Erikson, "the basic attitude of Satyagraha . . . depends on the militant recognition of a common humanity. . . ." [16] Erikson has recounted how Gandhi seemed to him to embody in theory, as well as action, a modernization of the Golden Rule: "one should choose to act so as to enhance the potentials of one's counterplayer's development as well as one's own." [17] Gandhi succeeded in India by meeting the British in terms of their own best Christian ideals. But as Erikson quotes Tom Mboya on the tactical limitations of the technique of nonviolence, "you can use it with the British but you can't use it with the Belgians." [18]

By establishing the impact of self-suffering, Gandhi illustrates Erikson's belief that "mastery over anger is less foreign to those who have learned to express anger in traditional and disciplined ways." [19] Nonviolence does not mean abstaining from what one could not manage anyway, but rather renouncing aggressive tactics one has learned how to use well. Therefore, Gandhi "felt that Indians would have to learn to fight before they could *choose* to be non-violent." [20] Erikson can in this way rationalize Gandhi's controversial backing of the British in drafting Indians for military service.

In Erikson's view, there need not be vindictiveness in Gandhi's kind of militancy. Erikson would dissociate the technique of Gandhi from that of student radicals, in the 1960s for example, who acted not to elicit the best in their opponents, but who rather set up provocations in order to mobilize the worst in their objects of hatred. Such tactics are a debasment, both of one's opposition and of Gandhi's method. Erikson is even uncomfortable with the description

of Gandhi's technique as "passive resistance," instead pre-
ferring much of the time to translate Satyagraha as "truth
force." [21]

To Erikson, Gandhi succeeded in combining politics with
religion, and there are many parallels here to his earlier view
of Luther. Both were reformers with special techniques
(prayer and truth force) which had their effects on the
masses. A kind of motto for *Young Man Luther* had been
Kierkegaard's diary entry about Luther being "a patient of
exceeding import for Christendom." [22] And a comparable
guiding principle for *Gandhi's Truth*, not cited until after
the middle of the book, was Nehru's statement that Gandhi
had given back to India its identity: Nehru said that what
Gandhi had achieved was "a psychological change, almost
as if some expert in psychoanalytic methods had probed
deep into the patient's past, found out the origins of his
complexes, exposed them to his view, and thus rid him of
that burden." [23]

As in his Luther book, the figure of Freud stands behind
what Erikson has to say about his biographical subject.
Gandhi was, like Freud, a man of visual inclination. (It is
striking, however, that Erikson includes no photographs or
portraits in any of his biographical studies; perhaps he is
himself so visual that he fears the reader's distraction from
the prose text.) Erikson remarks on the "superb clarity of
Gandhi's new and surprising insights," although to many
Gandhi's mysticism appears at odds with Freud's ideal of
writing clearly and simply. As Freud had selectively relied
on his own predecessors, so Gandhi "accepted" from men
like Tolstoy and Ruskin "only a sanction of and a vocabulary
for what was becoming articulate in him." It is reminiscent
of Freud's own self-assurance when Erikson tells us, in connection with Gandhi's alleged economy with words, that he
once said: "I do not recollect ever having had to regret any-

thing in my speech or writing." [24] Even for details in Gandhi's life, such as his endurance as a walker, Erikson draws parallels with Freud.

In the course of *Gandhi's Truth* Erikson maintained that his was the book of a psychoanalyst. Yet one wonders, in the midst of his romanticization of heroes, whether Erikson has not been using Gandhi to work himself free from Freud's clinical tradition. Erikson could not be more dutiful toward Freud as a mythical figure; yet he is conscious of not having set out to merely "apply" traditional psychoanalytic concepts to Gandhi's life.

It is characteristic of Erikson's method to describe his own emotional involvement in the collection of material about Gandhi. To express his feelings Erikson even punctuates the middle of his book with a twenty-five-page letter to Gandhi (although Erikson is not the passionate letter writer Freud was). Yet for all Erikson's direct introspective openness, which means that it takes a hundred pages in *Gandhi's Truth* before the hero gets born, he does not tell us exactly how he came to meet and get on with the family who played such a major part in his account of Gandhi, and whose estate he stayed on in India. Even more curiously, Erikson writes that his host, Ambalal Sarabhai, had once "visited Freud to see what kind of man he was and whether he could be trusted to help" a relative.[25] Erikson has been apparently so candid that one almost does not notice how odd it is that, with all his interest in Freud, we are not told any more about that clinical encounter. One of the dangers of psychohistory is that intimacy can too easily be used manipulatively; and perhaps this drawback stems from the cultural effect of psychoanalysis which, despite its individualistic aims, has helped undermine privacy by universalizing intimate dilemmas.

Many would agree that Erikson as a young man was very different from the person he later became. And as in his Luther study, Erikson is primarily interested in the earlier

Gandhi, before he became a celebrity, on the principle that his career afterwards is relatively well known. A biographer like Lytton Strachey, even though he could not have shared Erikson's attitudes toward either religion or hero worship, also, in his book on Queen Victoria, chose to "describe the long process by which the character of the queen was formed; once that character had crystallized, her actual life was of less significance to him." [26]

In his *Young Man Luther* Erikson had focused on the fit in the choir, and in *Gandhi's Truth* he chose to discuss a strike in 1918, which he dramatizes as "the Event." Erikson does not justify his selection of a single incident in Gandhi's life simply on the traditional psychoanalytic grounds of extracting as much meaning as possible from a limited amount of material. Nor does he concede that because his hosts in India had possessed special knowledge of this strike, it was an obvious mine for him to plumb. But unfortunately Erikson's case for the objective significance of the 1918 strike is weakened by Gandhi's own autobiography, in which he minimized the importance of the Ahmedabad incident—and most historians would today side with Gandhi's own view of the matter.[27]

Erikson, however, considers the Ahmedabad textile strike of 1918 to have been "the dramatic event by which labor unionism was founded in India." It was the first time Gandhi fasted on a political issue; a year later he led "the first nationwide civil disobedience and became forever India's Mahatma." [28] Yet what appeal could Gandhi's tactics have had for the approximately one third of the population of India who were then not Hindus but Moslems? It would be curiously future-oriented to see Gandhi solely in the context of post-partitioned India. (The partition was marked by violence and bloodshed.) [29]

Erikson claims that "all agree that the Event radically

changed labor relations in Ahmedabad and in India." But
if he has overstated material to which he merely had good
personal access, it is notable that Ahmedabad was different,
a "maverick" part of India, as late as July 1975. Erikson,
however, makes a case for his 1918 Event having "a central
position" not only in Indian labor history but in Gandhi's
life and in the fate of nonviolence as a technique as well.
Erikson may be unwilling to acknowledge the novelistic
character of his kind of biography writing; but he is clear
about his Christian moral purpose. For Erikson "the over-all
importance of the Ahmedabad episode had been the emergence and the investment of an almost spiritual belief in
reconciliation as a ritual." [30]

As a Freudian, Erikson was in an excellent position to
appreciate the "mythologizing that goes on in the writings
of the true followers." Gandhi succeeded in creating, like
Freud, a retinue which became a substitute for his real
family. In Erikson's view, "true saints" become "father and
mother, brother and sister, son and daughter, to all creation,
rather than to their own issue." [31] In interviewing Gandhi's
followers, whom Erikson calls his "witnesses" of the Event,
he wondered about the means which the leader of such a
movement employed to attract, select, and train his support-
ers. Yet in pondering the material given by these witnesses,
Erikson belatedly questioned whether he had the right to
interpret their unconscious motives.

In reading Erikson's account of Gandhi's adherents, one
is reminded of Erikson's own participation in Freud's movement. For these followers of Gandhi felt bound by the offer
of a vocation. Like the early Freudians, Gandhi's disciples
felt themselves to be "a self-chosen group making history
together." Erikson is clearly thinking in terms of the experience of his colleagues in psychoanalysis. For each disciple, "a new convert" with "a total commitment," serving
Gandhi as a master meant complete devotion to a cause

which provided a "sense of purpose." In the course of Gandhi's recruitment and indoctrination of his adherents, he necessarily had to be concerned "with the relationship of his prospective followers to their parents, or their guardians." [32]

Gandhi, we are told, "elected sons and daughters in his ascetic settlement. . . ." Erikson says that "it would always be Gandhi's explicit intention to incorporate a follower's marriage into his orbit if"—and what follows is not like Freud—"he could not prevent it." But, again like Freud, Gandhi "assumed without delay prerogatives of the utmost consequence in any new follower's life." [33] Erikson concludes that any "educator must become, in varying combination, both father and mother to his students. . . ." Here Erikson may be confusing a possible role of a therapist with the tasks of a teacher. But he might have been thinking of Freud when he wrote about Gandhi's "passionate search for sons who would be worthy disciples and for disciples who would be ideal sons." [34]

In keeping with his earlier interest in the nature of great men in history, Erikson is on the lookout for patterns of greatness. For he foresees "a time when man will have to come to grips with his need to personify and surrender to 'greatness.'" Erikson is enigmatic about how he judges the implications of this supposed need. He infers that "greatness depends on the preservation and continued corroboration of something most ex-children lose," implying his admiration for historical success. And he thinks that "special men . . . *have* to become their own fathers and in a way their fathers' fathers while not yet adult." [35] Once again we are back with Erikson's theme of self-creation, a legitimate concern for all people of talent.[36] Gandhi, we are told, "eventually would justify the trust of all his older brothers only by becoming great in his own way." Yet whatever the merits of his general comments on greatness, or its relevance for understanding Gandhi's life, when Erikson cites the example of "boys of future prominence" it is hard not to conclude that he is not aware of the dangers of what sounds like an ethics of success.[37]

In *Gandhi's Truth* Erikson described a period of pre-adolescent testing in which Gandhi experimented with delinquency in league with a friend, Sheik Mehtab, who for Erikson is the personification of Gandhi's negative identity. Of Gandhi's stay in England, Erikson writes that it was a genuine moratorium. In London, Gandhi was a dandy, and he violated traditional Hindu taboos: "away from home and not as yet constrained to be self-sufficient . . . he must test what he has brought along. His father . . . is dead; and yet some deep determination to compete with his memory by wielding power in a new way will and must emerge only gradually." Erikson writes of Gandhi's two-decade stay in South Africa, where he developed Satyagraha, as though it were part of a continued detour. For a time Gandhi could sucessfully project his negative identity, "like the driven devil, on his alter ego, his Muslim friend." [38] But as Gandhi found himself he broke this tie, and according to Erikson such identity solutions can result in splits between former friends.

Erikson's Gandhi is not without inner conflicts; Erikson speaks of repeated depressions, and of how Gandhi fasted in order to fight despair. (Traditional psychoanalytic thought would look upon such abstinence less positively, as part of symptomatology.) Doubtless Gandhi's most devoted followers would be offended by Erikson's explanation of Gandhi's dietary struggles in terms of his relationship with his mother. But Erikson tries, in conceiving of greatness, to avoid too conformist a view of human dilemmas: "even a great man may be only as great as the degree of despair he can allow to himself—and admit to a few others." Citing Freud, Gandhi, and St. Augustine, Erikson says that many great intro-spective writers reach their peak "in middle age and at the threshold of lonely greatness." [39]

Yet Erikson recognizes Gandhi's propagandistic purpose, since any great confession is only in part self-exploration. In particular, he is impressed with how Gandhi adopts an "accustomed role of pleading guilty." For Erikson, Gandhi was a "saintly politician," and one "frankly conscious . . . of being crafty and cunning as well as saintly." Erikson quotes Gandhi's refusal to let a disciple join him in a fast: " 'Leave this to me,' he said. 'Fasting is *my* business.' " [40]

Throughout his study of Gandhi, Erikson resists excessively simple Freudian interpretations. Gandhi's father, for example, was accidentally injured while on his way to his son's wedding; and then later the father died while Gandhi was making love to his wife, who was by then pregnant. When the child aborted, Gandhi considered it fitting: he felt he should have been attending to the nursing of his dying father instead of having intercourse. But Erikson does not reduce Gandhi's later attitude toward sex to this trauma of his father's death.

Erikson sees in Gandhi's autobiographical account that "a desperate clinging to the dying father and a mistake made at the very last moment represented a curse over-shadowing both past and future." [41] Erikson refuses to re-duce this problem to an oedipal conflict. He found as a typical theme, either for Indians in general or for Gandhi's followers in particular: "a *deep hurt* which the informant had inflicted on one of his parents or guardians and could never forget, and an intense wish *to take care of abandoned creatures*, people or animals, who have strayed too far from home." [42]

If his account of Gandhi is largely hagiographical, in a few places Erikson is starkly realistic, for example in des-cribing the suffering of Gandhi's suicidal eldest son, Harilal.

Erikson considers that in general "Gandhi's letters to his sons are often moralistic in a vindictive way, as though his sons had to be doubly good for having been the issue of that early marriage." Erikson presents Harilal's dilemma from the point of view of the progeny of greatness: "nothing is left for the son to correct or complete, nothing to live out which in the old man's life remained recognizably unlived as a mourned or abandoned potential—except the old man's negative identity, his 'murdered self.'"[43] One might consider, though, that a life marked by sexual fulfillment and rich family relationships was still an open possibility.

Gandhi could write to his eldest son that one of his loyal adherents had replaced him, while Harilal determined, for his own part, "to get even with his moralistic father." Harilal eventually "became a Muslim and a derelict who within a year after the Mahatma's assassination, was found in a coma 'in some locality.'" (The locality was, according to an earlier account by Erikson, a brothel, but he seems to find the circumstances of Harilal's death too sordid for more explicit description in *Gandhi's Truth.*) Despite Erikson's general emphasis on the positive, he movingly tried to account for the failure in Gandhi's relationship with his eldest son: "from his own sons, Gandhi demands the most and expects the worst—that is, he associates his sons with what is worst in himself."[44]

In this account of Gandhi's struggles, Erikson looks for the resolution of identity conflicts. This can partly be a matter of dress, discovering what kind of clothes make one feel like oneself. In Erikson's view, however, there cannot be an identity without ideology, and it is the "new gospel" sanctioning Gandhi's acts which interests Erikson most.[45] In contrast to his study of Luther, with Gandhi he was less interested in the methodology of psychohistory and more concerned with the ethical substance of his hero's teachings.

Gandhi's doctrine of "ahimsa" (noninjury) held that "the only test of truth is action based on the refusal to do harm," and Erikson interprets this dogma broadly as "a determination not to violate another person's essence." Gandhi's position was that "*that action alone is just which does not harm either party to a dispute.*" Erikson infuses Gandhi's philosophy with his own special concern for mutual activation, what he calls the "leverage of truth": "ethically speaking . . . a man should act in such a way that he actualizes both in himself and in the other such forces as are ready for a heightened mutuality." [46] But before considering what Erikson's ideal of mutuality amounts to, it is necessary to assess his version of what might be meant by psychological normality.

CHAPTER 9

Normality

Although at times Freud explicitly repudiated Christian ethics, on the whole the new morality he stood for can only be inferred from his life and thought. As a matter of doctrine, Freud proposed that analysts not preach or give advice; patients should be relied upon to determine their own goals. But Freud could safely confine the analyst's moralizing only because he chose to restrict his kind of therapy to a special category of sufferer. Regardless of his theoretical intentions, with patients he admired Freud could be therapeutically activist. In practice, analysis in Freud's view was an ethical endeavor; to be "cured" was proof of one's "worthiness."

Yet Freud was so eager to separate his psychology from past philosophical systems that he was not particularly interested in discussing what so-called normality might entail. Erikson has referred to the oral tradition among analysts on this point, citing approvingly Freud's "shortest saying" in response to an inquiry about the nature of psychological health: " 'Lieben und arbeiten' (to love and to work). It pays to ponder on this simple formula; it gets deeper as you think about it."[1] Again and again Erikson has quoted Freud's maxim as the standard of what a normal person should be able to do well.[2]

Erikson understands that in the past psychoanalysis popularized the ideal of genitality. He thinks, however, that "even where a person can adjust sexually in a technical sense and may at least superficially develop what Freud called genital maturity, he may still be weakened by the identity problems of our era." Erikson has increasingly questioned whether genitality and health can be identical. (Wilhelm Reich probably took this equivalence to its furthest extreme; for him the capacity to experience orgasm was inconsistent with the existence of neurosis.) Instead, Erikson has proposed generativity not only as a further developmental stage, but as a part of psychosexuality; generative "frustration results in symptoms of self-absorption."[3]

In another context, however, Erikson treats mature sexuality as an aspect of generativity; and he defines generativity as meaning "to generate in the most inclusive sense . . . children, products, ideas, *and* works of art."[4] An activity is generative as long as it contributes "to the life of the generations."[5] Erikson believes that psychoanalysis will have to go beyond considering normality negatively, as an absence of childhood conflicts. He regards it as one of Freud's limitations that "he was merely concerned with freeing the adult capacity to love from infantile remnants."[6]

Erikson knows that part of the bias inherent in psychoanalysis stems from its traditional therapeutic task; in "the typical medical report," he reminds us, "the frequent occurrence of the word 'negative' denotes the fact that the patient enjoys positive good health."[7] But too often a psychoanalytic concept of health seems wholly out of place—as, for example, in talking about an innovator like Luther. Freud did at times hint at the great diversity among healthy persons. In practice, he could accept therapeutic outcomes that were, even by our own standards today, unconventional. But it is the theory he bequeathed and the clinical tradition that has grown up in his name that have been influential. And it is the psychoanalytic approach to normality that is questionable.

For someone genuinely creative, the ideal of being somewhat like other people may represent a desirable check on one's own eccentricities. But unfortunately the use of normality as a standard tends to make even the least impressive personalities feel superior. As Erikson well knows, it is too much to demand of creative people that they fulfill prefabricated norms. Yet without some explicit standard of normality, therapists would be in danger of simply supporting pre-existing social expectations.

In Erikson's earliest writings adulthood played little role. Increasingly, however, he has had to ask himself: "What, really, *is* an adult?" [8] In his attempt to understand adulthood, Erikson has wondered what we might like children or young people "to become, or even what we would like to be—or to have been." He has cited the example of some American Presidents as illustrations of what he has had in mind. Jefferson was, we are told, "a man of rare adult stature, caring intensely and competent to take care of what he undertook—publicly and privately." [9] Yet evidently the best Jefferson could do for the many children he seems to have fathered by one of his slaves was to permit them quietly to leave his plantation, becoming part of white America.

Whatever the merits of Erikson's version of Jefferson, the principle that "adulthood is generative" is worthy of attention, for according to Erikson it is in adulthood that "you learn to know what and whom you can *take care of*." [10] In his quest for what it might mean to be fully developed as a human being, Erikson has cited the life of Abraham Lincoln; Erikson asked Huey Newton: "would you say Lincoln was a reasonably adult man?" [11] Yet how much of an ethical burden can the concept of normality bear? To describe Lincoln as an adult may amount to the diminution (and degradation) of a politician as much a saint as Gandhi. And how inadequate it is of Erikson to describe Hitler as a "fanatically unadult leader." [12]

A key part of Erikson's version of normality hinges on his notion of leverage: an individual is most grown-up when he can provide "leeway" not only for himself but for those who are in interplay with him. Erikson holds that "each identity cultivates its own sense of freedom. . . ." [13] As elsewhere, he does not adequately distinguish between a subjective feeling and an objective condition. Society has its role to play in creating leeway for the individual, to the degree that identity development depends on social confirmations. Freedom, the "capacity to make informed choices," [14] is an aspect of a healthy ego. Although he prides himself on having been on the periphery of every field he has worked in, Erikson chooses to stress the ego's need not to feel alienated. [15] Recently he has written of *"inner liberation"* and "the courage to stand alone," as opposed to those inner obstacles to humanity's efforts to free itself. [16]

Erikson stresses the existence of "a quality in all things alive, namely the restoration and creation of a *leeway of mastery.*" The deprivation of such freedom can have, Erikson thinks, dire consequences; frustrated people may struggle at the expense of deadly harm to themselves or others. [18] Erikson, like Freud, has long viewed the aim of psychotherapy as that of restoring a patient's capacity for choice. But Erikson warns us that any leeway accomplished in the past, however revolutionary it may have been, may become oppressive today. With characteristic ambivalence, however, he goes on to maintain that "the method of yesterday can also become part of a wider consciousness today." [19]

Erikson has complained that "psychoanalysis has revealed the irrational thinking which hinders reality testing, but has not given its due to actuality." [20] It is typical of his kind of reverence for Freud that Erikson reports that "the German word *Wirklichkeit*" was "often implied in Freud's use of the word *Realität* . . ."; Erikson would like to believe that Freud's concept of reality included what Erikson now means by actuality as opposed to factuality.[21] But Erikson's discussion of actuality is designed to emphasize what he thinks is missing in traditional psychoanalytic thinking: "if reality is the structure of facts consensually agreed upon in a given stage of knowledge, actuality is the leeway created by new forms of interplay." [22]*

Freud assumed a split between the inner world of fantasy and the outer world of external reality; instead of adopting a static view of the environment as a given, from which inwardly people more or less depart, depending on their rationality, Erikson wants to loosen up the rigid separation between the supposedly verifiable external world and less reliable inner distortions. His concept of actuality is designed to highlight the way fantasy can be constructive, overcoming neurosis to energize unexpected social sources of support.

Erikson links his ideas about actuality with his convictions about greatness: "the great adults who are adult and are called great precisely because their sense of identity vastly surpasses the roles foisted upon them, their vision opens up new realities, and their gift for communication revitalizes actuality." [24] For Erikson, true identity formation has to be confirmed by what he has recently called the three aspects

* In a different context Herbert Marcuse has also criticized the limitations of what he has called Freud's "performance principle." [23]

of reality—factuality, sense of reality, and actuality. "Only this threefold anchoring of a given world image in facts and figures cognitively perceived and logically arranged, in experiences emotionally confirmed, and in a social life cooperatively affirmed, will provide a reality that seems self-evident." [25] In Erikson's view, mutual activation lies at the heart of health. He fears that people will base their reality testing solely on the issue of mastery over factuality, ignoring the possibilities of what can be cultivated by mutual interplay.

Erikson's way of conceiving the healthy personality has been in terms of ego strength, in spite of his once having said that the whole energetic viewpoint in psychoanalysis meant little to him. [26] A "strong" ego reconciles contradictions. But such strength need not imply uniformity, for Erikson believes that "to have the courage of one's diversity is a sign of wholeness in individuals and in civilization. But wholeness, too, must have defined boundaries." [27] Erikson's version of the life cycle presupposes that the higher the level of personal integration, the greater the tolerance for conflict and diversity. As he puts it,

> I shall present human growth from the point of view of the conflicts, inner and outer, which the healthy personality weathers, emerging and re-emerging with an increased sense of inner unity, with an increase of good judgment, and an increase in the capacity to do well, according to the standards of those who are significant to him. [28]

Doing well has to be seen, according to Erikson, in terms of cultural relativity.

No feature of society is more critical to emotional health than work. Erikson believes that human beings, to survive psychosocially, "must acquire a 'conflict-free,' habitual use of a dominant faculty, to be elaborated in an occupation. . . ." [29] Impressed by "the curative as well as the creative role of work," Erikson rightly thinks that "probably the most neglected problem in psychoanalysis is the problem of work, in theory as well as in practice. . . ." [30] Even in the case of children, Erikson believes that they gain ego strength "only from wholehearted and consistent recognition of real accomplishment." [31]

It is striking that in his endorsement of Freud's maxim "to love and to work," Erikson did not feel it necessary to add what Freud so significantly omitted—namely, play. The Freudian tradition has encouraged in Erikson an unnecessarily bourgeois view of the child: play serves functions of balance for the child; play is the child's "most serious occupation." [32] Purposefully hard at work in play, the Eriksonian child does not seem to have much fun. Erikson's whole model of the life cycle looks like hard work, as one envisages the stages to be successfully surmounted as one grows older. Yet theoretically Erikson holds that man is most human at play. He likes to contrast neurotic childishness to "childlikeness, which to regain in the complexities of adult life, is the beginning of the kingdom." [33]

Erikson has gone so far as to maintain that for Freud "the *via regna* to mental life had been the dream. For me, children's play. . . ." [34] The child's ego is already capable of synthesizing, in its ability to achieve self-cure in play. By play Erikson has in mind "*free movement* within *prescribed* limits." It is like Erikson to try to find whatever indirect support he can from Freud for a theory of play. Even in describing the nature of Freud's achievement, Erikson claims that "Freud, in freeing the neurotics of his repressed era from the onus of degeneracy, invented a method of playful communication called 'free association'. . . ." [35] In terms of his own view of the life cycle, Erikson observes that Freud gave "the dominant 'complex' of the play age the name of a tragic hero: Oedipus." [36] Nevertheless, Erikson has more recently acknowledged his need to innovate within psychoanalysis.[37]

Erikson has interpreted the child's play, following Freud's lead, as "the infantile form of the human ability to deal with experience by creating model situations and to master reality by experiment and planning." [38] Erikson believes that by observing children at play it is possible to learn what they are nonverbally concerned with; play in childhood constitutes "an intermediate reality in which purposefulness can disengage itself from fixations on the past." [39] Play is precious to Erikson because it "gives a sense of divine leeway, of excess space." In play therapy a child is able "to regain some play peace. . . . For to 'play it out' is the most natural self-healing measure childhood affords." [40] Disturbances in a child's play can be considered the best index to unconscious conflicts.

Erikson regards instances of daytime disruption of play as parallel to anxiety dreams during sleep. And "the antithesis of play disruption is play satiation, play from which a child emerges refreshed as a sleeper from dreams which 'worked.' " [41] Although his model of the life cycle is differentiated into separate stages, Erikson does not distinguish the meaning of play in, say, a two-year-old as opposed to a four-year-old. As long ago as 1937, in his own most traumatological phase of thinking, Erikson complained of this theoretical inadequacy.[42] Yet his continued lack of specificity may be a telling sign of the essentially ideological commitment behind his interest in play. He is more concerned with the theory of play than with its psychology. He holds that the play of children is "an infinite source of what is potential in man." [43] An adult at play "steps sideward into another, an artificial reality; the playing child advances forward to new stages of *real mastery*." [44]

One of Erikson's earliest publications had to do with his observations of pre-adolescent children at play. He asked each child to construct on a table "an exciting scene out of an imaginary moving picture." He saw that girls and boys treated space in significantly different ways. In the play constructions of these eleven-, twelve-, and thirteen-yearolds, he thought he could detect a language of representations in space. For example, "the most significant sex difference was the tendency of boys to erect structures, buildings, towers, or streets; the girls tended to use the play table as the interior of a house, with simple, little, or no use of blocks." [45]

In contrast to the "static interiors" built by the girls, the boys' play tended to express the contrasts of "height and downfall . . . strong motion and its channeling arrest." [46] And Erikson proposed that these differences had diagnostic significance; for example, in a boy's play "extreme height . . . reflects a trend toward the emotional overcompensation of a doubt in or a fear for, one's masculinity, while the varieties of 'lowness' express passivity and depression." [47]

Erikson's use of play constructions constituted a projective test, and he concluded that in view of the contrasts in the way boys and girls use space "sexual differences in the organization of a play space seem to parallel the morphology of genital differentiation itself. . . ." [48] If "the girls emphasized inner and the boys outer space," this was for Erikson an indication that "a profound difference exists between the sexes in the experience of the ground-plan of the human body." [49] It would seem that for all his efforts to emancipate himself from traditional psychoanalysis, Erikson remained committed to a psychology still claiming to see "clearly biological determinants" in these play constructions. [50]

Erikson has extended his interest in play to different societies; for instance, he observed how Indian play performances were different from what he has seen in the West. Nonetheless, Erikson had earlier written without cultural qualifications: "in our unconscious and mythological imagery," he once wrote, for example, "tasks and ideals are women. . . ." [51] Erikson broadened Freud's outlook on female psychology into the assertion that "anatomy, history, and personality are our combined destiny," [52] yet this was in support of, rather than in contradiction of, Freud's famous claim that anatomy is destiny. It was entirely in keeping with Freud's own sexually reactionary doctrine for Erikson to refer to "man's intrinsic abhorrence of femininity." [53] As for the "biological differences between the sexes," Erikson considers that "they are decisive from the beginning" of life.[54]

Erikson's conviction that experience is anchored in the ground plan of the body—a less direct approach than saying we are biologically determined—has been challenged by many in the women's liberation movement. Erikson has noted that such women distrust his work, but he sees himself as coming to "conclusions concerning women's very special superiorities" based "on the claim that there are (some) sexual differences." [55] He might turn out to be right; but if such differences are observed in children already as old as eleven, twelve, and thirteen, can that not be at least partly explained by the particular upbringing of traditional Western society? Moreover, Erikson has emphasized that special methods can bias conclusions, and therefore both clinicians and historians can influence what they observe; although he has become skeptical of the so-called neutrality of the traditional psychoanalytic treatment setting, he remains curiously oblivious to the built-in social tilt in his own observation of play constructions. As Kate Millet pointed out, "It must have been difficult for American girls to 'imagine' themselves 'motion picture directors' . . . since their society totally deprives them of such role models." She thinks that "Erikson's whole theory is built on psychoanalysis' persistent error of mistaking learned behavior for biology." [56]

Erikson has protested that the " 'leading' women are all

too often inclined to lead in too volatile, moralistic, or sharp a manner . . ." and that "feminist suspicion watches over any man's attempt" to describe these problems.[57] He has tried to defend himself against such criticism: he discerns in the women's liberation movement a "moralistic projection of erstwhile negative self-images upon men as representing evil oppressors and exploiters."[58] He maintains that a commitment to the reality of uniqueness does not entail any support for inequality.[59] Erikson says he is among those interested in preserving "a sexual polarity, a vital tension, and an essential difference" that otherwise might get "lost in too much sameness, equality, and equivalence. . . ."[60] So despite his disclaimer, it may be that emphasizing uniqueness does help support inequality.

As opposed to the Freudian theory of castration anxiety, which in women is supposed to take the form of penis envy, Erikson thinks that "the existence of a productive inner-bodily space safely set in the center of female form and carriage has . . . greater actuality than has the missing external organ."[61] Although to some it has seemed that Erikson is bigoted about women, within the context of psychoanalytic thought he relegated penis envy to a more limited role. He has tried to focus on the way women's inner space participates in the development of a positive identity. In regard to psychopathology specific to women, Erikson believes it follows that the "*fear of being left* empty, and more simply, that of *being left*, seems to be the most basic feminine fear, extending over the whole of a woman's existence."[62] He does not, however, consider the social dependency of women which may have contributed to such a syndrome. Instead, he isolates "a specific sense of loneliness . . . a fear of being left empty or deprived of treasures, of remaining unfulfilled and of drying up. . . . an 'inner space' is at the center of despair even as it is the very center of potential fulfillment. Emptiness is the female form of perdition. . . ."[63]

In Erikson's view, "the feminine ego has a very specific task to perform in integrating body, role, and individuality." [64] In pointing to "the procreative function of genital activity" for understanding female psychology, Erikson insists that we "face it right now: it is the idea of being unconsciously possessed by one's body, rather than owning it by choice and using it with deliberation, which causes much of the most pervasive anger" of feminists. Like many temperamental conservatives, Erikson believes that conventional conflicted feelings about sexual identities and social roles "call not only for liberty in socio-economic matters, but also for emotional liberation—whatever comes first." [65]

Like many men of his period, Erikson finds women in some ways superior: he suggests that "it may be that woman has a finer touch, a finer sense of texture, finer discrimination for certain noises, a better memory for most immediate experience, a greater capacity to empathize immediately and emotionally. . . ." [66] Women have, according to this theory, uniquely "learned to respond to the measure of the developing child, to the measure of the child in the adult, and to the measure of manageable communalities within wider communities." [67] Again, for all his attention to social and cultural factors elsewhere in his writing, Erikson curiously fails to consider the extent to which these sexual differences may be culturally conditioned.

One wonders whether it is science or ideology that supports the generalization that "the infant must be suckled or, at any rate, raised within a maternal world best staffed at first by the mother. . . ." [68] At least at times Erikson has too readily accepted traditional Western male-female stereotypes; he once argued, for example, that "whatever developmental, whatever accidental factor may have delighted or disturbed the child, he is sure to have experienced it in relation to his mother." [69] This contention is so strange that one is tempted to look for autobiographical sources; in Erikson's own earliest years, of course, his father was entirely absent.

Erikson genuinely admires what he regards as certain traditional feminine strengths. He feels uncomfortable with the term "passivity" when it is applied clinically to feminine aspects of men. (Yet he does not reject the idea that passivity is a peculiarly feminine quality.) "Paradoxically, many a young man . . . becomes a great man in his own sphere only by learning that deep passivity which permits him to let the data of his competency speak to him." Erikson then ritualistically invokes the founder of psychoanalysis, quoting from a letter of Freud's to Fliess: " 'I must wait until it moves in me so that I can perceive it. . . .' " [70] Erikson's cultural breadth, and his acquaintance with a society as different from ours as India, have convinced him that it is possible for men to become "caricatures of their one-sided masculinity." [71] The Western male must learn to change his stereotyped aims, lest they lead to an unduly mechanical restriction of ego possibilities.

Erikson has himself called for a new kind of historical understanding which would overcome the prejudice that woman must remain what she has been in the past. He anticipates that "women may yet contribute something specifically feminine to so-far masculine fields. . . ." [72] He feels confident that women will play a great role in the future, and in particular he has pointed to those "prejudices which keep half of mankind from participating in [political] planning and decision-making. . . ." [73]

Erikson questions whether we should continue to confront the danger of human self-annihilation without having mothers represented "in the councils of image-making and decision," and he suggests that "they might well add an ethically restraining, because truly supranational, power to politics in the widest sense." [74] He looks forward to women assuming their share of political leadership. In one of his earliest references to Gandhi's philosophy, Erikson proposed that "it may well be that war cannot be banned until women, for the sake of a worthwhile survival, dare to recognize and to support the as yet undeveloped power of unarmed resistance." [75]

Erikson has regretted that traditional psychoanalysis has ignored the political dimension in human relationships. [76] Yet it is unrealistic to expect women in politics to serve the kind of purposes Erikson has in mind for them. Are "birth control" and "arms control" anything like, as he suggests, "two corresponding technological developments"? [77] It is not hard to detect a patronizing or at least a sentimentalizing tone when, in an essay on female psychology, Erikson concluded on a note of "mankind's" need for "a guiding vision" and for the humanization of its inventions. [78] The examples of Golda Meir in Israel and Indira Gandhi in India, not to mention various great women in history, are not reassuring as to the realism of Erikson's expectations of women as leaders in nonviolence. Nor is it obvious how the moral task of humanization cannot fail to reinforce women's historical social inferiority.

To his credit, Erikson has shown an interest in the meeting points of psychology and politics. He is well aware of the dangerous personal latitude accorded to American Presidents and their entourage, and he has even suggested that psychoanalysis "may yet play a part in questions of war and peace." [79] Essentially, however, Erikson remains morally hostile to the traditional instruments of political power.

CHAPTER 10

Morals and Ethics

Erikson began his career within the Freudian school, which fostered in him the ideal of analytic neutrality. "To interpret," he has recently said, "should mean to be objective, beyond approval or condemnation." Unfortunately he has "seen psychoanalytic explanations used as weapons—either of offense or defense—only too often. . . ." [1] At times he has been tempted to define the model analyst as a trained clinician free of private susceptibilities or preferences. When invited once to contribute a paper on the nature of clinical evidence, he chose first to discuss the topic as if he had been asked to reveal how a clinician works; only late in the essay did he explain that the question he had really been set to answer was how a *good* clinician works, which must call for a more subjective response.

Erikson can be modest about what psychoanalysis has achieved. For instance, it has not succeeded in giving very reliable advice on how we should raise our families, but "it has attempted at least to formulate what should *not* be done to children, and there are . . . any number of avoidances which can be learned from the study of the life cycle." [2] He sees himself as having tried to contribute an outlook, not a set of conclusions. If Freud could take morality for granted, this can be at least in part traced to the social position of early psychoanalysis. As long as Freud and his followers were themselves on the outside they could hardly be accused of advocating conformism. They could even afford to evade certain intellectual issues.[3]

Yet within the psychoanalytic framework lie important moral commitments. Erikson is right, for example, in seeing in Freud the implication that childhood is "the model of all oppression and enslavement, a kind of inner colonialization, which forces grown-ups to accept inner repression and self-restriction." [4] Psychoanalysis's traumatology is appropriate given the childhood roots of potential human exploitability. Regardless of his protestations of neutrality, Erikson is willing to affirm the belief that "the most deadly of all possible sins is the mutilation of a child's spirit. . . ." [5]

Erikson is not disposed to think ill of people, except for "those who misuse youth." [6] He ascribes to psychoanalysis "the persistent humanist intention, beyond the mere adjustment of patients to limited conditions, to apply clinical experience to the end of making man aware of potentialities which are clouded by archaic fear." [7] One of the reasons for Erikson's contemporary significance is that he is willing to entertain broader questions which earlier analysts hoped to avoid.

It is hard not to see in Erikson's work, as in his dedication to *Childhood and Society*—"To our children's children"—an implicit utopianism, not alien to a millennial strain within psychoanalysis. For Erikson the problem is not the existence of evil, which poses a constant and inescapable threat to human life and institutions, but rather our "sense of evil," [8] which can supposedly be minimized by proper child rearing. "In order to ban autocracy, exploitation, and inequality in the world," Erikson thinks, "we must first realize that the first inequality in life is that of child and adult."⁹ The fact that Erikson is morally on the side of the angels does not mean that he is using psychoanalysis as a "weapon" any less than those whose efforts he chooses to regret. Psychoanalysis has long sought to uncover unintentional biases. More explicitly than Freud, Erikson has tried to specify "some prime dangers to man's freedom," such as "the bondage of man to such fear of radical otherness that he must annihilate or suppress others; and the corresponding bondage of feeling so endangered by his own nature that he will attempt to unduly repress it."¹⁰ As in his treatment of the sources of racial oppression, Erikson believes that in general psychoanalysis can function as a criticism of "wasteful" social change.¹¹

In an effort to examine some of the moral implications of psychoanalysis, Erikson has explored the functioning of the superego, the part of the mind that Freud regarded as the so-called agency of moral values. Also like Freud, Erikson cites the need to counteract the danger of an excessively oppressive conscience, but unlike Freud, he also considers the superego in an evolutionary perspective. By "evolutionary" Erikson means that there are stages in the development of conscience. As conscience evolves, it also grows—and Erikson feels he can speak in terms of an improvement over time. He cites Shakespeare's Hamlet, for example, as a man who "advanced . . . beyond the legal concepts of his time. . . ."¹² Erikson does not see tragedy in terms of an ultimate conflict between mutually contradictory, but equally valid, values; rather, tragedy for him is due to a kind of developmental lag: "the fact that human conscience remains partially infantile throughout life is the core of human tragedy."¹³ Implicit in Erikson's position is a morally optimistic view of the life cycle; he insists, for example, on "the wisdom of the ground plan." [14]

Central to Erikson's evaluative statements is his effort to distinguish between morals and ethics. For even though he has admitted his "wordiness" and his tendency to play with words, Erikson has increasingly drawn attention to the significance of "the difference between infantile morality, adolescent ideology and adult ethics." [15] In his conception of the development of the life cycle, ethical strength differentiates itself from the ideological conviction of adolescence and childhood's feelings of moral obligation. To Erikson "morality can become synonymous with vindictiveness and with the suppression of others"; therefore he considers "*moral rules* of conduct to be based on a fear of *threats* to be forestalled," whereas "*ethical rules*" rest "on *ideals* to be striven for. . . ." [16] He is interested in "a new mankind" and "a new ethics"; but for him ethics are adult, morality is childish. [17]

For Erikson the central problem with morality, and one of his grounds for distinguishing it from ethics, is that to him morals necessarily connote moralism. For he claims to be particularly on guard against righteousness and prejudice. He explains that "a clinician may be forgiven for questioning the restorative value of an excessive dose of moral zeal." [18] Too often such excessive moralism only succeeds in perpetuating infantile dependencies. The mistakes of "patriarchal moralism" have convinced him of the present "necessity for a more universal and more mature ethics." [19] He clearly dislikes "moralistic fervor, puritan or radical." His distaste for "moralistic outrage" stems from his suspicion that "you can always be sure that the loudest moralists have made deals with their own consciences. . . ." [20] Too often such moralistic fervor outlasts changing historical circumstances.

In attempting to understand varieties of conscience, Erikson has differentiated between "a *premoral* position that denies any need for morality; . . . an *amoral* position that

flaunts [*sic*] accepted norms; . . . an *anti-moral* position
that militantly negates all authority; and . . . an *anti-author-
itarian* and yet *moralistic* position that condemns the adult
world with righteous fervor. . . ." [21] None of these alternatives, however, fits Erikson's call for a new worldwide ethics.
He thinks "it is more important to gain painful insights into
our common evolutionary and developmental corruptibility
than an easy moral superiority over our dead heroes." Of
America after its formal withdrawal of combat troops from
South Vietnam, Erikson thought that "at this point in history
this country must come to grips with its own awareness of
historical guilt, over having transgressed against humanity
and nature"; but "to find culprits is more our style. . . ." [22]

When he proposes that an ethical orientation should replace moralism, it is because he believes that the latter is
"outdated"; for he defines ethics as meaning, "psychologically speaking, a moral discipline based on insight and informed assent." [23] He has applied his epigenetic principle to
what he sees as the development of conscience:

> I will speak of *moral learning* as an aspect of childhood; of
> *ideological experimentation* as a part of adolescence; and of
> *ethical consolidation* as an adult task. As we know from the
> study of psychosexuality, the earlier stages are not replaced,
> but develop according to an epigenetic principle—that is, they
> are absorbed into a hierarchic system of increasing differen-
> tiation. [24]

Erikson has departed so far from Freud's efforts at ignoring the question of the relationship of psychology to moral
values that, on the model of Freud's own interest in the
psychopathology of everyday life, he now speaks of "the
ethicality of everyday life." [25] Erikson finds ethical involve-
ments inevitable; and in this regard he parts company with
"some scientific pretensions" of psychoanalysis. [26] Long ago
he remarked that the psychoanalyst "in analogy to a certain
bird . . . has tried to pretend that his values remained

hidden because his classical position at the head of the 'analytic couch' removed him from the patient's visual field. We know today that communication is by no means primarily a verbal matter. . . ." [27] In contrast to many others in his profession, Erikson believes that "any psychotherapist . . . who throws out his ethical sentiments with his irrational moral anger, deprives himself of a principal tool of his clinical perception." [28]

Erikson has clearly undertaken the philosophizing Freud so often feared. (Yet despite having once dismissed some of Jung's writings as the work of a prophet rather than a scientist, Freud himself was capable of composing books of social prophecy.) In his earlier writings on the life cycle Erikson was aware that he had "come close to overstepping the limits (some will say I have long and repeatedly overstepped them) that separate psychology from ethics." [29] He has become convinced, however, that mankind possesses "a truly ethical potential," and therefore "to study the psychological foundation of this potential may be one of the more immediate tasks of psychoanalysis." [30]

In his essays on Thomas Jefferson, Erikson indulges his tendency to idealize those who personify his conception of greatness. It is also true that he discusses specific symptoms, such as Jefferson's migraine attacks. Yet if one reads Erikson on Jefferson for purposes of psychohistorical understanding, one is bound to feel disappointed by the paucity of new empirical data. Erikson was really composing an ethical treatise. He singles out, for example, "Jefferson's assumption and that of his friends that there is in man in principle a moral core that, if given leeway to manifest itself in mutual activation with others will tend to make ethical and rational choices," which for Erikson "represents a basic developmental truth." [31]

In presenting his version of the life cycle Erikson had feared that his model of human development might read "shockingly virtuous in a way reminiscent of moralistic values." [32] But he felt inclined not to apologize, since his account of such virtues meant to him a schedule of human strengths. Erikson's concept, for instance, of postadolescent 'virtue' " was intended "to represent a minimum evolutionary requirement rather than a maximized ideal." [33] It is not inconsistent of Erikson to maintain that his concepts imply unconscious ethical strengths as well as unconscious potentialities for destructiveness.

Erikson defines the meaning of "ethical" in terms of "a *universal sense of values assented to.*" [34] For him "universally convincing means, above all, credible in the eyes of youth." [35] In the end he singles out the maxim "love thy neighbor as thyself" as the basic universal Christian principle. Erikson has not sought to invent an ethical code out of thin air. But he has tried to update the Christian golden rule by placing it in a contemporary context: ethics "can only emerge from an informed and inspired search for a more inclusive human identity, which a new technology and a new world image make possible as well as mandatory." [36] Old moralities become "expendable only where new and more inclusive ethics prevail." [37]

Like Erich Fromm in his attempt to appeal to past religious truths, Erikson thinks that the superiority of a universal ethics "is the wisdom that the words of many religions have tried to convey to man." [38] He believes that the golden rule, as reformulated in his work on Gandhi, represents "a theme hidden in the sayings of great thinkers." [39] In aiming at a universally applicable ethical standard, Erikson has sought to understand what it means to be human in the interest of furthering "what must eventually become the identity of one mankind." [40] He believes he has found the bedrock of ethics in human infancy: "for the basic fact that will always keep and bring us all closer together is the nakedness and helplessness of the newborn human child." [41] And he is uncomfortable with any doctrine which might separate private and public values. [42]

Many writers in the history of ideas have insisted precisely on the incompatibility of individual and social ethics, or at least on the legitimacy of the possible tensions between public and private virtues. It is doubtful how much help even a universal belief in the preciousness of the infant can be in reconciling concrete social and political conflicts. Not for Erikson the skeptical temperament of a Henry Adams, who bemoaned that "the stupendous failure of Christianity tortured history." [43]

One does not have to be altogether cynical to suspect that even if everyone were to agree on the meaning of human love, it might not help much in alleviating painful social conflicts, the Arab-Israeli struggle for instance. Contending conceptions of the good life have been the stuff of all known history. Yet Erikson would rather ignore competing schools of thought, and instead cite a mythical consensus among the "sages of old." [44] It is enough for him, in order to support "a concept of the life cycle which clearly determines man's responsibility toward his own life as well as toward that of all those fellow beings to whom he grants equality," to rely on "its formulation in the wisdom of the ages, which must be rediscovered and reformulated by each new generation." [45]

If Erikson wanted to find an alternative to his own brand of Christian ethics, he need only have gone to Freud himself. Regardless of what Erikson has tried to argue exists implicitly within Freud's system of thought, the founder of psychoanalysis saw himself as a radical vis-à-vis traditional Western ethics; at times he could even identify himself with the devil. The love of mankind, in Freud's view, rested on sublimated homosexuality, and to a large degree Freud shared the conventional distaste for perversions. He openly espoused the conviction that "not all men are worthy of love." The commandment which, even more than "thou shalt

love thy neighbor as thyself," seemed to Freud "incomprehensible and arouses still stronger opposition in me" was " 'love
thine enemies.' " But then Freud qualified his comparison,
withdrawing the idea that the second commandment was an
even "greater imposition" than the first. For "at bottom it is
the same thing"; one's neighbors are one's enemies.[46]

Far from Gandhi's ethics of reconciliation, Freud liked to
quote Heine: "One must, it is true, forgive one's enemies—
but not before they have been hanged." [47] Once Freud even
went so far as to maintain: "It really seems as though it is
necessary for us to destroy some other thing or person in
order not to destroy ourselves." [48] It may be fortunate, from
Erikson's point of view, that Freud's passages on Christianity* were dropped, according to Bullitt's account, from their
study of Wilson. Erikson does note that, in the case of the
injunction "love thy neighbor as thyself," Freud "took this
Christian maxim deftly apart as altogether illusory, thus
denying with the irony of the enlightenment what a maxim
really is. . . ." Yet he still wishes to believe that Freud's denial should not outweigh the Christianity which he hopes
Freud's technique "may really stand for." [50]

Erikson's own name for what he calls "the secret of love"
is "mutuality," "devotion forever subduing the antagonisms
inherent in divided function." [51] In the end he prefers this
standard to the Freudian "genitality." In his clinical reflections Erikson has emphasized the necessary interaction between the therapist and patient, although such give and take
was not part of Freud's stated intentions. (In his study of
Gandhi, Erikson highlighted "counterplayers" to his hero.)
Most psychotherapists assume, and Erikson has made it explicit, a distinction between a higher and a lower self; but

---

* Freud once published the following oedipal interpretation of
Jesus: "The 'redeemer' could be none other than the most guilty person, the ringleader of the company of brothers who had overpowered
their father."[49]

he has his own way of stating the difference between more and less worthy actions: "it is best to do to another what will strengthen you even as it will strengthen him—that is, what will develop his best potentials even as it develops your own." [52] Erikson takes for granted a natural harmony of human needs, hence his praise for "consistent values." [53] (He had stressed the "confusion" involved in identity crises.) Freud, however, had recognized the potential incompatibilities between human goals and aspirations.

Erikson has rephrased the Christian golden rule in conformity with his view of mutuality. He advises that "what is hateful to yourself, do not to your fellow man." [54] Erikson says that his "base line is the Golden Rule, which advocates that one should do (or not do) to another what one wishes another to do (or not do) to him." [55] At bottom Erikson has been working toward ensuring that Christian ethics seem relevant. As he puts it in terms of his identity concept, we should "always . . . act in such a way that the identities of both the actor and the one acted upon are enhanced." [56] A truly ethical act for Erikson would be one which enhanced the "mutuality between the doer and the other." [57]

Erikson has tried to present his position as the contributions of a healing outlook to the field of ethics. Only recently has he appealed to the sayings of Jesus (another of his great leaders with followers), and in particular to the Sermon on the Mount. In commenting on Jefferson's version of the New Testament, however, Erikson complains of missing "all reference to Jesus' healing mission"; of one Biblical cure Erikson believes that it was a woman's "faith in his mission that had made her whole." But for Erikson, Jefferson is a hero because he stood for the "informed love of humanity—in others, in himself, and in his children." [58] Some time ago Erikson cited approvingly a prayer of St. Francis': "for it is in giving that we receive"; according to Erikson, "the cured patient, to speak with Saint Francis, would not so much seek to be loved as to love, not so much to be consoled as to console, to the limit of his capacity."[59] (Erikson's wife has written a book about St. Francis.) Erikson's concept of mature love is as much Christian as specifically Freudian.

Erikson's ethical concern has grown out of his great respect for religion; "there is a religious element," he believes, "to all true transvaluations of values. . . ."[60] For Erikson, even superstitions are not to be seen as neurotic obsessions, as Freud saw them, but rather as a means of collectively mastering the unknown. Religion, with its awareness of death and its concern for eternity, can help us attain a consciousness of our limitations. In terms of ego psychology this can be experienced as "an ego-chill, a shudder which comes from the sudden awareness of our nonexistence."[61] By such means Erikson has been able to express within psychoanalytic terminology that which he finds of value in religion.

As so often in Erikson's work, what is apt to look like neurotic failure from a classical psychoanalytic point of view is treated as a potential source of human development. For example, instead of focusing on the "symptomatic 'rituals' of isolated neurotics," Erikson considers what he calls "ritualization" as "a *special form of everyday behavior*."[62] In distinguishing between "obsessive symptomatology" and "creative ritualization" Erikson finds an empirical analogy to his ideal of mutuality, for "what may at first look like a shared symptom can claim to approach the mutuality of fruitful ritualization."[63] Erikson's kind of ritualization involves interplay which is repeated and has adaptive functions for the egos of the participants. Unlike Freud, who saw man as beset by powerful and contending instinctual drives, Erikson believes that "there is much to suggest that man is born with the need for such regular and mutual affirmation and certification. . . ."[64] Ritualization has sources which are nonrational, yet it has constructive purposes. Such interplay helps overcome ambivalence, which can be especially troublesome "in situations which have strong *instinctual* components."[65] For Erikson ritualization is the process which binds energies into patterns of mutuality. Teasing would be an example of a "spontaneous ritualization."[66] Erikson even sees signs of "a new ritualization of warfare," and he cites ethological evidence for "pacific propensities on the part of beasts."[67]

Ritualization has the emotional effect "a sense of *separateness transcended*, and yet also of *distinctiveness confirmed*." It involves a "numinous element, the sense of a hallowed presence." At the same time, ritualization includes a distinction "between the sanctioned and the out-of-bounds, the holy and the profane, the elect and the damned." A successful ritual promotes renewal. But the breakdown of these patterns can mean trouble, leading to "an alternation of impulsivity and compulsivity, of excess and self-restriction, of anarchy and autocracy." [68]

One of the sources of current discontent which Erikson perceives is the well-known decline in reassurance from traditional ritual ceremonies. For him a distinctive feature of psychoanalysis is its creation of a new "professional ritualization"; and for all the differences between Freud and Gandhi, the technique of Satyagraha is for Erikson another new ritualization.[69] Creative ritualizations are one way of mastering conflicts which earlier psychoanalysis would not have adequately appreciated. In tune with Erikson's interest in the confirmation of ego strengths, he has been searching for new ways "of thinking about and affirming our common humanity." [70]

The two modern ritualizations Erikson is most familiar with, Gandhi's and Freud's, are notable twentieth-century correctives to what Erikson calls the "pseudo-species" mentality. Many groups—tribes, clans, castes, nations, classes, religions, creeds, ideologies—"provide their members with a firm sense of God-given identity—and a sense of immortality"; but they each "behave as if they were separate species created at the beginning of time by supernatural intent." [71]

Each of the pseudo-species believes that it represents the sole fulfillment of human possibilities. Nationalism may only be the most notorious instance of peoples tempted to think that they constitute the human race.

Processes of cultural "pseudo-speciation" account for a dangerous feature in all group identities. For any dominant pseudo-species also harbors its own negative identity, and therefore the possibility exists for the moralistic treatment of others as embodiments of unacceptable ego tendencies. According to Erikson, "as long as the core of any collective identity is a pseudo-species idea, it is going to be oppressive."[72]

Among the specimens of pseudo-speciation, Hitlerian Germany is prominent on Erikson's list. Even before he worked out his latest terminology, he had considered that "extreme nationalism . . . is one of the indicators of the fear that a budding identity may be prevented from finding completion and may miss its historical period."[73] Teleology has been proposed before in the history of social thought; recently Erikson has referred to "that reactionary pseudospeciation which found (we hope) its climax in Hitler."[74] Yet Erikson thinks that it is extremely important not to denigrate the human tendency toward pseudo-speciation by using clinical terminology to describe it.

Erikson's purpose, he claims, is not a moralistic one. Therefore he can, attempting to bridge the gap between facts and values,* refer to what he calls "the fact and the obligation of

---

* The naturalistic fallacy of deriving values from facts is enduringly attractive. A psychoanalytically informed anthropologist, Clyde Kluckhohn, believed that "in principle, a scientific basis for values is discoverable. Some values appear to be as much 'given' by nature as the fact that bodies heavier than air fall. No society has ever approved suffering as a good thing in itself—as a means to an end, yes; as punishment, as a means to the ends of society, yes. We don't have to rely upon supernatural revelation to discover that sexual access achieved through violence is bad. This is as much a fact of general observation as the fact that different objects have different densities."[75]

man's specieshood."[76] He considers the question of man's universal identity to be what he calls an evolutionary problem,[77] implying that the course of history may be able to solve what others would deem a strictly ethical dilemma. Ethics does not, for Erikson, involve a confrontation with divergent goals, nor does it entail for him the kind of costly choices Jean-Paul Sartre has dramatized.

Yet oddly enough Erikson has criticized behaviorist psychology for offering "a utopia of conduct so scheduled by implanted controls that ethical conflict is altogether unnecessary."[78] In keeping with his special view of tragedy, he believes "a choice is free when it can be made with a minimum of denial and of guilt and with a maximum of insight and conviction."[79] But on what grounds, save utopian ones, can one expect free choices to be made without a considerable degree of acceptance of guilt? For Erikson future identities rest, not as for Freud on the ruins of past failures, but on a combination of historic liberations.

In this process the United States has for Erikson played a key role. For he has the "faith" that "each pseudospecies and each empire in some dialectical way added new elements to a more universal sense of humanity." Erikson has perceived that all is hardly perfect in America; he has recently noted that "obviously . . . something is crumbling in the whole American system, a change in America's sense of itself. . . ."[80] Supposedly the American heritage was a different and more glorious one. Erikson thinks that America has made an exceptional effort not to be ideological; this was part of the melting-pot phenomenon. The United States as a nation represents for Erikson the most notable example of an attempt to forge a new, broader identity out of the fragments of European identities.[81]

But should one be willing to abandon all ethical convictions in the face of changing facts? One can grant the relevance of the empirical world to our making value judgments. But it may still be the essence of a moral value to be incapable of being fully realized in history.

Erikson believes that "factors have inevitably forced the American to lead the way in a development which sooner or later will and must include the whole world." [82] America endorsed the ideal of the self-made man; and the struggle for a universally inclusive identity, in conflict with negative identities, is for Erikson the main contest in our world. Ever since the Founding Fathers in the eighteenth century, the "psychological fascination of the American dream" has lain in its "world image" of "a new man, self-made in an America dedicated to natural labor . . . guaranteeing a reciprocation of rights." [83] Yet Erikson ignores the extent to which the Founding Fathers necessarily had to rely on past colonial experience, and he understates the darker side of their beliefs and actions, in order to highlight their commitment to unlimited progress.

Erikson's standard of value, which he believes to be evolving in history, is that of universalism. For example, he holds that child training can be improved "only where the universal trend toward larger cultural entities is sustained." [84] Broader identities are to be encouraged; Erikson's conception of the psychoanalyst's task leads him to think he is apt to be especially sensitive to the emergence of more inclusive identities. At the same time the growth of any such broader identities can be in itself threatening; and Erikson argues that "psychoanalysis, at this juncture, must remain vigilant in regard to the anxieties and rages aroused where a wider identity will endanger existing styles of instinctuality and identity and traditional visions of morality and reality." [85] It follows politically for Erikson that "the best leader is the one who realizes what potentials can be activated in those led, and most of all, what more inclusive identities can be realized." [86]

Erikson favors the polarity of relativity and universality. Any interpreter must include himself in an interpretation, since his ideas remain subject to the influence of his own life history and that of his intellectual ancestry. But as much as Erikson emphasizes such "relativities," he has sought for a new vision of "a more universal speciation." [87] He has written of the need for a new model of man, and for him "that means a new and wider and more inclusive identity." [88] One instance of "superidentity" that he cites is "the worth of the human infant." [89] Yet by his late writings the concept of identity had itself come to have an ethical meaning: Erikson now suggests that "identity means what the best in you lives by, the loss of which would make you less human." [90]

Erikson has for a long time seen mankind working toward a better future—"more rational, more conscious, and more universal." [91] We live, he believes, in "a world of universally expanding identities," and he is convinced that this is not mere wishful thinking but that "a more universal, more inclusive human identity seems forcefully suggested by the very need for survival." [92] Erikson does not think it is possible to fabricate identities; what he desires seems to him built into our situation. He has repeatedly maintained his confidence in the expansion of the "image" of humanity in our era. [93]

Along with what Erikson sees as ethical progress, he detects a long-term increase in human self-awareness. Modern history seems to him to display "a wider trend in the scrutiny of human motivation ranging from Darwin's discovery of our evolutionary animal ancestry and Marx's uncovering of classbound behavior to Freud's systematic exploration of the unconscious." [94] With insight must go, in Erikson's view, better ethical convictions; he speaks of "our slow and zigzagging road toward the realization of specieshood," "mankind's painfully slow progress towards unity," and it is partly because of technology that "the creation of an American identity" [95] seems to Erikson such a significant model. For him "an all-inclusive identity must be part of the anticipation of a universal technology." [96] He believes in such a new ethical system, "not as a utopia, but as a necessity." [97]

Erikson recognizes the possibility, however, of retrogression; and Hitler's Germany is an illustration of how "advancing civilization is potentially endangered by its own advance. . . ." [98] But perhaps such supposed advances in human culture are more illusory than Erikson would care to admit. Despite what he sees as "an irreversible humanist sense of world community," [99] Erikson can acknowledge that America in recent years has behaved as a technological pseudospecies in trying to annihilate so-called less advanced peoples.

Perhaps the essence of Erikson's proposed new ethics lies in a greater consciousness of what any generation owes to every other generation. The ideal of maturity becomes "the symbolic guarantor of a universal adulthood," which constitutes the fullest development of the human personality.[100] For all his idealism, a humanitarianism at odds with early Freudian skepticism, Erikson at times can be more cautious; it is sometimes clear to him that his ideal of universality *is* a utopia. At one point he can even express reservations about the implications of an ideal of being human; for "while this strange phraseology of being 'human beings' may at times represent a genuine transcendance of the pseudospecies mentality, it often also implies that the speaker, having undergone some revelatory hardships, is in a position to grant membership in humanity to others." [101] Aware of the danger of the "extremes of too narrow and too wide identities," [102] even if it be utopian Erikson is willing to stand behind the ideal of an ethics of a universal identity. It may not be possible to tell whether such an ethics can encompass all the possible diversities; still he is sure "that history points to more inclusive identities as the only remedy for . . . political and psychological anxieties." [103] But such a solution, which proposes no institutional changes, is idealist; and it may well convince many that, despite the millennial strain in his thought, Erikson's fundamental outlook is conservative.

CHAPTER 11

The Future of Depth Psychology

PHILOSOPHICAL CONTROVERSY AND FREUD'S INFLUENCE

It is at least an open question what effects Erikson's kind of philosophizing can be expected to have. He has attempted to elaborate a Christian ethics that will be meaningful to his contemporaries. His ethical concern comes up not only in his concepts of mutuality and generativity, as well as in his theory of the life cycle, but in his commitment to the purity of the technique of nonviolence. As we have seen, Erikson's ideas of ego strength and identity, as well as his specific social outlook, have implications that cannot be verified or falsified empirically. He has chosen as an ultimate value the sacredness of human infancy.

Such moral positions have a philosophical basis. Freud taught us that throughout childhood we introject into our superegos the values of our parents and other authority figures. These standards and beliefs, however, do not form a neatly harmonious system. If only because we have as models both fathers and mothers, our aspirations are bound to be in conflict. The past rarely presents us with a monolithic hierarchy from which we can deduce answers to such questions as "What ought I to do?" or "How ought I to live?"

Generally people turn to history for value judgments; previous elaborations of ethics are helpful to us in making choices. One of the merits of studying social and political thought, as well as great imaginative literature, is that it broadens our horizons, showing us possibilities of human life that we need not experience ourselves in order to know them. History can be seen as a vast compendium of values, from which we pick and choose. We may in fact decide to construct new ethical systems, but our point of departure should be the past. It is worth remembering that not every age, nor every individual, holds to an identical set of ethical ends throughout a lifetime. And despite Erikson's insistence on continuities, the reality of change in moral life also needs emphasizing.

All values, however, are not of the same range; some are more inclusive than others. Specifically political norms, for instance, can usually be expressed in the form of a rule: for instance, that "governments derive their just powers from the consent of the governed." Even Jesus' ethic finds expression in a maxim like "love thy neighbor," or that of rendering unto Caesar the things that are Caesar's and unto God the things that are God's. And although it may be extremely difficult to express certain values in the form of a rule, even catchall values denoted simply as "love" or "spontaneity" serve the function of helping us to decide between differing, but more narrow, rules.

Moral principles are not always binding. Even if we all agree on the significance of justice, we may find that in a particular concrete case it conflicts with another value, such as human welfare. We proceed on the assumption that an ethical precept is binding until it conflicts with other principles; each is always relevant while not conclusive.[1] When we defend an act by referring to an ethical rule, we are doing more than explaining why we have so behaved. We are also announcing that we are affirming an end which we approve, and exhorting others to adhere to it as well.

We can accept such ethical ends as intuitions, in the sense that they are unprovable. We do not—and should not—characterize someone who advocates inequality or even the maximization of social coercion in the way we might consider unbalanced a person who is suffering from gross perceptual distortions or who is on the verge of suicide. We should say of Mussolini, for instance, not that he was mad—although he might conceivably have been so—but that he was wrong, evil, worthy of blame. Any reasons we give for an ethical judgment can be objectively discarded as irrelevant or clumsy, but can be called bad (in the moral sense) only in terms of some other rule, precisely because the rules themselves are the sources of our knowledge of good and bad. If we are asked why we hold to a certain principle, we may have to clarify our adherence or reiterate our beliefs. But in principle we cannot be pushed beyond what we deem logically ultimate, since that point constitutes the justification of less inclusive positions.

Now such a viewpoint need not exclude tolerance. We are not prepared to uphold all ethical principles with equal force. On some occasions it is proper to abandon toleration, or even go to war. But it is the process of discussion, the nature of ethical arguments, that deserves more attention. For we do not simply grunt our approval, affirm or deny principles, or just preach to one another. Even if we do not, like Erikson, undergo religious conversion, as individuals we do discuss, and even alter, our values; and societies as a whole have been regularly known to change their commitments.

Most social and political discussions assume an ethical context. Perhaps there are some values common to all human beings; but even if anthropologists could settle the question, the mere fact of such agreement should never by itself satisfactorily establish ethical values. It may be that there are some moral principles agreed upon by all Westerners. One explanation for why force is not even more often resorted to is that an ethical framework exists within which disputes arise.

In any particular situation, some values need not be considered since they will be inapplicable. In the midst of a great economic catastrophe, it would seem odd today to discuss whether unemployment compensation would damage the moral fiber of the nation. Middle-class parents would feel justified in going to any expense to help their desperately ill child.* Given a particular empirical context, some ethical inquiries are inappropriate. But in clarifying an ethical position, one is apt to justify an adherence to a principle by referring to a higher value. Any commitment has to be understood, though, in terms of a concrete situation, for no principle necessarily entails the specific means for applying it.

One difficulty with Erikson's contribution to ethics is that the kinds of propositions that are most often the subject of dispute are of a less ultimate character than his form of Christianity. "Love thy neighbor" and Erikson's ideal of "mutuality" are often of little help in settling most social conflicts. Indeed, most social conflicts do not involve basic ethical disagreement of the kind that ultimate values might help resolve. The social sciences can hope at least to settle questions of an empirical nature. But fundamental ethical

---

* The same family may be, nevertheless, remarkably callous about suffering inflicted on other people's children.

issues can be resolved to the satisfaction of our consciences only because we have already decided upon our moral premises. It is an indication of Erikson's cast of mind that any discussion of the logic of ethical precepts would make him uncomfortable.

It is mistaken to think that it is possible to solve all ethical dilemmas at any one stroke. By and large Erikson and others who argue that it is possible to infer values from human nature have chosen a particularly genial picture of mankind to work with. In appealing to the wisdom of the ages Erikson has selectively scanned the history of ideas. The Western tradition alone, for example, offers a great variety of possible values, and an investigation of other cultures would yield even more ethical possibilities. Ethical values endure because of human choices, even though none of them may be hallowed by God, sanctioned by science, or justified by the future.

A confusion between facts and values can lead to two different, and undesirable, consequences. On the one hand, there is the danger of utopianism. Out of hopefulness it is possible to blind oneself to the practical means of implementing ethical commitments; desiring something in the future need say little about the likelihood of its ever coming to pass. On the other hand, there is the danger of conservatism. Many writers have been inclined to throw a moral wrap over the pre-existing world, endorsing everything that already "is" with an ethical glow.[2]

Erikson may have fallen into both utopianism and conservatism. His message communicates too much of what we want to hear. It is reassuring to be addressed with high-minded thoughts. (Although no one, including Erikson himself, can feel at ease being measured by such lofty standards.) His version of the Golden Rule is likely to make us feel a little better about ourselves. But his faith in the world's progress toward more inclusive identities lacks the cutting edge of a critical challenge. The troubling question is whether or not, for all the attractive features of Erikson's ethical position, he has not served in the end to reinforce the social status quo.

A Pollyanna is defined by the dictionary as "one characterized by irrepressible optimism and a tendency to find good in everything." Erikson believes, for example, that "radically new assumptions may, because they must, emerge from the matrix of traditional configurations of thought"; and he contends that Freud anticipated the "source of a new morality, based on the mutuality of function, which in our time may well (again, because it must) evolve from psychoanalytic and ecological considerations." [3] But such hopefulness is in Erikson's thought too often allied to social conservatism. He is not sufficiently skeptical, and therefore does not really confront the possibility that there may be very few social groups worth being "integrated" with.

The preachiest features of Erikson's work have emerged relatively recently. It is undoubtedly better for a thinker to make explicit his commitments, rather than for latent convictions to exert an unwitting influence. But as one reflects on the implications of Erikson's ego psychology, with its deferential attitude toward the benefits of pre-existing social institutions, a consistent ethical mood does emerge: marriage, heterosexuality, and the raising of children are unquestionably part of what he takes the good life to consist of.

But on what grounds can one say that such norms are universally valid? Some people are better off not married. The demand for so-called normal sexual activity can be a new kind of moralistic injunction. A marriage as unique as that between talented writers like Harold Nicolson and Vita Sackville-West may be at least as worthy, if not exemplary, as many more run-of-the-mill arrangements; yet they often lived apart, he slept with men and she with women, and neither took much part in the early upbringing of their sons. [4]

The recent middle-class ideal of the nuclear family consisting of parents raising children by themselves is historically a highly unusual one. An important cultural goal should be to appreciate the variety of possible social patterns, rather than try to assimilate them to the scale of one model of the life cycle. Erikson may have unwittingly lent support to a new form of ego restriction.

In contrast to Erikson's kind of conformism, Freud—despite the scope of his ambitions—saw himself in the minority; he sought long-range approval through his distance from many widely accepted standards of his own day. In terms of everyday life Freud seemed an ordinary middle-class physician of his era. But his lack of conventionality was shown by the originality of his work, the power of his writing, and his boldness of spirit. Like Nietzsche, Freud knew the way altruism can mask aggressive purposes. In contrast to post-Freudians, however, Freud had little taste for uttering moral platitudes.

Undoubtedly there were conservative implications in Freud's thought, and in particular in his view of reality in contrast to fantasy. A black patient in North America, for instance, confronted by racial discrimination, would be expected to live by his wits, like traditional Jewish outsiders, without counting on changes in the external world, or without being encouraged to help bring about such changes. But Freud also had, at least in his attacks on religion, utopian hopes for the future. He aimed to protect individual autonomy from unconscious threats. By means of rational insight, Freud sought to treat neurotic suffering; at the turn of the twentieth century that meant trying to help the emotional have-nots. In contrast to Erikson's concern with greatness and success, one of the attractive features of the earlier psychoanalytic viewpoint was its respect for disability and failure.

It is unnecessary to romanticize, as Herbert Marcuse has done, the political implications of Freud's standpoint.[5] In his old age Freud supported a clerical and authoritarian regime in Austria which put down the socialists in a civil war. Not only could Freud flatter Mussolini by inscribing to him a copy of *Why War?* but he even maintained the hope that one of his Italian disciples had direct access to the Italian dictator. Moderate and pro-establishment, Freud remained an old-fashioned liberal. In *The Interpretation of Dreams* he had expressed his sympathy for the aristocratic leaders of the *ancien régime* who suffered from the French reign of terror. Freud was a relative innocent in the public affairs of his maturity, but he could excessively admire others who were rich and successful; Marie Bonaparte and William Bullitt, whatever social insecurities they may have felt, represented to Freud status and international political connections.

From today's perspective Freud is bound to seem old-fashioned even when it comes to sex. He did not doubt the merits of male supremacy or the soundness of patriarchal family life. As a husband he was faithful, although increasingly dissatisfied with what he saw as inadequacies in his wife's personality. As a father he was not active in the day-to-day care of his six children; for instance, they could not even go walking with "Papa" until toilet training was completed. When his sons inquired about "the facts of life," Freud sent them to 'a family doctor. (Of course, to say that Freud was different from ourselves does not denigrate him, but rather makes him more worthwhile to study.) Freud remained the official head of his family; children, in-laws, aunts, uncles, nieces, nephews, and cousins were closely knit together. His family mattered a great deal to him, and he was always ready with money or advice.

These personal traits in Freud were of a piece with the culture of his time, and in particular with traditional Jewish patterns. In his treatment of women patients, it is no surprise that Freud was not eager to encourage them to act contrary to conventional social roles. He was horrified by Wilhelm Reich's attack on the traditional bourgeois family and his use of Marxism in psychoanalysis. Reich tied radical social change to sexual liberation; and Freud wrote his *Civilization and Its Discontents* as a reply. Freud partook of the conformism that to some degree everyone shares, for the psychological and philosophical ideas of every thinker, whether Erikson or Freud, cannot exist entirely apart from their social context.

Yet although psychoanalysis reflects the era of its origins, another strain in Freud's thought ultimately helped to undermine traditional masculine culture. His own sexual problems led him to declare that all neurotic symptomatology represents an expression of repressed infantile sexual life. His gnawing uncertainties about his own adequacy were shared by male patients as well, and many of them came for treatment because of potency disturbances. As puritanical about sex as Freud often was, he could also be emancipated from conventional pieties.

As a matter of doctrine Freud sought to break down some of the artificial lines between masculinity and femininity. Whatever has own private distaste for homosexuality, he tried to be tolerant and search for its sources. For all the notorious anti-feminine biases in his thought (he even blamed women for men being "asocial" [6]), Freud created a profession in which women have been able to attain a certain fulfillment. The success of women analysts (evidently more in demand than male colleagues) may be due to sexually reactionary biases, which have accustomed women to respond to emotional nuances, and men to be sensitive to the external world of power.

Although for a time Freud helped to reinforce patriarchalism, in the long run his ideas have helped to topple many of the stereotypes that he shared with others of his era.

Freud forged some of the tools for contemporary doubts and self-questioning. He himself held that women had weak superegos, and were incapable of a man's sublimations or intellectual superiority; but in the end women used psychoanalytic concepts as a means for elucidating such patterns of discrimination. Our image of human nature can never be the same after Freud. But probably no one would be more surprised than he at some of the specific uses to which his work has been put.

Although Freud liked to think that his concentration on sex brought him ill-repute, without that aspect of his work it is hard to believe his ideas would have had the same impact. (Freud might justifiably turn a charge of puritanism against some of his psychoanalytic successors; for it is writers like Erikson who think in terms of an individual's mediating with the environment via ego processes, whereas Freud stressed how little life would be worth if instincts did not bring us in contact with the outside world.) In the course of his self-analysis in the 1890s Freud proposed that the source of his patients' difficulties was a childhood sexual trauma, inflicted on them by a parent, family member, or servant. By 1897, however, Freud abandoned this view, and instead treated his patients' troubles as an expression of their inner world. Rather than believing that children were seduced into sexuality, Freud now held that they were themselves sexual beings. Freud interpreted tales of seduction as the product of unconscious infantile desires, mobilized in the therapeutic context.

It took years for Freud publicly to admit his error, which may have helped him acquire a dubious reputation in Viennese medicine. He appeared to many as an unreliable sexologist, unaware of his potential for misleading patients. But Freud's special perspective was that of a psychologist; through studying memories and false recollections he aimed to explore his patients' past. However Freud modified his own theories, the public has appropriately responded to his interest in sex. As a scientist he was an opponent of hypocrisy. Throughout his clinical practice Freud thought neurosis had a physical basis in dammed-up sexuality. Sex remained for Freud a prime source of neurotic anxiety.

Freud's power has also rested on his interest in another area of enduring human concern, aggression. His theory of the death instinct may be untenable, but no one can doubt that he understood the human potentiality for evil. Freud understood the inevitability of limits in human life, and always tied human gains to past losses. He had an acute sense of tragedy. Under certain conditions the sacrifice of neurosis, Freud held, was morally more worthy than the freedom of health. Philosophically he was sophisticated; he knew at least some of the dangers inherent in linking freedom to self-realization. Unlike Erikson, Freud did not think that all human goals could be harmoniously reconciled.

In contrast to the contemporary conviction, especially in North America, that neurosis is curable and unhappiness therefore unnecessary, Freud's final approach to suffering was more stoic. Whatever his initial hopes, in the end he held that ambivalence and tension were inevitably part of the human lot. One wonders, for example, if the suicide rate among analysts would have been so high if a greater awareness of the range of human troubles, and greater tolerance toward varieties of normal conflicts, had been promoted.[7] A fulfilled life does not consist in the extirpation of neurosis.

Nevertheless, there was an idealistic side to Freud which encouraged the hope that through analysis it might be possible to be purified of conflicted feelings. Freud was a rationalist who set out to help people change. He thought his "science" had discovered truths that were previously unknown. In *The Interpretation of Dreams* he declared that "impressions from the second year of life, and sometimes even from the first, left a lasting trace on the emotional life of those who were later to fall ill. . . ." [8] Even by World War I, Freud was uncompromising: "The little creature is often completed by the fourth or fifth year of life, and after that merely brings gradually to light what is already within him." [9]

In contrast to many of his successors in psychoanalysis, Freud prided himself on telling people what they did not want to hear; as a scientist he felt entitled to attack common sense. And he thought he had evolved rules of therapeutic "technique" that would enable the psychoanalyst to rival the surgeon's precision. If Freud's kind of rationalism tempted him as well as others to try to do more than was humanly possible, these excesses were sanctioned by his rationalist premises. Freud's own clinical efforts may have been largely patch-up jobs. But his ideas encouraged the notion that subsequently became popular, especially in North America, that psychoanalysis involves not mere tinkering with personality, but psychological destruction and re-creation.

Freud's high expectations for mankind often led him to disillusionment. And so his utopianism was intimately connected to misanthropy. "Worthless" was an important concept for Freud. As he once wrote,

> I do not break my head very much about good and evil, but I have found little that is "good" about human beings on the whole. In my experience most of them are trash, no matter whether they publicly subscribe to this or that ethical doctrine or to none at all. . . . If we are to talk of ethics, I subscribe to a high ideal from which most of the human beings I have come across depart most lamentably. [10]

He could even declare: "I have never done anything mean or malicious and cannot trace any temptation to do so. . . ." But "other people are brutal and untrustworthy. . . ." [11] Freud also wrote: "In the depths of my heart I can't help being convinced that my dear fellow men, with few exceptions, are worthless." [12] His attitude had class overtones, since by "good-for-nothing" he often implied society's "rabble" or "riffraff." He often considered the problems he dealt with clinically as the filth of human life. When he referred in passing to "a person even of only moderate worth," [13] he was affronting Christian culture, which has at least paid lip service to the sanctity of each human soul. (Nor did he subscribe to any barriers against speaking ill of the dead.[14]) When he refers to one patient as "an excellent and worthy person," [15] the reader is left wondering how Freud would treat someone who fell outside that category designated as superior.

It is still surprisingly threatening for many to acknowledge Freud as the man of multiple contradictions that he was. Yet if we are to understand the sources of his historical triumph, and the extent of his influence, it is necessary to appreciate how much at odds the Freud of history was from current stereotypes of his genius. Erikson's kind of idealizations about Freud are unnecessary; such sanctification imposes a deadening hand on him. Freud lived in a world alien to anything we can have experienced. It is a miracle how he emerged from his own family background. The historical Freud, at odds with his own surroundings, is a model of originality and brilliance; but he has been used to serve the bureaucratic needs of the psychoanalytic movement. Freud was undoubtedly a leader with great organizing powers. And in the end his political talents, by achieving an unrealistic degree of loyalism, may have swallowed up his search for heirs who would be psychologically original.

THE IMPLICATIONS OF PSYCHOTHERAPY

A difficulty arises when we try to translate Freud's philosophically attractive cosmopolitanism into a viable doctrine of psychotherapy. It is relatively harmless for a social thinker to indulge in stinging denunciations; societies are so tough that they often envelop and absorb even the most radical pronouncements. Freud did, in fact, succeed in helping reform many standard Western norms. But how much negativism can a vulnerable patient be expected to take? Here Erikson's hopefulness may be more productive for a therapist than Freud's own brand of skepticism.

Erikson proposes, for example, that "you can test the truth (or the healing power inherent in a situation) . . . by action which maximizes mutual insight and minimizes violence, coercion, or threat." [16] The distinguished British analyst Donald Winnicott commented about a visit Erikson once made to a clinic for troubled children that he had pointed out (without invention) genuine positive traits in the patients. [17] In the course of my own limited personal contact with Erikson, while I was interviewing Freud's patients, pupils, and relatives who were still alive, I found that often Erikson did not want to hear the worst of what I had discovered; but he was helpful in getting me to think about my material in a different and constructive light.

One does not have to share all of Erikson's values, such as his belief in progress, to appreciate the gentleness of spirit conveyed by his concepts. To counteract Freud's overstatements, at times Erikson has swung too far in the other direction. In practice Freud took for granted that patients need support. During therapy he might have seemed to be a relentless scrutinizer, but he could be actively helpful. Freud considered such therapeutic moves entirely apart from analytic technique. He knew about more than self-deception. He saw that patients had recuperative powers, which he often tried to mobilize through humor. He not only shared with his patients an extensive collection of humorous anecdotes but wrote a theoretical book on wit and its relation to the unconscious.

It was the id, however, that Freud sought to uncover. Only in passing could he comment about aspects of ego development, for example when he observed how important clothes are to a child. Erikson has tried, like other post-Freudians, to center his concern on the more reassuring side of development and therapy. And from this perspective he is right in seeing the potential usefulness of society as a support.

Erikson's ego approach, devoid of Freud's own ambivalences about ego psychology, has had clear advantages for initiating changes in therapy. For example, although few would contest Freud's contention about the psychological meaningfulness of neurotic symptoms, Freud's belief that such problems could be traced to repressed infantile sexuality can scarcely be justified today. Nor can a so-called symptom like masturbation be seen as the vice Freud was inclined to deem it. Freud's concept of the unconscious was unduly one-sided; he could consider all of Goethe's works, for instance, as a means of self-deception.[18]

Freud's expectations, like those of Karl Marx, were excessive. Marx saw the state as the agent of the ruling class; he therefore predicted that once a classless society arose, the state, then a temporary dictatorship of the proletariat, must as a matter of definition wither away. Freud defined symptoms as the product of unconscious conflicts; he predicted that once such conflicts are raised to consciousness they must, as a matter of logic, cease to exist. But such neat resolutions by Marx and Freud of difficulties we now know to be more intractable testify to the inadequacies of the internal consistency of closed systems.

According to a Central European limerick which Freud must have been familiar with, a centipede was once asked how it knew when to put forward which foot next; the centipede was then so distracted that it was unable to walk again. Self-consciousness may bring difficulties all its own. And as Franz Alexander pointed out, rational insight gained in therapy may be less a cause of personal change than an outcome of emotional growth.

Although Freud proposed that in the future psychoanalysis should become a profession of lay "curers" of souls, he was not by intention a healer. He wrote that he had unwillingly undertaken the study of medicine, and lacked, as he put it, "a genuine medical temperament"; "I became a therapist against my will. . . ." [19] Freud liked to consider himself an observer and discoverer. His patients could mean a great deal to him personally, and especially in his earlier years he could be therapeutically outgoing. And unlike many contemporary "orthodox" analysts, Freud could chat with patients, lend them books, and otherwise be supportive.

But psychoanalysis mattered most of all to Freud for its efficacy as a research instrument rather than for its therapeutic power. In his old age Freud once went so far as to describe his interest in psychotherapy, medicine, and natural science as a lifelong *"détour"* from his earliest fascination with "cultural problems." [20] Freud had a striking understanding of the way opposites go together, and he explained his not having had "any craving in . . . early childhood to help suffering humanity" in terms which are still startling: "My innate sadistic disposition was not a very strong one, so that I had no need to develop this one of its derivatives." [21]

Many of Freud's ideas, however, had less scientific standing than he liked to think. He increasingly expressed concern less his therapy destroy his science. But the objectivity of many of Freud's. "findings" has to be considered questionable. His stature in intellectual history is assured; many of his ideas, however, have proved either incapable of testing or have actually been proven false. Freud was right in old age to question the value of his earlier work, but his doubts need to be extended. When he wrote in favor of the broadscale application of psychoanalytic therapy, he said this would involve alloying "the pure gold of analysis freely with the copper of direct suggestion. . . ." But the "most effective and most important ingredients" of such future uses of his work would remain "those borrowed from strict and

untendentious psychoanalysis." [22] Freud as a scientist overlooked, however, the degree to which so-called strict psychoanalysis is itself "tendentious." For not only do the personality and training of an analyst have a suggestive impact,
but, as Erikson has insisted, the apparently neutral psychoanalytic situation has its own biases. We now know, for instance, that traditional psychoanalysis is apt to contain hidden regressions, on the analyst's part as well as the patient's.

Freud's concept of transference may not really point to
unconscious fantasy life, or even to patients' past real-life experiences. The context of the psychoanalytic treatment setting has been inadequately studied for its special impact.
Stress will bring out human infantilism; Freud was correct,
we all have a child still living within us. But the creation of
transference neuroses, centering on the person of the analyst,
tells as much about the consequences of psychoanalytic technique as about the nature of the human psyche. On the one
hand, a patient's regression makes possible a loosening up
which may ultimately permit better personality organization. However, as Jung long ago pointed out, mobilizing
such transference reactions in patients can also have dangerous consequences for therapy. The difficulty with psychoanalysis is more subtle than the possibility of straightforwardly misleading patients, as in the instance of Freud's
mistake about the seduction tales. The analogy he drew between psychoanalysis and surgery had its own suggestive
impact, encouraging passivity in patients rather than the
analytic ideal of self-reliance. Erikson is the first analyst to
my knowledge to liken analysis as therapy to sensory deprivation. But if he is right, then how patients behave during
psychoanalytic treatment tells us less about normal psychology than Freud himself supposed.

One of the sources of Freud's power, and at the same time
a means by which he was able to mislead himself as to the

scientific status of his psychology, was that he tended to interpret what were personal transferences as independent confirmations of his ideas. In extreme old age he admitted that at the outset he had not been wary enough to look for latent negative transferences. (In the 1920s Reich made that technical innovation into a therapeutic program.) It was too easy for Freud to see any patient's criticism as a sign of emotional resistance to self-understanding, and also to treat even the most lavish praise as tribute appropriate to his genius.

Idealizations of Freud too often went uninterpreted. Out of devotion to the master, and living off the profession he created, disciples proselytized Freud's message and treatment procedure. The almost hypnotic hold he had on his followers was partly a consequence of the impact of suggestion in the analytic therapeutic setting. In the face of outside criticism that threatened the way they had reorganized their egos, ex-patients of Freud and the early analysts could react with the vindictiveness associated with cultism.

Like Luther in Erikson's account, Freud not only contributed to the growth of human consciousness but unfortunately also helped to reinforce authoritarianism. Freud was not solely a great enlightening influence. Nor did his power rest only on his great capacities as a writer. Irrational forces, partly stemming from infantilism aroused in therapy, have also played a role. Perhaps Freud was not fearful enough of the deleterious aspects of religion, for psychoanalysis succeeded in becoming for many a surrogate religion.

Patients have been known to undergo analytic treatment for long periods, in extreme instances for ten or fifteen years. After such an enormous expense of time and money it would be hard to expect from either patient or analyst a rational evaluation of therapeutic gains or intellectual insights. Such extended therapy can encourage not individualism but narcissism. And if such massive support is needed, should psychoanalysis have been the preferred method of treatment at the outset? Freud tended to attract foreign pupils in his last years, during which he endured sixteen years of cancer of the jaw; but it was during his most aloof phase, when it hurt him to talk, that his followers acquired the technique now most closely identified with "orthodox" treatment.

The limitations of Freud's preferred technique of therapy have implications of a broader nature. Philosophers, for example, are prone to worry about the difficulties of finding psychoanalytic propositions that can be disproved. But in their search for independent verifiability, such philosophers have not been concerned enough with what any scientific psychology must insist on—the problem of the credulity of patients. For even if someone accepts almost anything an analyst proposes, this may still not mean that the interpretations are correct. Nor need such so-called inexact interpretations fail to have a constructive therapeutic effect. An analyst could tell a lie to a dying patient, to take only one example, and still be comforting.

In reflecting on the more general implications of the practice of psychoanalytic psychotherapy, one has to question how much in the end the healthy and the sick do form a continuum. Freud only belatedly separated off the clinical understanding of psychoses from his theories about neurosis. And by the end of his life he acknowledged, at least in private, the therapeutic limitations of truth-telling. There is no surefooted rule, however, for separating tactfulness from evasiveness or lying. But the therapeutic obstacle is not just that the worse off people are the more they are apt to have difficulty listening to what they do not want to hear; one also has to doubt how much objective truth is likely to be uncovered or communicated in a traditional psychoanalytic situation.

So-called normal psychology, however, may have little appropriateness for the understanding of cases of real abnormality. Freud and most of his early followers had little experience with the treatment of classic psychiatric cases. Freud tried to hold himself aloof from psychiatric problems, although he was interested in what other analysts had found out. Supposedly, psychotics were too self-involved to form the kind of transferences suitable for psychoanalysis. Today, however, instead of dismissing such patients as excessively "narcissistic," they can be more humanely seen as suffering from ego weakness, from deficiency rather than excess. Freud held out the hope for the future that ego psychology might make the so-called narcissistic neuroses accessible to psychoanalytic therapy. In his clinical writings Erikson has tried to show the specific sources of psychopathology in ego defects. Undoubtedly a psychogenic component plays a substantial part in the precipitation of psychosis; but specialists are increasingly inclined to hypothesize that cases of severe mental illness are at least also the outcome of chemical, biological, or even genetic processes, which find psychological expression.

It is even doubtful that Freud's approach to neurotic suffering is unchallengeable. Much has been properly written, for example by Thomas Szasz, about the misuses of institutional psychiatry in the West. (Even more notoriously, under both Tsarism and Communism the Russians have used hospital facilities for political purposes.) But one has to consider what ordinary neurotics are like when they come for therapy. For whatever purposes they may have originally undertaken treatment, once they have been put into a regressive situation it may be unrealistic to consider them able to "terminate" treatment at will. And it may conflict with the economic interests of analysts to keep reminding patients of the rational objectives of therapy. Freud ruled out psychotics from psychoanalytic treatment on the grounds of their inability to form a transference. But did he adequately understand the nature and sources of so-called neurotic transferences?

Traditional psychoanalytic standards of approach may unknowingly manipulate a patient's dependencies. Anna Freud once described an analyst listening to a patient's free associations: she remarked that "the dreamer's psychic state differs little from that of the patient during the analytic hour." [23] She knew that the analytic situation was an artificial one, resembling in its effects the ego-curtailing of hypnosis. From this point of view the ego's awakening is looked upon as an antagonism, a "resistance," instead of a sign of health. Her view on ego defenses was in line with Freud's own last formulations. According to him, "the crux of the matter is that the defensive mechanisms directed against former danger recur in the treatment as *resistances* against recovery." Such defenses were seen by Freud as "resistances not only to the making conscious of contents of the id, but also to the analysis as a whole, and thus to recovery." [24] Erikson's ego approach instead emphasizes the constructive side of expressions of ego activity.

If Freud's conception of analysis involves putting a patient's ego to sleep, then an analyst's interpretations can be licensed to be, if not a sadistic attack, an assault on the dignity of the patient's whole being. Freud conceived of the patient as opposed to the analyst in terms of a contrast between the passive and active "partner in the analytic situation." [25] Jean-Paul Sartre has bluntly declared that "the psychoanalytic relationship is, *by its very nature,* a violent one. . . ." * There is an inevitable difference in authority between an analyst and patient; but one worries about what in traditional psychoanalytic training alerts the analyst to

---

* Sartre's conception of psychoanalysis should be contrasted with Erikson's attempt to utilize Gandhi's doctrine of "ahimsa." See Ch. 8, p. 134.

the possible misuses of his power. Sartre believes that because of the lack of reciprocity between the reclining patient and the out-of-sight analyst, "the road to independence (facing up to one's fantasies, and to other people) cannot pass via a situation of absolute dependence. . . ." [26]

It is hard to know what to recommend to people who feel in need of therapeutic help. Too often they are so distraught as to be unable to "shop around" before finally choosing a therapist. But here old-fashioned psychoanalytic advice can be seriously misleading; Lawrence Kubie, for example, once advised in a well-known handbook that patients who initially react badly to an analyst should persevere regardless of what their common sense tells them. (Kubie later adopted liberal views,[27] but retained his specific textbook principle.*) I think that patients would be better advised to trust to their own experience, whatever their self-doubts; if an analyst responds to one's sense of humor that may be as good an index as any that a favorable rapport will be possible. But I have not encountered in clinical conferences (or in the relevant literature) any discussion of the route by which patients arrive at particular analysts; interpretations of such psychologically significant material might undermine the prospect for prolonged treatment.

All too often there is a gulf between practitioners devoted to analytic psychotherapy and those committed to physical means of treatment. If one has ever witnessed the catastrophe of serious mental collapse, it is hard to scoff at the prospect of symptomatic recovery. Nor, if one has seen how frequently suicidal patients can change their minds, often

---

* "[A] patient's positive or negative feelings about his analyst arise predominantly out of unconscious fantasies which the patient brings preformed into the analytic situation and then drapes around the analyst. Therefore whether the patient likes or dislikes an analyst is intrinsically of little significance to the outcome of the treatment."[28]

after it is already medically too late, can one indulge in the abstract luxury of entertaining lightly the right to kill oneself. A suicide attempt may be a warning signal, to family or therapist; and it can be part of an illusory search for immortality. There are, nonetheless, occasions when a suicide may be rationally in order. But human life is sacred and everyone has the right to be protected against himself in an extremity.

Freudian doctrine holds as a matter of theory as well as of practice that human suffering is inevitable. Yet there are inadequacies to such stoicism. Of course there should be limits set to meddling in other people's lives; Freud thought that the couch ensured neutrality, whereas it had misleading biases all its own. In the past there have been roughly two kinds of therapists who have dealt with the mentally most troubled; on the one hand, some psychiatrists have used psychotic clinical material for the most theoretical purposes, while others, who may be able to hear psychological grass growing, are unable to explain exactly how it is that they are best able to help individual patients. The solution need not be mysticism, although successful therapy depends very much on the qualities of the people interacting. One should not give up on trying to educate therapists better, but success in treatment may in the end have little to do with the analyst's prior training.

It may be that the best a therapist can do is to stick with his patient until natural recuperative forces take over. Therapists may, at least at the outset of their training, find they need fancy theories to rely on as a crutch. But seasoned clinicians will admit to the hand-holding component in their work. Once such rapport gets established, however, it becomes a problem how to disengage the bond—without its being a terrible loss to the patient, or his otherwise remaining infantilized.

As a matter of psychoanalytic ideal, therapists are committed to leaving the status quo of a patient's life alone.

Although this may sound conformist, seriously disturbed patients may therapeutically be most in need of stability. It does not sound defensible as a social goal, but for many people the ability to function tolerably well in everyday life constitutes a significant achievement. It ought to be possible to appreciate such limited human capacities without committing oneself to broad-scale social quietism.

Critics have charged that psychoanalytic reformist practices have threatened to replace the best features of Freud's original theories. According to one formulation of this view, a dialectical tension should exist between theory and therapy; this disjunction is supposedly required by the peculiarities of the social problems of our era. To bring theory and therapy in too close alignment might blunt psychoanalysis's critique of Western society, and make it one more instrument of social domination and adjustment. The standard of "authentic" human relationships may result in spiritualizing social injustices.[29]

But there is a difference between therapy and radical politics. And whether or not our society is as unfree as, say, Marcuse thinks, it should still be possible to distinguish between decent therapy and poor therapy. Any proposed contradiction between theory and therapy, whatever its hypothetical social advantages, can lead to a hypocritical gap between what "orthodox" analysts profess and what they are sometimes willing to do in practice. In fact, no intelligent therapist can be entirely happy with existing clinical results. The literature is hardly littered with examples of effective therapeutic approaches, and, unfortunately, therapeutic failures are almost never written about. Even if it could be proven that the real sources of a patient's trouble were not in his own past experiences but in large-scale social factors, pragmatic success in helping the victims of the world as we know it is no minor matter.

It is still true that certain classes of mental patients are being unjustly treated by others, including doctors—as if they were, to paraphrase Erikson, a separate, Freudian species. Patients are sometimes described as if they were doomed[30]—psychologically if not genetically. One has to question the value of a psychotherapeutic interpretation, for prophecies, as we know, can be self-fulfilling. Rational insight can itself be a considerable support. But to understand unconscious conflicts in terms of wish fulfillment in accord with a Freudian view of the unconscious may also make a patient worse, guiltier about the past and less free toward the future. An analyst's sadism can feed a patient's masochism or depressive need for martyrdom. But to interpret a dream as a compensation from the unconscious, or as a gift of insight, as Jung and Erikson might be inclined, can be a valuable reassurance.

Clinical and social fashions influence both what patients expect and what analysts consider themselves entitled to do. Freud's own clinical intolerances, and his arbitrary personal preferences, have exerted an exceptional influence. For whatever the genius Freud was in the context of his own time, it is necessary to reflect on the uses to which his ideas have been put. For example, only toward the very end of Freud's life did he comment on what kind of model the analyst can be expected to be: displaying "mental normality and correctness," the analyst "must possess some kind of superiority, so that in certain analytic situations he can act as a model for his patient and in others as a teacher." On the whole Freud wanted to believe that psychoanalysis as a technique could be effective independent of the individual practitioner. Perhaps this helps explain the unsatisfactory condition that, although many patients have undergone therapy with different analysts, the literature is sparse about such cases. Freud himself commented of switching analysts that "such a change will involve a fresh loss of time and abandoning fruits of work already done." [31]

Freud might take his own exceptional capacities as a model for granted. But he would no doubt be distressed by the generally narrow kinds of people now attracted, at least in North America, to the practice of his profession. He had not wanted psychoanalysis to become a mere auxiliary to psychiatry. It was reported not long ago that, in an "orthodox" training center in one of America's larger cities, the most common symptom in those accepted for analyses at low fees by analysts-in-training was the inability of the patients to complete their Ph.D. dissertations. One hopes this would not be the kind of problem considered suitable for psychoanalytic therapy in old Vienna, but in any event it is hard to believe that the contemporary analyst-in-training has any special qualifications to be of help on this particular issue.

In most centers of psychoanalysis, however, once an analytic training has been completed there is little opportunity for further supervision. Clarence P. Oberndorf, an analyst who got on badly as a patient in treatment with Freud, suggested in 1942 that it become customary for any case which had been in psychoanalytic treatment four or five hours a week for over three hundred hours to be reviewed by an outside consultant or a panel of analysts.³² The dangers of fantasies of omnipotence can be harmful in other treatment procedures as well. But the tradition of the autonomy of the medical practitioner has flourished in analysis as elsewhere, and Oberndorf's valid proposal has not been institutionalized.

Unlike many clinical writers, Erikson has had his doubts about the bases of much clinical evidence. On this issue Freud was not skeptical enough. He knew that therapeutic improvement was not necessarily a test of science, but he did not realize that analysis's sensory deprivation could lead in "normal" people to disorientations about an analyst's genius or deviltry. It is true that Erikson has not had enough distance from Freud to realize the special congeniality of the traditional psychoanalytic situation for Freud personally. But, at least lately, Erikson has not shared much of the credulity toward the so-called findings of psychoanalysis in the past.

Erikson has tended to take the medical analogy of a psychoanalytic "cure" [33] for granted. Such a metaphor may have its advantages, especially for dealing with the most seriously disturbed patients. But one does not have to be a romantic to think that some personal upheavals, even acute ones, may in the long run be better than unthinking conformism. Laing's point of view, which tends to glorify those who are now worst off, is an extreme perspective that has disadvantages of its own; but one can still argue that Erikson's ideal of ego strength, keeping oneself together and functioning for others, may be had at too great a price. Even temporary madness may sometimes be better, which may have been implied by Freud's dictum about the moral need for neurosis under certain conditions. Clamorous symptomatology may be constructive.

Freud would not have stressed the way a neurotic pattern may represent a legitimate challenge—to a family, therapist, or other social setting—and thereby be a positive step for the individual. He once pointed out, though, in the case of a recovering schizophrenic reported to him, that the reappearance of an oedipal conflict can be a sign of health. [34] Neurosis, he came to believe, can defend against more primitive disorders. [35] Neurotic problems represent, from a developmental point of view, a high level of personal civility. Instead of ensuring that clinical terms not be used to reinforce social stereotypes, Freud was inclined to foster the idea that health involves serenity. But inner harmony can be an illusion; and Laing is right if he can be taken to mean that "solutions" to inner conflicts can be at the expense of other goals. In his discussion of adolescence Erikson warned against premature "foreclosures" of identity problems.

Whatever the conservative aspects to his work, Erikson has at least expressed reservations about past clinical evidence. "Every student of psychotherapy is (or should be) impressed with the hiatus between the unfathomable richness of the data and the stingy parsimony of theorizing." [36] Erikson has done his most original work in the course of memorable case histories, dream interpretations, and biographical studies. He has theorized as a therapist, and whatever the disadvantages to such a starting point he has brought forward some of the most important implications of the practice of psychotherapy. Society's power over the individual can be for good as well as evil. Originally a child analyst, Erikson could not ignore the role of the environment in personality functioning. He may have too often appealed to the possibilities of human growth and integrity, instead of looking for social injuries within the individual psyche. But an earlier generation of analysts dismissed the social level as superficial and unsuitable for an analyst's inspection.

In spite of the limitations in Erikson's approach, at least it is unlike the rarefied air of so much recent psychoanalytic conjecturing. From his historical writings and clinical illustrations, at least one can examine the grounds for his beliefs and criticize what he has said. In contrast, the premise of psychoanalytic metaphysics, like so much of Heinz Hartmann's work, is that past empirical knowledge will on the whole suffice.

Undoubtedly Erikson could have gone much further in drawing revisionist implications from his developing point of view. But here he was hampered by past psychoanalytic sectarianism, which remains a menace to the future of depth psychology. For previous psychoanalytic controversies, instead of having had enlightening consequences, too often have resulted in new barriers of fear. [37] Robert Coles has commented of his own training experience in Boston that none of his psychoanalyst hospital supervisors assigned, for example, any of Karen Horney's books or articles; she was already outside the pale.[38] It is still taboo among Freudians to have any good word to say about Jung.

These historical issues are not narrow academic ones. For if one can say that often the early analysts did not know what they were doing therapeutically, too many of them even today cannot acknowledge that it once was so. But then that makes one wonder how much they now know what they are doing. Even after medicine has long begun to reconsider earlier psychotherapeutic errors, the psychoanalytic sectarian spirit has been imbibed in literary, philosophical, and historical circles.[39] It is very difficult to get a genuine debate on what alternatives to Freud, either philosophical or psychological, might be available.

In the course of the twentieth century psychoanalysis has changed, so that now ideas of earlier "deviants" are, usually without acknowledgment, often accepted and incorporated without any admission of prior doctrinal error. Psychoanalysis, for instance, now aims to be a general psychology instead of an abnormal one, fulfilling one of the hopes of Alfred Adler. And if psychoanalysis now shares that goal, that may represent genuine growth and not merely the "watering down" of original insight.

Despite all the Freudian emphasis on the principle of the importance of the past, psychoanalysis as a field has not yet achieved much historical awareness. Its ideals were bourgeois; and the sacredness of individual human freedom may not represent the wave of the future. But the scholasticism of so much psychoanalytic writing can never succeed in putting Freud in proper historical perspective.

Too often left-wing writers have been inclined to dismiss psychoanalysis as decadent soul-searching. John Strachey wrote in 1933 that because Freud had not asked Marxist questions he remained, "for all his great intellectual powers, the last major thinker of the European capitalist class, unable to step outside his class limitations." In this perspective *Civilization and Its Discontents* becomes "nihilistic pessimism." [40] It may be that service to some higher goal is required for the future of mankind, or that only by losing self-preoccupation can the individual find real fulfillment. But the reflections of someone like Georg Lukács are not encouraging; he lived for a time in Freud's Vienna, and in commenting on his own lack of interest in psychoanalysis for Marxist social thought, Lukács once said: "I can say that I have never felt frustration or any kind of complex in my life. I know what these mean, from the literature of the twentieth century, and from having read Freud. But I have not experienced them myself." Even more chilling in terms of the future of humanity are other of his recorded remarks: "What preserves me is that I have no inner life. I am interested in everything except my soul." [41] However distressing such a perspective may be, one ought not to confuse the future of Freud's individualistic aims with the survival of civilization itself.

In his resistance to orthodoxy, and his idealistic commitments, Erikson has innovated in his search for the bases of real strength, and this was in contrast to the earlier Freudian quest for the sources of weakness. Freud learned that "psychoanalysis brings out the worst in everyone," [42] but if no one ends up looking good under such inspection then there must be something wrong with Freud's methodological assumptions. Erikson's divergence from Freud has been in the direction of a new emphasis on health as opposed to neurosis. Long ago Erikson wrote programmatically that "mutual genital love faces toward the future." [43] The kind of transformation of past material under the impetus of new experiences which Erikson stresses may represent precisely those normal processes of development which are barred to the neurotic by virtue of his problems. But the difference of emphasis is also a difference of focus.

To the degree that psychoanalysis was an outgrowth of Freud's own experience, Erikson has found it possible to use the model of Freud's life as an alternative to some of Freud's doctrines. Whatever the inevitable human limitations of the early Freudians, and the weaknesses in their ideas, the significance of their impact makes them enduringly fascinating as figures. Erikson's own career has fulfilled one of the central convictions of Freud's old age: psychoanalysis cannot survive as a medical specialty, but needs the infusion of interdisciplinary contributions. Perhaps the most valuable lesson in the growth of Erikson's independent work, his incorporation of past knowledge into an individual vision of human existence, can best remind us of the truth of the maxim: every man his own psychologist.

Notes

ABBREVIATIONS

CS, 1st   Erik H. Erikson, *Childhood and Society,* 1st ed. (New York: Norton, 1950).

CS, 2nd   Erik H. Erikson, *Childhood and Society,* 2nd ed. (New York: Norton, 1963).

Dialogue   Richard I. Evans, *Dialogue with Erik Erikson* (New York: Harper, 1967).

Dimensions   Erik H. Erikson, *Dimensions of a New Identity: The 1973 Jefferson Lectures in the Humanities* (New York: Norton, 1974).

GT   Erik H. Erikson, *Gandhi's Truth: On the Origins of Militant Nonviolence* (New York: Norton, 1969).

Identity   Erik H. Erikson, *Identity: Youth and Crisis* (New York: Norton, 1968).

ILC   Erik H. Erikson, *Identity and the Life Cycle: Selected Papers,* with a Historical Introduction by David Rapaport (New York: International Universities Press, 1959).

IR   Erik H. Erikson, *Insight and Responsibility: Lectures on the Ethical Implications of Psychoanalytic Insight* (New York: Norton, 1964).

IS   *In Search of Common Ground: Conversations with Erik H. Erikson and Huey P. Newton*, with an Introduction by Kai T. Erikson (New York: Norton, 1973).

LH   Erik H. Erikson, *Life History and the Historical Moment* (New York: Norton, 1975).

YML   Erik H. Erikson, *Young Man Luther: A Study in Psychoanalysis and History* (New York: Norton, 1958).

PREFACE

1. "Greatness Finding Itself," reprinted in W. H. Auden, *Forewards and Afterwards* (London: Faber and Faber, 1973), pp. 86, 79.

2. Robert Coles, *Erik H. Erikson: The Growth of His Work* (Boston: Little, Brown, 1970). In his preface Coles noted that his was "only one of several books that could be written about Erikson and his writings" (p. xvii).

Cf. also Don S. Browning, *Generative Man: Psychoanalytic Perspectives* (Philadelphia: Westminster Press, 1973), Chs. 6–7; Harry Guntrip, *Psychoanalytic Theory, Therapy, and the Self* (New York: Basic Books, 1971), Ch. 4; Irving Howe, "Gandhi and Psychoanalysis," in *The Critical Point: On Literature and Culture* (New York: Horizon Press, 1973), pp. 190–202; Robert Jay Lifton, with Eric Olson (editors), *Explorations in Psychohistory: The Wellfleet Papers* (New York: Simon and Schuster, 1974); Lewis Lipsitz and Herbert M. Kritzer, "Unconventional Approaches to Conflict Resolution: Erikson and Sharp on Nonviolence," *Journal of Conflict Resolution*, XIX (Dec. 1975), 713–33; Lucian W. Pye, "Personal Identity and Political Ideology," in *Political Decision Makers*, ed. Duane Marvick (New York: Free Press, 1961), pp. 290–313; Daniel Yankelovich and William

Barrett, *Ego and Instinct: The Psychoanalytic View of Human Nature—Revised* (New York: Random House, 1970), Chs. 8–9.

3. *Time,* March 17, 1975, p. 76. Cf. also the cover story in *Newsweek,* Dec. 21, 1970, pp. 84–89.

4. Frederick Crews, "American Prophet," *The New York Review of Books,* Oct. 16, 1975, p. 9. Contrast this essay about Erikson with earlier remarks in Frederick Crews, *Out of My System: Psychoanalysis, Ideology, and Critical Method* (New York: Oxford University Press, 1975), pp. 21, 29, 173, 174, 190, 196, 206.

5. Cf. Paul Roazen, *Brother Animal: The Story of Freud and Tausk* (New York: Knopf, 1969; London: Allen Lane, 1970; New York: Vintage, 1971; London: Penguin, 1973), and Paul Roazen, *Freud and His Followers* (New York: Knopf, 1975; London: Allen Lane, 1976; New York: Meridian, 1976). (Subsequent citations refer to the pagination in the American editions.)

6. Cf. Paul Roazen, *Freud: Political and Social Thought* (New York: Knopf, 1968; London: Hogarth, 1969; New York: Vintage, 1971), and Paul Roazen (ed.), *Sigmund Freud* (Englewood Cliffs, N.J.: Prentice-Hall, 1973). (Subsequent citations refer to the pagination in the American editions.)

7. Cf. Paul Roazen, "Psychology and Politics: The Case of Erik Erikson," *The Human Context,* VII (Autumn 1975), pp. 577–87. Cf. also Paul Roazen, "Book Review of Erikson's *Dimensions of a New Identity,*" *The Nation,* June 7, 1975, pp. 697–98.

CHAPTER 1: FREUD

1. *LH,* p. 29.

2. *IR,* p. 210.

3. LH, p. 24.

4. Erik Homburger, "Psychoanalysis and the Future of Education," *Psychoanalytic Quarterly,* IV (1935), 50–68. For his change of last name from Homburger to Erikson, see the biographical discussion in Ch. 6, and in particular pp. 98–99.

5. *LH,* p. 33.

6. *Dialogue,* p. 81.

7. *YML,* p. 90.

8. *GT,* p. 440.

9. *Ibid.,* pp. 44, 85, 61.

10. Erik H. Erikson, "Psychoanalysis and Ongoing History: Problems of Identity, Hatred and Nonviolence," *The American Journal of Psychiatry,* CXXII (Sept. 1965), 242. Reprinted in Roazen (ed.), *Sigmund Freud,* p. 32.

11. *GT,* p. 86.

12. "Recommendations to Physicians Practising Psychoanalysis," *The Standard Edition of the Complete Psychological Works of Sigmund Freud,* ed. James Strachey (London: Hogarth, 1953–74), Vol. 12, p. 116. Cf. Henri Ellenberger, *The Discovery of the Unconscious* (New York: Basic Books, 1970), p. 719.

13. Interview with Erik H. Erikson, March 21, 1966. Cf. Roazen, *Freud and His Followers,* pp. 438–40.

14. Erik Homburger, "Configurations in Play–Clinical Notes," *Psychoanalytic Quarterly,* VI (1937), 167.

15. *LH,* p. 38.

16. *Ibid.,* pp. 40, 99.

17. Letters from Anna Freud to Ernest Jones, Jan. 10, 1956, Nov. 2, 1952, Nov. 15, 1950; letter from Felix Deutsch to Ernest Jones, Jan. 31, 1956 (Jones archives).

18. Erik Homburger Erikson, "The Dream Specimen of Psychoanalysis," in *Psychoanalytic Psychiatry and Psychology,* ed. Robert Knight and Cyrus Friedman (New York: International Universities Press, 1954), pp. 148, 159; letters from Anna Freud to Ernest Jones, Dec. 25, 1952, April 5, 1955 (Jones archives).

19. Letter from Abraham Brill to Ernest Jones, Nov. 17, 1933 (Jones archives).

20. Letter from Henry Murray to the author, Sept. 1972. Interviews with Henry Murray, April 27, 1965, and Nov. 10, 1965. Cf. Roazen, *Freud and His Followers,* p. 296.

21. *ILC,* p. 64.

22. *LH,* pp. 81, 109; *ILC,* p. 99.

23. *YML,* p. 16.

24. *ILC,* p. 159; *CS,* 2nd, p. 87; *YML,* p. 50.

25. *IR,* p. 62.

26. *Ibid.,* pp. 42, 78, 166.

27. *CS,* 2nd, p. 207; *IR,* p. 56.

28. *CS,* 2nd, p. 45.

29. Homburger, "Psychoanalysis and the Future of Education," p. 67.

30. *IR,* p. 178.

31. *GT,* p. 246.

32. *Ibid.,* p. 247.

33. *YML,* p. 153.

34. *Dialogue,* p. 95.

35. *LH,* p. 96. Cf. Roazen, *Brother Animal,* pp. 177–91; and Roazen, *Freud and His Followers,* Ch. IV.

36. *CS,* 2nd, p. 63.

37. *Identity,* pp. 275, 150; *Dialogue,* p. 81.

38. *Identity,* p. 201.

39. Erik H. Erikson, "The Ontogeny of Ritualization," in *Psychoanalysis—A General Psychology: Essays in Honor of Heinz Hartmann,* ed. Rudolph Loewenstein, Lottie Newman, Max Schur, and Albert Solnit (New York: International Universities Press, 1966), p. 619; *CS,* 2nd, p. 281; *ILC,* p. 101; *Identity,* pp. 20–21; Erik H. Erikson, "The Concept of Identity in Race Relations: Notes and Queries," *Daedalus,* XCV (Winter 1966), p. 148; Erik H. Erikson, "Identity, Psychosocial," *International Encyclopaedia of the Social Sciences* (New York: Macmillan, 1968), VII, 61.

40. *Identity,* p. 203.

41. Erikson, "The Dream Specimen of Psychoanalysis," p. 168.

42. *LH,* p. 56.

43. *IR,* p. 38. Cf. Ilse Bry and Alfred Rifkin, "Freud and the History of Ideas," in *Psychoanalytic Education,* ed. Jules H. Masserman (New York: Grune & Stratton, 1962), pp. 6–36.

44. Compare Erik H. Erikson, "The Strange Case of Freud,

Bullitt, and Woodrow Wilson: A Dubious Collaboration," *The New York Review of Books*, Feb. 9, 1967, pp. 3–5, with Erik H. Erikson, "A Questionable Cooperation: The Wilson Book," in *LH*, pp. 81–97.

Erikson's second thoughts are worth highlighting. At several points Bullitt now gets praised and patted on the back: new passages are inserted telling us of Bullitt's modesty about helping Freud to escape from Vienna, of Bullitt's "rare knowledge of international personalities and power struggles," and Bullitt's resignation from Versailles is cited as showing "besides personal irritation, . . . courage and foresight. . . ." Two sentences are dropped entirely: (1) "Bullitt's preface obscures, even as it offers to clarify, the history of the manuscript," and (2) "For me and for others it is easy to see only that Freud could have 'written' almost nothing of what is now presented in print."

Rather than saying, as he did originally, "One might even concede that some of the formulations are reasonable facsimiles of Freud's early theories," now Erikson says, instead of "might," "must." Erikson adds a fresh sentence before quoting some particularly dreary parts of the book: "even as Bullitt's mechanization of psychic forces only caricatures a trend which does exist in the literature, so do the following excerpts only render more obviously absurd a kind of formulation not always absent from newer applications of psychoanalysis to history." Instead of working to rebut what to others "appears to be genuine Freud," Erikson now sees his opponent as what "appears as genuine Freudian history." Whereas once Erikson was so offended by the text that he doubted the veracity of the collaboration ("something like this seems to have been in Bullitt's mind when the 'collaboration' started"), now he is obviously changing ground ("something like this seems to have been in Bullitt's mind when he convinced Freud of the desirability of collaboration"). Most striking of all is Erikson's change in his more general assessment of the book. Eight years earlier he thought: "The only point to be made here is that the text now printed must be ascribed to Bullitt, because he either transcribed or wrote, translated or caused to be translated, every word of it." Now, however, Erikson writes: "The main point to be made here is that Bullitt either transcribed or wrote, translated or caused to be translated, every word of the bulk of the book." The ambiguities of the fresh wording—"every word of the bulk of the book"—reveal Erikson's own new hesitations.

Cf. Paul Roazen, "Erik H. Erikson: Psycho-Historian as Mythologist," *Reviews in European History* (forthcoming in Sept. 1976). For an important contribution to our understanding of Woodrow Wilson, cf. Edwin A. Weinstein, "Woodrow Wilson's Neurological Illness," *Journal of American History*, LVII (1970), 324–51.

45. *YML*, p. 46.

46. *LH*, p. 77.

47. Sigmund Freud, *The Origins of Psychoanalysis: Letters to Wilhelm Fliess, Drafts and Notes: 1887–1902*, ed. Marie Bonaparte, trans. Eric Mosbacher and James Strachey (London: Imago, 1954), p. 227.

48. *LH*, p. 48. Cf. Erik Homburger Erikson, "Freud's *The Origins of Psychoanalysis*," *The International Journal of Psychoanalysis*, XXXVI, Part I (1955), 1–15. Whereas once Erikson thought it relevant that "after all, Fliess had not undergone an analytic process," now that sentence begins: "After all, Fliess had not cultivated the correspondence for purposes of self-analysis . . ." In 1906 Fliess had helped publish some letters of Freud's in relation to the Weininger-Swoboda incident. In 1955 Erikson thought Fliess was displaying "a clearly paranoid public defense of his priorities"; but now Erikson has softened that judgment to "a more paranoid public defense of his priorities."

49. *Dimensions*, p. 116.

50. *Dialogue*, pp. 43–44.

51. *Identity*, p. 226.

52. *Dialogue*, pp. 84–85.

53. *GT*, pp. 64, 378.

54. *Dialogue*, p. 14; *CS*, 2nd, p. 64.

55. *IR*, p. 145.

CHAPTER 2: THE EGO

1. "New Introductory Lectures in Psychoanalysis," *The Standard Edition of the Complete Psychological Works of Sigmund Freud*, Vol. 22, p. 60.

2. *CS*, 2nd, p. 403.

3. *Dimensions*, p. 102.

4. *LH*, p. 185.

5. *Dimensions*, p. 86; *GT*, p. 113.

6. *YML*, p. 8.

7. *IR*, p. 77.

8. *CS*, 2nd, p. 414.

9. *IR*, p. 146.

10. *CS*, 2nd, p. 282.

11. *Ibid.*, pp. 11, 17.

12. For example, cf. *Identity*, pp. 209, 211, 213, 217, 222–23.

13. *Ibid.*, pp. 9, 209; *LH*, p. 37. For Tausk's origination of the concept of ego boundaries, cf. Bertram Lewin's obituary of Federn, *The Psychoanalytic Quarterly*, XIX (1950), 296.

14. Erik H. Erikson, "Autobiographic Notes on the Identity Crisis," *Daedalus*, XCIX (Fall 1970), 739. Erikson later greatly modified this passage. Cf. *LH*, p. 37.

15. *Identity*, p. 10.

16. *CS*, 2nd, pp. 193–94.

17. Erik Homburger, "Review of Anna Freud's *Psychoanalysis for Teachers and Parents*," *The Psychoanalytic Quarterly*, V, (1936), 292–93.

18. *ILC*, p. 46.

19. *IR*, p. 150.

20. *Ibid.*, p. 44.

21. *CS*, 2nd, p. 68.

22. *Dialogue*, p. 100.

23. *CS*, 2nd, pp. 406–07.

24. *Ibid.*, p. 64.

25. *LH*, p. 19.
26. *Dialogue*, p. 28.
27. *CS*, 2nd, p. 279.
28. *ILC*, p. 102.
29. *Dimensions*, pp. 92, 27.
30. *ILC*, p. 37.
31. *Identity*, p. 209.
32. *ILC*, p. 149.
33. *CS*, 2nd, p. 261.
34. *IR*, p. 147.
35. *Identity*, p. 276.
36. *CS*, 2nd, p. 241.
37. *Identity*, p. 276.
38. *CS*, 2nd, p. 414.
39. *Ibid.*, p. 240.
40. *ILC*, p. 93.
41. *CS*, 2nd, pp. 68, 240, 43.
42. *YML*, p. 113.
43. *ILC*, p. 90.
44. Quoted in *Identity*, p. 19.
45. *IR*, pp. 200, 198, 200.
46. *Ibid.*, p. 69.
47. *LH*, p. 164.
48. Erik H. Erikson, "On the Sense of Inner Identity," in *Psychoanalytic Psychiatry and Psychology*, ed. Knight and Friedman, p. 362; *YML*, p. 102.
49. *CS*, 2nd, p. 244.

CHAPTER 3: SOCIETY

1. *CS*, 2nd, p. 325; *Identity*, p. 44.
2. *CS*, 2nd, p. 67.
3. *Identity*, p. 49.

4. Erikson, "On the Sense of Inner Identity," p. 363.

5. *ILC*, p. 42.

6. *CS*, 2nd, p. 282.

7. *ILC*, p. 221.

8. Erik H. Erikson, "Reflections on the Dissent of Contemporary Youth," *Daedalus*, XCIX (Winter 1970), 160.

9. *LH*, p. 105.

10. *ILC*, pp. 20, 39, 19.

11. Erikson, "Reflections on the Dissent of Contemporary Youth," p. 160.

12. *Identity*, p. 87.

13. *ILC*, pp. 20–21.

14. Erikson, "The Dream Specimen of Psychoanalysis," p. 158.

15. *CS*, 2nd, p. 277.

16. *IR*, p. 116.

17. *Dialogue*, p. 26.

18. *Identity*, p. 83.

19. *ILC*, pp. 64–65.

20. Erikson, "On the Sense of Inner Identity," p. 353.

21. Erik H. Erikson, "Wholeness and Totality—A Psychiatric Contribution," in *Totalitarianism*, ed. Carl J. Friedrich (Cambridge: Harvard University Press, 1954), p. 164.

22. *YML*, p. 265; *Identity*, p. 134.

23. Erikson, "Wholeness and Totality," p. 164.

24. *ILC*, p. 38; Erikson, "Wholeness and Totality," p. 167.

25. *IR*, pp. 155, 213–14.

26. *CS*, 2nd, p. 418.

27. *IS*, p. 67.

28. *CS*, 2nd, p. 240.

29. *IS*, p. 89.

30. *CS*, 2nd, p. 282.

31. Geoffrey Gorer, in *Psychoanalysis Observed*, ed. Charles Rycroft (London: Constable, 1966), p. 41.

32. *IS*, p. 56.

33. Erik H. Erikson, "Environment and Virtues," in *Arts of the Environment*, ed. Gyorgy Kepes (New York: Braziller, 1972), p. 74.

34. *CS*, 2nd, p. 184.

35. *Ibid.*, pp. 111, 124.

36. *Ibid.*, p. 163.

37. Erikson, "Environment and Virtues," pp. 63–64.

38. *CS*, 2nd, p. 129.

39. *Ibid.*, pp. 137, 164, 160.

40. *Ibid.*, pp. 169, 167, 185.

41. Erikson, "On the Sense of Inner Identity," p. 356.

42. *CS*, 2nd, p. 138.

43. *Dialogue*, p. 62.

44. Erikson, "Autobiographic Notes on the Identity Crisis," pp. 754, 745.

45. *YML*, p. 151.

46. *Ibid.*, p. 16.

47. *IR*, p. 43.

48. *YML*, p. 21.

49. *IR*, p. 205.

50. *Identity*, pp. 68–69.

51. *ILC*, p. 44.

52. Erikson, "The Dream Specimen of Psychoanalysis," p. 157.

53. *IS*, pp. 54, 124.

54. *LH*, p. 25.

55. *Identity*, p. 36; *LH*, p. 42.

56. *LH*, p. 30.

57. *Identity*, p. 301.

58. *ILC*, p. 43; *IS*, p. 119.

59. Erikson, "Environment and Virtues," p. 76.

60. *ILC*, p. 23.

61. *Dimensions*, pp. 27–28.

62. Erikson, "The Dream Specimen of Psychoanalysis," p. 168.

63. Paul Robinson, *The Freudian Left* (New York: Harper, 1969), pp. 144–45. For a sound criticism of some of Roheim's work, cf. Erik H. Erikson, "Childhood and Tradition in Two American Indian Tribes," *The Psychoanalytic Study of the Child*, Vol. I (New York: International Universities Press, 1945), p. 330.

64. Cf., for example, *Minutes of the Vienna Psychoanalytic Society*, Vol. IV, ed. Herman Nunberg and Ernst Federn, trans. M. Nunberg (New York: International Universities Press, 1975), p. 136.

65. *CS*, 2nd, pp. 249–50.

66. Hannah Arendt, "Home to Roost: A Bicentennial Address," *The New York Review of Books*, June 26, 1975, p. 4.

67. Erikson, "Environment and Virtues," pp. 65, 67.

68. *Dimensions*, p. 94.

69. *YML*, p. 252.

70. *IS*, p. 86.

71. Erikson, "The Concept of Identity in Race Relations: Notes and Queries," p. 149. Cf. Hannah Arendt, *Eichmann in Jerusalem: A Report on the Banality of Evil* (New York: Viking, 1963), p. 112.

72. Erikson, "Reflections on the Dissent of Contemporary Youth," p. 155.

73. *Identity*, p. 293.

74. *CS*, 2nd, p. 412.

75. *Dimensions*, p. 110; *ILC*, p. 74; *Identity*, p. 195.

76. Erik H. Erikson, "Editor's Preface," *The Challenge of Youth* (New York: Anchor, 1965), p. xii.

77. *ILC*, p. 94; *CS*, 2nd, p. 399.

78. *CS*, 2nd, p. 318. For different attitudes toward Erikson's reflections on America, cf. David Gutmann, "Erik Erikson's America," *Commentary*, Sept. 1974, pp. 60–64, and Daniel Bell, *The End of Ideology*, Rev. ed. (New York: Collier Books, 1961), pp. 101–02.

79. *IS*, p. 142. For Erikson's long-standing conjecturing about

the two-party system, cf. Erik H. Erikson, "Ego Development and Historical Change," *The Psychoanalytic Study of the Child*, Vol. II (New York: International Universities Press, 1947), p. 381.

80. *LH*, p. 44.
81. *IS*, pp. 122, 131
82. *Ibid.*, p. 123.
83. *Dimensions*, p. 60.
84. *LH*, p. 204.
85. *CS*, pp. 293–94, 323, 322.
86. *IS*, p. 60.
87. Erikson, "Environment and Virtues," p. 74.
88. *IS*, p. 84.
89. *Ibid.*, p. 125.
90. *ILC*, p. 30.
91. *Dimensions*, p. 36.
92. *ILC*, p. 31.
93. *Dialogue*, p. 66.
94. *CS*, 2nd, pp. 329–30.
95. *Identity*, p. 192.
96. *Dialogue*, pp. 67–68.

CHAPTER 4: POST-FREUDIANISM

1. *CS*, 2nd, p. 424.
2. *Ibid.*, p. 355.
3. *CS*, 1st, p. 313.
4. *YML*, p. 153.
5. *Identity*, pp. 203, 228.
6. *IR*, p. 212.
7. *Identity*, p. 275.
8. *IR*, p. 77.
9. *Dialogue*, p. 105.

10. *Identity*, p. 267.

11. Erikson, "The Dream Specimen of Psychoanalysis," pp. 154–55.

12. *Ibid.*, p. 155.

13. *LH*, pp. 96, 84.

14. *Identity*, p. 164.

15. *ILC*, p. 99.

16. *Identity*, p. 163.

17. *YML*, pp. 117–18.

18. *Identity*, p. 277.

19. *Dialogue*, p. 27.

20. *Identity*, pp. 30–31.

21. *LH*, p. 39.

22. *Identity*, p. 197.

23. *YML*, p. 142.

24. Erikson, "The Dream Specimen of Psychoanalysis," pp. 139, 163.

25. *ILC*, p. 154.

26. *IR*, p. 195.

27. Erikson, "The Dream Specimen of Psychoanalysis," pp. 133, 156, 170.

28. *Ibid.*, p. 167.

29. *Dialogue*, p. 24.

30. *CS*, 2nd, p. 91.

31. Erik H. Erikson, "Psychosocial Development of Children," in *Discussions on Child Development*, Vol. III, ed. J. M. Tanner and Bärbel Inhelder (New York: International Universities Press, 1958), p. 180.

32. Erikson, "Autobiographic Notes on the Identity Crisis," p. 744.

33. *LH*, p. 39.

34. *Ibid.*, p. 82.

35. *Dialogue*, pp. 92, 13.

36. Erik H. Erikson, "Gandhi's Autobiography: The Leader as a Child," *The American Scholar*, XXXV, No. 4 (Autumn 1966), 646.

37. *IS*, p. 105.

38. *Identity*, p. 320.

39. *Ibid.*, pp. 227–28.

40. *ILC*, p. 147.

41. *Identity*, p. 45.

42. *LH*, p. 101.

43. *Identity*, pp. 124, 303; Erikson, "Childhood and Tradition in Two American Indian Tribes," p. 339.

44. *Identity*, p. 225.

45. *Ibid.*, pp. 58, 283; *ILC*, p. 31; Erikson, "Ego Development and Historical Change," p. 372. Cf. Roazen, *Freud and His Followers*, pp. 290–94.

46. *Identity*, p. 59.

47. Erik H. Erikson, "Reflections on Dr. Borg's Life Cycle," *Daedalus*, CV (Spring 1976), p. 2.

48. *Identity*, p. 82.

49. Erik H. Erikson, "Inner and Outer Space: Reflections on Womanhood," *Daedalus*, XCIII (Spring 1964), p. 586; *YML*, p. 18.

50. *GT*, p. 98.

51. *Dialogue*, p. 74.

52. Homburger, "Configurations in Play—Clinical Notes."

53. Erik H. Erikson, "Play, Vision, and Deception," Godkin Lectures, p. 36.

54. *CS*, 2nd, p. 37.

55. *IS*, p. 84; Erikson, "Autobiographic Notes on the Identity Crisis," pp. 754–55.

56. *CS*, 2nd, p. 60.

57. Erikson, "Psychosexual Stages in Child Development," in *Discussions on Child Development*, Vol. IV, ed. J. M. Tanner and Bärbel Inhelder (New York: International Universities Press, 1960), p. 136.

58. *Minutes of the Vienna Psychoanalytic Society,* IV, 21.

59. *Ibid.,* p. 161.

60. *CS,* 2nd, pp. 63–64.

61. *Dialogue,* p. 86.

62. *GT,* pp. 65, 244–45.

63. *Identity,* p. 199.

64. *YML,* p. 73.

65. Erik H. Erikson, "Play and Actuality," in *Play and Development,* ed. Maria W. Piers (New York: Norton, 1972), p. 156.

66. *IS,* p. 117.

67. *Minutes of the Vienna Psychoanalytic Society,* IV, 254.

68. *Ibid.,* p. 235.

69. *ILC,* p. 40.

70. *Ibid.,* p. 129.

71. *CS,* 2nd, p. 64.

72. *GT,* p. 429.

73. *IR,* p. 176.

74. *IS,* p. 119.

75. Erikson, "Wholeness and Totality," p. 156.

76. *Identity,* pp. 77, 17; Erikson, "Wholeness and Totality," p. 158.

77. *YML,* p. 18.

78. Homburger, "Configurations in Play—Clinical Notes," p. 214; *IR,* p. 72.

79. *IR,* p. 52.

80. *CS,* 2nd, p. 422.

81. Erikson, "The Dream Specimen of Psychoanalysis," p. 131.

82. Erikson, "The Ontogeny of Ritualization," pp. 619.

83. *YML,* p. 154; *Identity,* p. 164.

84. *ILC,* p. 43.

85. *Dialogue,* p. 94.

86. *Ibid.*

87. *IR,* p. 166.

88. *Identity,* p. 253.

89. *YML,* pp. 151–52.

90. *Ibid.,* p. 154; *Dialogue,* p. 104.

91. *IR,* p. 175.

92. *Dialogue,* p. 97.

93. *LH,* p. 35.

94. *Dialogue,* p. 96.

95. Erikson, "Play and Actuality," pp. 138–39. Cf. John P. Zubek (ed.), *Sensory Deprivation: Fifteen Years of Research* (New York: Appleton-Century-Crofts, 1969).

96. Erikson, "Play, Vision and Deception," p. 30.

97. "The Future of an Illusion," *The Standard Edition of the Complete Psychological Works of Sigmund Freud,* Vol. 21, p. 53.

98. "An Autobiographical Study," *The Standard Edition of the Complete Psychological Works of Sigmund Freud,* Vol. 20, p. 42.

99. *LH,* p. 115.

100. *Ibid.,* p. 105.

101. Erik H. Erikson, "The Golden Rule and the Cycle of Life," in *The Study of Lives: Essays in Honor of Henry A. Murray,* ed. Robert White (New York: Atherton, 1963), p. 425. Cf. also *LH,* p. 34.

102. *Dialogue,* p. 95.

CHAPTER 5: PSYCHOHISTORY

1. *Dimensions,* p. 12.

2. *LH,* p. 88.

3. *IR,* p. 36.

4. *CS,* 2nd, p. 16.

5. *LH,* p. 84.

6. *CS,* 2nd, p. 112.

7. *YML,* p. 108.

8. *Ibid.,* pp. 150, 9; *IR,* p. 202; *YML,* p. 15; *IR,* p. 203.

9. *Dimensions,* p. 55.

10. *YML*, p. 218.

11. *GT*, p. 363.

12. *Dimensions*, pp. 13–14.

13. *GT*, p. 113.

14. *YML*, p. 252.

15. *Ibid.*, p. 196.

16. *Ibid.*, p. 65.

17. *LH*, p. 40.

18. Cf. Erich Fromm, *Escape from Freedom* (New York: Holt, 1941), and Norman O. Brown, *Life Against Death* (New York: Random House).

19. *YML*, p. 249.

20. Cf. Paul Roazen, "Psychology and Politics: Biographies of Leaders," *Contemporary Psychoanalysis*, XII, No. 1 (Jan. 1976), 144–57.

21. *YML*, pp. 16, 15.

22. *Ibid.*, pp. 94, 131, 97, 129.

23. *Ibid.*, pp. 148, 150.

24. *Ibid.*, pp. 201, 198–99.

25. *Ibid.*, pp. 54, 15, 234.

26. *Ibid.*, pp. 71, 229.

27. "Civilization and Its Discontents," *The Standard Edition of the Complete Psychological Works of Sigmund Freud*, Vol. 21, pp. 102, 109–12, 114, 142–43; "Why War?," *The Standard Edition of the Complete Psychological Works of Sigmund Freud*, Vol. 22, p. 212.

28. *YML*, p. 212.

29. *Ibid.*, pp. 135, 219, 175, 193–94.

30. *Ibid.*, pp. 220, 214, 39.

31. *Ibid.*, pp. 205, 237, 206, 252.

32. In his old age Luther wrote "dreadful antisemitic pamphlets." He proposed "that the Jewish schools and synagogues, where their doctrines were disseminated, be burnt down; that their books should be taken away and their rabbis forbidden to

teach . . . ; that they should be made to work on the land and debarred from practising usury . . . , prevented from moving about, dispossessed so as to live all together 'in one barn like Gypsies,' in the hope that they might at last learn their lesson. But as he wrote on Luther became doubtful even of this method, and concluded with a fiery exhortation to drive out the Jews altogether—shipping them to Palestine lock, stock and barrel was one suggestion—unless they would desist from calumny and usury 'and become Christians.' " Some of Luther's followers protested against his anti-Jewish pamphlets. Cf. Edith Simon, *Luther Alive* (London: Hodder & Stoughton, 1968), pp. 346, 348. Cf. also Leon Paliakov, *The History of Anti-Semitism: From the Time of Christ to the Court Jews,* trans. Richard Howard (New York: Schocken Books, 1974), pp. 216–26, and Roland H. Bainton, *Here I Stand: A Life of Martin Luther* (New York: New American Library, 1955), pp. 296–98.

33. *YML,* 210, 197.

34. *Ibid.,* pp. 50, 176.

35. Roland H. Bainton, "Psychiatry and History: An Examination of Erikson's *Young Man Luther," Religion in Life,* XL, No. 4 (Winter 1971), 470. Cf. also Roger A. Johnson, "Psychohistory as Religious Narrative: the demonic role of Hans Luther in Erikson's saga of human evolution," forthcoming.

36. *YML,* p. 91.

37. *Ibid.,* p. 67.

38. *Dialogue,* p. 66.

39. *LH,* p. 47.

40. *Dimensions,* p. 14.

41. Richard Ellmann, *Golden Codgers* (New York: Oxford University Press, 1973), pp. 7–9.

42. *YML,* pp. 23, 37.

43. *GT,* p. 97.

44. *IS,* p. 123.

45. *YML,* p. 139. Cf. Ernst Kris, "The Personal Myth," *Journal of the American Psychoanalytic Association,* X, No. 4 (Oct. 1956), 653–81.

CHAPTER 6: YOUTH AND IDENTITY

1. *ILC,* p. 161.

2. Anna Freud, *The Ego and the Mechanisms of Defence,* trans. Cecil Baines (London: Hogarth, 1937), Chs. 11–12. The new foreword to a "revised edition" says that the original book has been left intact. Cf. "Foreword to the 1966 Edition," *The Ego and the Mechanisms of Defense, The Writings of Anna Freud* (New York: International Universities Press, 1966), p. vi. The account of "a young governess" in chapter 10 may be Anna Freud's autobiographical conception of herself.

3. *Identity,* p. 156.

4. *ILC,* p. 110; *Identity,* p. 127.

5. *Identity,* p. 156.

6. *YML,* p. 43.

7. *CS,* 2nd, pp. 262–63.

8. *Identity,* p. 128.

9. *GT,* p. 147.

10. *YML,* pp. 261–62.

11. Erikson, "The Dream Specimen of Psychoanalysis," p. 169; Heinz Hartmann and Rudolph M. Loewenstein, "Notes on the Superego," *The Psychoanalytic Study of the Child,* Vol. XVII (New York: International Universities Press, 1963), p. 77.

12. *YML,* p. 143.

13. *Identity,* p. 37.

14. *YML,* p. 140.

15. Erik H. Erikson, "Insight and Freedom" (University of Cape Town, 1968), p. 16.

16. *ILC,* p. 92.

17. *YML,* p. 34; *Identity,* p. 167.

18. *LH,* p. 173; Anna Freud, *The Ego and the Mechanisms of Defense,* Ch. 12, "Conclusion."

19. *YML,* p. 14.

20. Erik H. Erikson, "Memorandum on Youth," *Daedalus,* XCVI (1967), 864.

21. *Identity,* pp. 188, 235.
22. *ILC,* pp. 122–23.
23. *Dialogue,* p. 65.
24. Fromm, *Escape from Freedom,* p. 184.
25. *ILC,* p. 141.
26. *Identity,* p. 166.
27. *Ibid.,* p. 163.
28. *Ibid.*
29. *LH,* p. 22.
30. *IR,* p. 90.
31. *IS,* pp. 117–18; *Identity,* p. 184.
32. *Identity,* p. 184.
33. *Dimensions,* p. 125.
34. *Identity,* p. 219.
35. *IR,* pp. 96, 92.
36. *Identity,* p. 303.
37. *Ibid.,* p. 308.
38. *Dialogue,* p. 41.
39. *Identity,* p. 314.
40. *IS,* p. 129.
41. *LH,* p. 152.
42. Cf. Marshall Berman, *The New York Times Book Review,* March 30, 1975, p. 22.
43. *LH,* p. 26.
44. Compare *LH,* p. 26, to Erikson, "Autobiographic Notes on the Identity Crisis," p. 742.
45. *LH,* p. 27.
46. "The Childhood Genesis of Sex Differences in Behavior," in *Discussions on Child Development,* Vol. III, ed. Tanner and Inhelder, p. 16.
47. *LH,* p. 31.
48. *Ibid.,* p. 125.
49. *The New York Times Book Review,* March 30, 1975, pp. 12, 22; *ibid.,* May 4, 1975, pp. 56–58.

50. *LH*, p. 27.

51. Coles, *Erik H. Erikson*, pp. 180–81.

52. *LH*, p. 28.

53. Coles, *Erik H. Erikson*, p. 181.

54. Martin Jay, *The Dialectical Imagination: A History of the Frankfurt School and the Institute of Social Research 1923–1950* (Boston: Little, Brown, 1973), p. 33.

55. *LH*, pp. 31, 22.

56. Coles, *Erik H. Erikson*, p. 181.

57. *ILC*, p. 27.

58. *IS*, p. 51.

59. Coles, *Erik H. Erikson*, p. 181.

60. *LH*, pp. 100, 29.

61. Coles, *Erik H. Erikson*, p. 181.

62. "The Childhood Genesis of Sex Differences in Behavior," p. 17.

63. Compare Erikson, "Autobiographic Notes on the Identity Crisis," p. 739, with *LH*, p. 37.

64. Erik H. Erikson, "Youth: Fidelity and Diversity," *Daedalus*, XCI, No. 1 (Winter 1962), 8, 11.

65. Erik H. Erikson, "The Syndrome of Identity Diffusion in Adolescents and Young Adults," in *Discussions on Child Development*, Vol. III, ed. Tanner and Inhelder, p. 151.

66. *LH*, p. 31.

67. *Ibid.*, p. 29.

68. *Dimensions*, p. 115.

69. *IR*, p. 204.

70. Erikson, "On the Sense of Inner Identity," p. 359.

71. *ILC*, p. 132.

72. *Identity*, p. 176.

73. *Ibid.*, p. 213.

74. *ILC*, p. 133.

75. Erikson, "The Concept of Identity in Race Relations: Notes and Queries," p. 164.

76. *Dialogue*, p. 38.

77. Erikson, "Wholeness and Totality," p. 161.

78. *YML*, p. 84.

79. *IR*, p. 124.

80. *Ibid.*, p. 100.

81. *Dialogue*, p. 49.

82. *Identity*, pp. 242–43.

83. *LH*, p. 221.

84. *Identity*, pp. 179, 132.

85. *Dialogue*, p. 40.

86. *Identity*, pp. 179, 174.

87. *Dialogue*, p. 56.

88. *IR*, p. 65.

89. *YML*, p. 17.

90. *Identity*, p. 214.

91. *Dialogue*, p. 31.

92. *IR*, p. 95; *YML*, p. 17.

93. *IR*, p. 170.

94. Cf. Elizabeth Janeway, "On 'Female Sexuality,'" in *Women and Analysis: Dialogues on Psychoanalytic Views of Femininity*, ed. Jean Strouse (New York: Grossman, 1974), pp. 57–70.

95. *YML*, pp. 124–25.

96. *IR*, p. 97.

97. Freud rightly, I believe, put forward a view at odds with much of what became fashionable in twentieth-century education: he mentioned the "duty" of secondary schools "of providing a substitute for the family and of arousing interest in life in the world outside . . . The school must never forget that it has to deal with immature individuals who cannot be denied a right to linger at certain stages of development and even at certain disagreeable ones. The school must not take on itself the inexorable character of life: it must not seek to be more than a *game* of life." "Contributions to a Discussion on Suicide," *The Standard Edition of the Complete Psychological Works of Sigmund Freud*, Vol. 11, p. 232.

98. Erikson, "Identity, Psychosocial," p. 63.

CHAPTER 7: THE LIFE CYCLE

1. *Dialogue,* p. 21.
2. *ILC,* p. 52.
3. *GT,* p. 38.
4. Erikson, "The Ontogeny of Ritualization," p. 618.
5. *Dialogue,* p. 68.
6. *Ibid.,* p. 97.
7. *IR,* p. 114.
8. *ILC,* p. 100.
9. *Identity,* p. 96.
10. *IR,* pp. 138–39.
11. *CS,* 2nd, pp. 270–71.
12. *Identity,* pp. 162–63.
13. *YML,* p. 254.
14. *CS,* 2nd, p. 246.
15. Erikson, "The Dream Specimen of Psychoanalysis," p. 155.
16. *CS,* 2nd, p. 46.
17. *ILC,* p. 56.
18. Erik H. Erikson, "Life Cycle, The Human," *International Encyclopaedia of the Social Sciences* (New York: Macmillan, 1968), IX, 287.
19. *IR,* p. 175.
20. *Ibid.,* p. 139.
21. *Dialogue,* p. 17.
22. *Identity,* p. 232.
23. *CS,* 2nd, p. 80.
24. *Dialogue,* p. 17.
25. *Ibid.,* p. 55.
26. *Identity,* p. 105.
27. *Ibid.,* p. 83; Erikson, "On the Sense of Inner Identity," p. 353; Erikson, "Wholeness and Totality," p. 164; *CS,* 2nd, p. 250.
28. *IR,* p. 153.

29. *Identity*, p. 106.

30. *Ibid.*, pp. 108–109.

31. *Dialogue*, p. 20.

32. *ILC*, p. 68.

33. *Identity*, p. 113.

34. *GT*, p. 132.

35. *LH*, p. 163. Cf. the brilliant article by Karl Mannheim, "The Problem of Generations," in his *Essays on the Sociology of Knowledge*, ed. Paul Kecskemeti (London: Routledge & Kegan Paul, 1952); pp. 276–320.

36. Erikson, "Life Cycle, The Human," p. 289.

37. *IR*, p. 123.

38. Erikson, "Life Cycle, The Human," p. 289.

39. Erikson, "Reflections on the Dissent of Contemporary Youth," p. 172.

40. *Identity*, p. 126.

41. *YML*, pp. 40–41.

42. Erik Homburger Erikson, "Problems of Infancy and Early Childhood," in *An Outline of Abnormal Psychology*, ed. Gardner Murphy and Arthur Bachrach (rev. ed.; New York: Random House, 1954), p. 12; *YML*, p. 259.

43. *YML*, p. 225.

44. *Identity*, p. 139.

45. Erikson, "Life Cycle, The Human," p. 291.

46. *ILC*, p. 98.

47. Erikson, "Reflections on Dr. Borg's Life Cycle."

48. *Ibid.*, pp. 23, 17.

49. *IR*, p. 229.

50. Erikson, "Life Cycle, The Human," p. 286.

51. *IR*, pp. 134, 156.

52. *ILC*, p. 97; Erikson, "On the Sense of Inner Identity," p. 352.

53. Erikson, "Life Cycle, The Human," p. 292.

54. *ILC*, p. 61.

55. *Dialogue,* p. 15.

56. *ILC,* p. 61.

57. *IR,* p. 208; *Identity,* p. 235.

58. Erikson, "Life Cycle, The Human," p. 292.

59. *Dialogue,* pp. 17, 30.

60. *Identity,* p. 232.

61. Erikson, "Life Cycle, The Human," p. 292.

62. *Ibid.*

63. *IS,* p. 104; Erik H. Erikson, "The Roots of Virtue," in *The Humanist Frame,* ed. Sir Julian Huxley (New York: Harper, 1961), p. 162.

CHAPTER 8: GANDHI'S "NONVIOLENCE"

1. *LH,* pp. 175–76.

2. *Identity,* p. 299; *Dimensions,* p. 78.

3. *GT,* p. 248.

4. *LH,* p. 178.

5. *Dimensions,* p. 114.

6. *Identity,* 138.

7. *LH,* p. 85.

8. *GT,* p. 438.

9. Erikson, "Gandhi's Autobiography," p. 637.

10. *GT,* pp. 244, 424–25.

11. *LH,* p. 188.

12. *GT,* p. 236.

13. Erikson, "The Golden Rule and the Cycle of Life," p. 421.

14. Erikson, "Insight and Freedom," p. 14.

15. *LH,* pp. 129, 147.

16. *Ibid.,* pp. 181, 183.

17. *Dialogue,* p. 72.

18. *IS,* p. 114. Cf. Geoffrey Gorer's review of *Gandhi's Truth* in the London *Observer,* Jan. 4, 1970.

19. *GT*, p. 335.

20. *IS*, p. 113.

21. *Dialogue*, p. 76.

22. Quoted in *YML*, p. 13.

23. Quoted in *GT*, p. 265.

24. *GT*, pp. 374, 162; quoted in *ibid.*, p. 92.

25. *GT*, p. 72.

26. Michael Holroyd, *Lytton Strachey and the Bloomsbury Group: His Work, Their Influence* (Middlesex, Eng.: Penguin, 1971), p. 265. Cf. also Michael Holroyd, *Lytton Strachey: A Biography* (Middlesex, Eng.: Penguin, 1971), p. 911.

27. For a conception of Gandhi rather different from Erikson's, cf. Lloyd I. Rudolph and Susanne Hoeber Rudolph, *The Modernity of Tradition: Political Development in India* (Chicago: University of Chicago Press, 1967), Part II. Cf. also Susanne H. Rudolph, "Review of *Gandhi's Truth*," *Contemporary Psychology*, August 1970, pp. 484–86. I am grateful for Lloyd Rudolph's calling my attention to David G. Mandelbaum, "The Study of Life History: Gandhi," *Current Anthropology*, June 1973, pp. 177–96.

28. *LH*, pp. 117, 119.

29. For his understanding of India, I am indebted to Gorer's review of *Gandhi's Truth* in the London *Observer*, Jan. 4, 1970.

30. *GT*, pp. 418, 46, 86.

31. *Ibid.*, pp. 111, 399.

32. *Ibid.*, pp. 409, 312–13, 307.

33. Erik H. Erikson, "On the Nature of Psycho-Historical Evidence: In Search of Gandhi," *Daedalus*, XCVII (Summer 1968), 717; *GT*, p. 312.

34. *GT*, pp. 239, 318.

35. *Ibid.*, pp. 99, 107, 102.

36. For Freud's own fantasies about self-creation (and his ambivalences about being Jewish), cf. Roazen, *Freud: Political and Social Thought*, pp. 176 ff.

37. *GT*, pp. 189, 117.

38. *Ibid.*, pp. 145, 174.

39. *Ibid.*, pp. 381, 401.

40. *Ibid.*, pp. 292, 79; *Dialogue*, p. 75; *GT*, pp. 352, 79; *LH*, p. 151.

41. *LH*, p. 163.

42. Erikson, "On the Nature of Psycho-Historical Evidence," pp. 716–17.

43. *GT*, pp. 118, 140.

44. *Ibid.*, pp. 369, 140, 320.

45. *Ibid.*, p. 345.

46. *Ibid.*, pp. 412, 342, 413.

CHAPTER 9: NORMALITY

1. *CS*, 2nd, pp. 264–65.

2. *Identity*, p. 136; Erikson, "Life Cycle, The Human," p. 290; Erikson, "Reflections on Dr. Borg's Life Cycle," p. 14.

3. *Dialogue*, pp 29, 52.

4. *Dimensions*, p. 122; *Dialogue*, p. 51.

5. Erik H. Erikson, "Once More the Inner Space," in *Women and Analysis*, ed. Strouse, p. 336.

6. *Dialogue*, p. 50.

7. Erikson, "Editor's Preface," *The Challenge of Youth*, p. xi.

8. Erikson, "Reflections on the Dissent of Contemporary Youth," p. 175.

9. *Dimensions*, pp. 121, 59.

10. *Ibid.*, pp. 123, 124.

11. *IS*, p. 85.

12. *LH*, p. 44.

13. *ILC*, p. 147.

14. *Dimensions*, pp. 108–109.

15. Erikson, "Play, Vision, and Deception," p. 27.

16. *Dimensions*, pp. 100, 104.

17. Erikson, "Play and Actuality," p. 133.

18. Erikson, "Play, Vision, and Deception," p. 40.

19. Erikson, "Play and Actuality," p. 165.

20. *Dialogue*, p. 92.

21. *IR*, p. 164; *LH*, p. 103.

22. Erikson, "Play and Actuality," p. 165.

23. Herbert Marcuse, *Eros and Civilization: A Philosophical Inquiry into Freud* (Boston: Beacon Press, 1955).

24. Erikson, "Play and Actuality," p. 163.

25. *Dimensions*, p. 79.

26. *Dialogue*, p. 86.

27. *Identity*, p. 90.

28. *ILC*, p. 51.

29. *Identity*, p. 150.

30. *YML*, pp. 8, 17.

31. *CS*, 2nd, p. 235.

32. Erikson, "Problems of Infancy and Early Childhood," p. 34.

33. *Dimensions*, p. 46.

34. *LH*, p. 39.

35. Erikson, "Play and Actuality," pp. 133, 163.

36. Erikson, "The Ontogeny of Ritualization," p. 614.

37. Erikson, "Play, Vision, and Deception," p. 32.

38. *CS*, 2nd, p. 222.

39. *IR*, p. 121. Cf. the well-known article by Donald W. Winnicott, "Transitional Objects and Transitional Phenomena: A Study of the First Not-Me Possession," *International Journal of Psychoanalysis*, XXXIV (1953), 89–97.

40. *CS*, 2nd, pp. 213, 222.

41. *Ibid.*, p. 229.

42. Homburger, "Configurations in Play—Clinical Notes," pp. 167–68.

43. Erikson, "Play and Actuality," p. 127.

44. *ILC*, pp. 85–86.

45. *CS*, 2nd, pp. 98, 102–103.

46. Erikson, "Once More the Inner Space," p. 326.

47. Erik H. Erikson, "Sex Differences in the Play Configurations of American Pre-Adolescents," in *Childhood in Contemporary Cultures*, ed. Margaret Mead and Martha Wolfenstein (Chicago: University of Chicago Press, 1955), p. 334.

48. *Identity*, p. 271.

49. "Inner and Outer Space," pp. 590, 592.

50. Erik H. Erikson, "Sex Differences in the Play Configurations of Preadolescents," *American Journal of Orthopsychiatry*, XXI (195 1), 690.

51. Erikson, "The Dream Specimen of Psychoanalysis," p. 162.

52. *Identity*, p. 285.

53. Erikson, "The Dream Specimen of Psychoanalysis," p. 165.

54. *IR*, p. 129.

55. *Dimensions*, p. 116.

56. Kate Millet, *Sexual Politics* (New York: Avon, 1971), pp. 214–15.

57. *Identity*, p. 263.

58. Erikson, "Once More the Inner Space," p. 334.

59. *IR*, p. 235.

60. *Identity*, p. 264.

61. *Ibid.*, p. 267.

62. *CS*, 2nd, p. 410.

63. *Identity*, p. 278.

64. *Dialogue*, p. 47.

65. Erikson, "Once More the Inner Space," pp. 337, 322, 333.

66. *Dialogue*, p. 47.

67. *Dimensions*, pp. 123–24.

68. Erikson, "Inner and Outer Space," p. 598.

69. Erikson, "Problems of Infancy and Early Childhood," p. 22.

70. *YML*, p. 207.

71. *Dimensions*, p. 119.

72. *Dialogue*, p. 46.

73. *Identity*, p. 292.

74. *Identity*, pp. 261–62.

75. *CS*, 2nd, p. 411.

76. Erikson, "Play, Vision, and Deception," p. 31.

77. Erikson, "Once More the Inner Space," p. 338.

78. *Ibid.*, p. 339.

79. *Dialogue*, p. 90.

CHAPTER 10: MORALS AND ETHICS

1. *IS*, pp. 45, 100.

2. *Identity*, p. 113.

3. Cf. Paul Roazen, "The Impact of Psychoanalysis on Values," in *Moral Values and the Superego Concept in Psychoanalysis*, ed. Seymour Post (New York: International Universities Press, 1972), pp. 197–204.

4. *IS*, p. 52.

5. *YML*, p. 70.

6. *Dialogue*, p. 40.

7. *ILC*, p. 48.

8. *YML*, p. 263.

9. *ILC*, p. 100.

10. *LH*, p. 188.

11. Erikson, "Reflections on the Dissent of Contemporary Youth," p. 155.

12. *Identity*, p. 237.

13. *CS*, 2nd, p. 257.

14. *Identity*, p. 122.

15. *GT*, pp. 40, 180–81; *IR*, p. 227.

16. *Identity*, pp. 119–20; *IR*, p. 222.

17. *Identity*, pp. 259–60.

18. *Ibid.*, p. 304.

19. *LH*, p. 224.

20. *Dimensions*, pp. 114, 117, 108.

21. Erikson, "Reflections on the Dissent of Contemporary Youth," p. 165.

22. *Dimensions*, pp. 32, 111.

23. Erikson, "Insight and Freedom," p. 10.

24. *LH*, p. 206.

25. *GT*, p. 249.

26. *Dialogue*, pp. 105–106.

27. *CS*, 2nd, p. 424.

28. *IR*, p. 73.

29. *ILC*, p. 99.

30. Erikson, "Reflections on the Dissent of Contemporary Youth." p. 175.

31. *Dimensions*, pp. 95–96.

32. Erikson, "Inner and Outer Space," p. 586.

33. Erikson, "Play and Actuality," p. 145.

34. *LH*, p. 207.

35. *Identity*, p. 241.

36. Erikson, "The Golden Rule and the Cycle of Life," p. 418.

37. *Identity*, p. 260.

38. *Ibid.*

39. Erikson, "The Golden Rule and the Cycle of Life," p. 413.

40. *Identity*, p. 260.

41. *Dimensions*, pp. 81–82.

42. *IR*, p. 241.

43. Henry Adams, *The Education of Henry Adams* (New York: Random House, 1931), p. 472.

44. *IS*, p. 142.

45. Erikson, "On the Sense of Inner Identity," p. 363.

46. "Civilization and Its Discontents," pp. 102, 110.

47. *Ibid.*, p. 110.

48. "New Introductory Lectures in Psychoanalysis," p. 105.

49. "Moses and Monotheism," *The Standard Edition of the Complete Psychological Works of Sigmund Freud*, Vol. 23, p. 87.

50. *IR*, p. 221.

51. *Identity*, p. 219; Erikson, "Reflections on Dr. Borg's Life Cycle," p. 24.

52. *IR*, p. 233.

53. Erikson, "Once More the Inner Space," p. 333.

54. *IR*, p. 243.

55. Erikson, "The Golden Rule and the Cycle of Life," p. 413.

56. *Identity*, p. 316.

57. Erikson, "The Golden Rule and the Cycle of Life," p. 423.

58. *Dimensions*, pp. 47, 49, 71.

59. *IR*, pp. 232, 61.

60. *IS*, p. 49.

61. *YML*, p. 111.

62. Erikson, "Play and Actuality," p. 141; Erikson, "The Ontogeny of Ritualization," p. 603.

63. *GT*, p. 157.

64. Erikson, "The Ontogeny of Ritualization," p. 604.

65. Erikson, "Play and Actuality," p. 141.

66. Erikson, "Gandhi's Autobiography," p. 644.

67. *IS*, p. 48; *GT*, p. 46.

68. Erikson, "The Ontogeny of Ritualization," pp. 604, 612–13.

69. *Ibid.*, p. 620.

70. *LH*, p. 189.

71. *Ibid.*, p. 176; Erikson, "The Ontogeny of Ritualization," p. 606.

72. *IS*, p. 129.

73. Erikson, "On the Sense of Inner Identity," p. 362.

74. *IS*, p. 91.

75. Clyde Kluckhohn, *Mirror for Man* (New York: Fawcett, 1957), p. 218.

76. *Identity*, p. 298.

77. *LH*, p. 47.

78. *Ibid.*, p. 256.

79. Erikson, "Once More the Inner Space," p. 336.

80. *IS*, pp. 83, 127.

81. Erikson, "Play, Vision, and Deception," p. 35.

82. Erikson, "On the Sense of Inner Identity," p. 360.

83. *Dimensions*, pp. 76–77.

84. *CS*, 2nd, p. 165.

85. Erikson, "Play and Actuality," p. 166.

86. *Dialogue*, p. 70.

87. Erikson, "Play and Actuality," p. 155.

88. *IS*, p. 127.

89. *Identity*, p. 287.

90. *IS*, p. 128.

91. *CS*, 2nd, p. 186.

92. *ILC*, p. 40; *Identity*, p. 299.

93. Cf. *CS*, 2nd, p. 237; Erikson, "Childhood and Tradition in Two American Indian Tribes," pp. 344–45, 350; Erikson, "Ego Development and Historical Change," p. 362.

94. *Identity*, p. 302.

95. *Dimensions*, p. 98.

96. *Identity*, p. 42.

97. *Dialogue*, p. 108.

98. *CS*, 2nd, p. 327.

99. Erikson, "Environment and Virtues," p. 74.

100. *IS*, p. 61.

101. *Identity*, p. 316.

102. *Dimensions*, p. 104.

103. Erikson, "On the Sense of Inner Identity," p. 362.

CHAPTER 11: THE FUTURE OF DEPTH PSYCHOLOGY

1. J. D. Mabbott, "Moral Rules," *Proceedings of the British Academy*, XXXIX, (1953), 98.

2. I am indebted here to lectures at Harvard given years ago by Louis Hartz.

3. *LH,* pp. 63–64.

4. Nigel Nicolson, *Portrait of a Marriage* (London: Weidenfeld & Nicolson, 1973).

5. Marcuse, *Eros and Civilization.* Cf. Paul Roazen, review of Russell Jacoby's *Social Amnesia,* in *The American Scholar,* XLV, No. 2 (Spring 1976), 314–16.

6. *Minutes of the Vienna Psychoanalytic Society,* IV, 136.

7. Roazen, *Freud and His Followers,* pp. 435–36.

8. "The Interpretation of Dreams," *The Standard Edition of the Complete Psychological Works of Sigmund Freud,* Vol. 5, p. 451.

9. "Introductory Lectures on Psychoanalysis," *The Standard Edition of the Complete Psychological Works of Sigmund Freud,* Vol. 16, p. 356.

10. *Psychoanalysis and Faith: The Letters of Sigmund Freud and Oskar Pfister,* ed. Heinrich Meng and Ernst Freud, trans. Eric Mosbacher (New York: Basic Books, 1963), pp. 61–62.

11. Quoted in Ernest Jones, *The Life and Work of Sigmund Freud* (New York: Basic Books; 1955), II, 417–18.

12. Sigmund Freud, *Letters,* ed. Ernst Freud, trans. Tania and James Stern (New York: Basic Books, 1960), p. 390.

13. "Recommendations to Physicians Practising Psychoanalysis," p. 119.

14. Cf. Roazen, *Freud and His Followers,* p. 209; Roazen, *Brother Animal,* pp. 139–41.

15. "Analysis Terminable and Interminable," *The Standard Edition of the Complete Psychological Works of Sigmund Freud,* Vol. 23, p. 222.

16. Erikson, "Insight and Freedom," p. 16.

17. Interview with Donald Winnicott, Sept. 1, 1965.

18. Hanns Sachs, *Freud: Master and Friend* (London: Imago, 1945), p. 103.

19. "An Autobiographical Study," p. 8; "The Question of Lay Analysis," *The Standard Edition of the Complete Psychological Works of Sigmund Freud,* Vol. 20, p. 254; *Letters,* p. 232.

20. "An Autobiographical Study," pp. 71–72.

21. "The Question of Lay Analysis," p. 253.

22. "Lines of Advance in Psychoanalytic Therapy," *The Standard Edition of the Complete Psychological Works of Sigmund Freud*, Vol. 17, p. 168.

23. Anna Freud, *The Ego and the Mechanisms of Defense*, p. 15.

24. "Analysis Terminable and Interminable," pp. 238–39.

25. *Ibid.*, p. 249.

26. Jean-Paul Sartre, *Between Existentialism and Marxism*, trans. John Mathews (New York: Pantheon, 1974), pp. 202, 201.

27. Cf. Lawrence S. Kubie, "Unsolved Problems in the Resolution of the Transference," *Psychoanalytic Quarterly*, XXXVII (1968), 331–52; Lawrence S. Kubie, "Missing and Wanted: Heterodoxy in Psychiatry and Psychoanalysis," *The Journal of Nervous and Mental Disease*, CXXXVII (1963), 311; Lawrence S. Kubie, "Traditionalism in Psychiatry," *The Journal of Nervous and Mental Disease*, CXXXIX (1964), 6–19; Lawrence S. Kubie, *Practical and Theoretical Aspects of Psychoanalysis* (rev. ed.; New York: International Universities Press; 1975), pp. 3–12. Cf. also Leon J. Saul, *Psychodynamically Based Psychotherapy* (New York: Science House, 1972).

28. Kubie, *Practical and Theoretical Aspects of Psychoanalysis* (rev. ed.), pp. 99–100. Cf. also Lawrence S. Kubie, *Practical and Theoretical Aspects of Psychoanalysis* (New York: Praeger, 1960), pp. 63–64.

29. Cf. Russell Jacoby, *Social Amnesia: A Critique of Conformist Psychology from Adler to Laing* (Boston: Beacon Press, 1975). Jacoby ignores Erikson's name while including Erikson's concepts among those under attack. Cf. p. 47.

30. Kurt R. Eissler, *Talent and Genius: The Fictitious Case of Tausk Contra Freud* (New York: Quadrangle, 1971), p. 120.

31. "Analysis Terminable and Interminable," pp. 248, 219.

32. Clarence P. Oberndorf, "Failures with Psychoanalytic Therapy," in *Failures in Psychiatric Treatment*, ed. Paul H. Hoch (New York: Grune & Stratton, 1948), p. 19.

33. *CS*, 2nd, p. 76.

34. Herman Nunberg, *Memoirs: Recollections, Ideas, Reflections* (New York: The Psychoanalytic Research and Development Fund, 1969), p. 32.

35. Edoardo Weiss, *Sigmund Freud as a Consultant* (New York: Intercontinental Medical Book Corp., 1970), p. 50. For an illustration of a psychosis precipitated by the "successful" treatment of neurosis, cf. Edoardo Weise, *Agoraphobia in the Light of Ego Psychology* (New York: Grune & Stratton, 1964), p. 6. Cf. also Ruth Mack Brunswick, "A Supplement to Freud's 'A History of an Infantile Neurosis,'" in *The Psychoanalytic Reader*, ed. Robert Fliess (New York: International Universities Press, 1948), p. 101.

36. *LH*, p. 36.

37. For my reply to Eissler's attack on my *Brother Animal*, cf. Paul Roazen, "Reflections on Ethos and Authenticity in Psychoanalysis," *The Human Context*, IV (Autumn 1972), 577–87. Cf. also "Victor Tausk Issue," *American Imago*, (Winter 1973), and Victor Tausk, *Oeuvres Psychoanalytiques* (Paris: Payot, 1975).

38. Robert Coles, "Karen Horney's Flight from Orthodoxy," in *Women and Analysis*, ed. Strouse, p. 189.

39. For an exception to this trend, cf. the astute article by Joseph Frank, "Freud's Case-History of Dostoevesky," *Times Literary Supplement*, July 18, 1975, pp. 807–08.

40. John Strachey, *The Coming Struggle for Power* (New York: Covici-Friede, 1933), pp. 170, 172.

41. Quoted in Jacoby, *Social Amnesia*, p. 169.

42. "On the History of the Psychoanalytic Movement," *The Standard Edition of The Complete Psychological Works of Sigmund Freud*, Vol. 14, p. 39.

43. Erikson, "Ego Development and Historical Change," p. 381.

Index

234